Jira Core 8 Basics

A Beginner Guide for Novice Jira Administrators

Jira is a fantastic software product that helps organizations manage Issues, Tasks, Processes, and Projects.

Jira Core 8 Basics explains the fundamentals of Jira Core in non-technical, easy to understand language focused on the business user.

The book gives an excellent explanation of the various Jira elements, includes exercises for hands-on experience, and provides 'How to' scripts to help you customize Jira Core to meet your organization's needs.

JIRA CORE 8 BASICS

A BEGINNER GUIDE FOR NOVICE JIRA ADMINISTRATORS

RYNDER ROY KLOMP

Published by

KlompRS Publishing

Toronto, Canada

ISBN 978-1-988018-13-3

Dedication

As always, to my beloved wife Anna.

And to Philipp Sendek. Great advisor, and even better friend. Thank you for your support and for your invaluable guidance.

TABLE OF CONTENTS

Table of Contents

Introduction

Hello, and welcome to **Jira Core 8 Basics: Beginner Guide for Novice Jira Administrators**.

I am excited to introduce you to Jira, a fantastic product that helps organizations and users manage their issues, tasks, processes, and projects.

In today's business world where employees are asked to do more, in less time, with fewer resources there is a need to 'automate' and simplify wherever possible. Jira meets those requirements perfectly.

I stumbled across Jira when I was looking for software I could use for a project I was building. I wanted software that would let me 1) manage tasks, 2) allow field agents to complete the project's status forms remotely, and 3) have automated responses based on a condition in a status form (e.g. an automated emergency email to the business owner if the status form indicated the project would not meet its deadline). Basically, I wanted something that would let me manage the project from a beach in Bora Bora. While Jira isn't yet able to do the last item, it does really well at delivering on the first three, that is why I got involved with it. And am glad I did; I was able to build a Jira project that allows a client to rollout a new product nationwide faster and with fewer challenges than the current manual process.

Who Should read this Book?

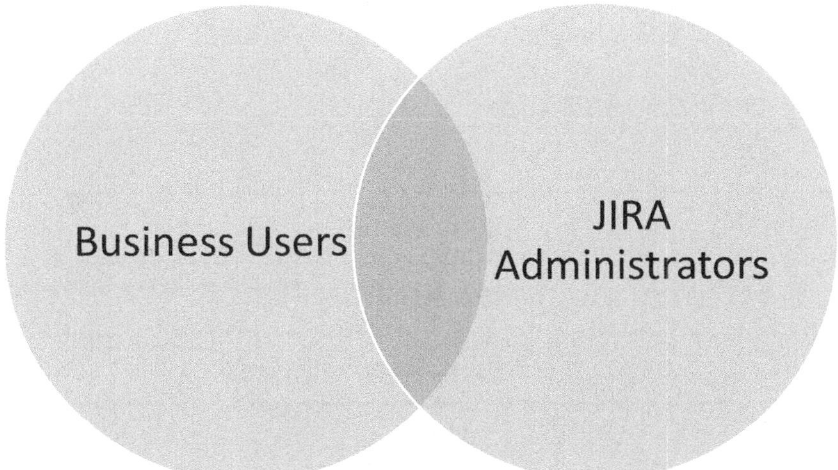

Business Users

There are a fair number of books and articles aimed towards the Jira user. While most of them are quite good, they are almost all written by Information Technology (I.T.) professionals targeting I.T. readers. In those books and documents, it is common to read something like, *"Next compact the parsnipial environment using a compound ambidextrous stacking algorithm. Here is a short 761 line example of how to do that using Bilingua Ascii Code. For your added enjoyment we have written the code in an obscure Western Mongolian Dialect that hasn't actually been spoken in 450 years."* This is great for I.T. individuals, but what about the rest of us?

This book is written for those who don't have I.T. backgrounds. It is written in non-I.T. language and is geared towards the business team member who either wants to work with Jira Core, or has been instructed to work with Jira (*"Sam, we've just bought 300 Jira Core licenses to improve our processes. Figure out how it works and build us a solution. Oh yeah, and do it by next Tuesday."*). So, if you are I.T. and are looking for help to manage Jira coding or databases; or, if you are searching for specific questions regarding macros or specialized installations, etc., this book is NOT for you. Of course, you are more than welcome to read the book, you may find it helpful.

JIRA ADMINISTRATORS

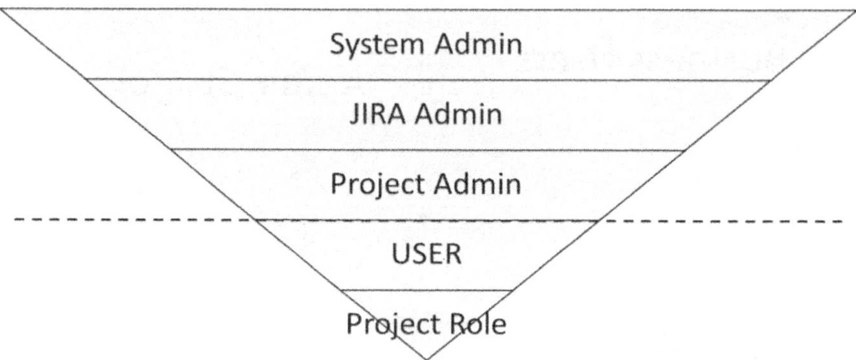

Jira Core has a number of security levels that allows or prevents access to various aspects of Jira. At the highest level is the Jira **System Administrator.** These folks (typically I.T.) have access to everything in Jira. Most of their work involves installing Jira or making sure it works with other software and hardware. This book is NOT meant for System Administrators.

Next is the **Jira Administrator**. These individuals have almost as much access as the System Admin but are typically prevented from access to the License details as well as areas that deal with making the program work with other software or hardware. The Jira Admin can build projects, screens, fields, workflow processes, etc. It is not necessary for the Jira Admin to be an I.T. individual.

Then we have the **Project Administrator**. This person usually has the same rights as the Jira Administrator, but is restricted to Jira 'projects' only (a project in Jira is defined as "a collection of Issues", or tasks).

Introduction

This book is written for Novice Jira Administrators and for Project Administrators.

Below the dotted line in the image are Users and, what are known as Project Roles. Users are people who are licensed to use the software, but do not have permission to modify the software. Project roles are licensed Users who are restricted to specific Jira projects. The whole purpose of Jira is to permit Jira Admins and Project Admins to build customized applications to be used by USERS. Most of this book deals with areas that the USER and Project Role will not have access; therefore, team members in those roles will probably find the book of limited value. We do, however, have on-line training courses available for novice Jira Core Users. They can be found at

https://www.torenois.com/product-category/jira-core-user/

What is Jira Core?

As I stated in the first paragraph, fundamentally Jira Core (which we will simply call Jira from now on) is a software program that helps organizations manage their issues, tasks, processes, and projects. However, it is 'smart software' because much of the tedious stuff related to issues, or tasks, or processes, or project management, can be automated fairly easily. Let's say you need to approve a product, or document, or whatever. You can set it up in Jira, so the approver just needs to click the "approved" button and messages are automatically sent to whom-ever needs to know that. If the thing is not approved, the approver can select from a predefined list of reasons for the rejection or can write an explanation, and again those messages are sent to the necessary individuals.

So what, you ask. I can do that already with emails or phone calls. Yes, you can. However, how many times have you intended to immediately write that email or make that phone call, only to be interrupted by life? Maybe you remembered a few hours later, or at the end of the day, that you needed to write that email. How many times did you recall it the next day, or forget completely until someone reminded you? Well, the benefit to Jira is that it is your silent 'admin assistant', and it automatically takes care of those tasks for you.

Jira started life in Atlassian (the parent company) as a way to track issues related to software 'bugs'. It wasn't long before additional features were added and it grew into a project management program with the ability to 'automate' a lot of the work that is necessary but provides little value, such as emailing or phoning a work colleague when a task is done and ready to be handed off.

It has, over the years, grown into a highly flexible and customizable tool to manage work activity. In addition, there are many 'apps' you can purchase at very reasonable prices that offer specialty solutions to specific challenges.

How does Jira Core Provides Value?

Here are three examples of how Jira Core provides business value to an organization.

Processes and Procedures

Jira excels in the area of repeatable *process procedures*. A process is a series of activities or tasks required to accomplish a goal. In other words, it describes *What* needs to be done. A procedure, in business, is the set of instructions which provides the steps and describes *How* to do the activities necessary to complete the process (not to be confused with an I.T. procedure which simply lists the detailed steps).

Many processes and procedures require checks (quality control or approvals), as well as handoffs to the area next involved in the process. These are often time consuming, and in the case of checks, provide no value-added to the customer. It is probably fair to say that in many situations just as much time is spent transferring a task for a check or for handoffs as is spent working on the task itself. Anything that can be done to reduce the time spend on these activities is of great value. On top of tracking the process tasks, Jira with its workflow component, is outstanding at managing the checks and handoff transfers.

For more business examples please see the 'Which Project Type to Select' section in Chapter 3.

JIRA APPLICATIONS

When you first go to the Atlassian web-site you are offered three Jira Programs: Jira Core, Jira Service Desk, and Jira Software. What is the difference between the three?

JIRA CORE

Jira started life as a means of helping software developers manage any software bugs that would show up in the course of writing a program. Any time the developer ran into a bug, the developer would create a Jira 'Issue' (a problem to be solved). This formed the basis for Jira. Slowly this evolved into the robust Jira Core program that can be used to manage tasks and processes. You must buy Jira Core if you want to use Jira Service Desk or Jira Software. That's because Jira Core is the 'engine' that allows Jira Service Desk and Jira Software to work.

JIRA SERVICE DESK

Jira Service Desk helps you manage a 'ticketing' process. Ticketing is any sort of work that involves a constant flow of incoming individual tasks or duties that must be assigned to a pool of resources.

A perfect example is an I.T. help desk. Any organization having more than three computers has an I.T. help desk. In small companies it may be Sam, and you get his attention by yelling across the room, "Hey, Sam, my printer has stopped working again." But, in large organizations there is usually a department dedicated to help employees with their I.T. issues. Whenever a help call comes in, a 'ticket' is created to track the issue until it is resolved. Jira handles this sort of thing perfectly. Tickets (called Issues) can be created and assigned by a manager, or can be created by any team member receiving a call or email.

Many organizations use 'ticketing' procedures where there is a flow of individual tasks that need to be assigned to workers. Insurance companies, delivery and taxi companies, repair companies, dry cleaning, etc. are examples.

With Jira you can also categorize your ticketing. Your I.T. help desk can create customized Issues (Tickets) for Printer Issues, PC Issues, Log on Issues, etc. In a transportation ticketing system two different types of Issues might be created depending on whether the product to be delivered needs a refrigerated truck or not.

Jira has developed the **Jira Service Desk** program for companies needing a ticketing solution. But in order to work with Jira Service Desk, you must first install Jira Core.

Jira Software

Many projects or processes involve accomplishing a number of related tasks within a defined time frame. You may have a list of 100 tasks needing to be accomplished. A pool of six team members decide, for example, they can accomplish *these* 17 (of the 100) items in the next 30 days. Each team member grabs one of the 17 items and works on it. Once complete s/he goes back to the pool and takes another of the remaining items and then works on that item; this continues until the workload of 17 items is complete. At which point they plan their next block of work.

The example above may be similar to the opening of a new store where 400 product categories (e.g. Peanut Butter) must be set up by a pool of 40 employees in 40 days. Each employee takes one category and when that product line is displayed properly s/he goes back and grabs the ticket for another category. Using the Jira program, the project manager can easily track the progress of the complete project.

Jira has developed the **Jira Software** program for companies needing an Agile project management delivery solution (and it is called Jira Software, because it is mostly used by Software teams). But, again, you need Jira Core in order for Jira Software to work.

WHY THIS BOOK?

'Process oriented' probably best describes me. Most of my work involves designing and implementing solutions for large companies. I love to design and build process solutions to a problem. While I have interacted with a lot of software and I.T. people, and indeed I am a partner in an I.T. company, I am not 'I.T'.

You know by now that there is often an 'understanding gap' between IT professionals and business people. Why? The terms and definitions that IT people use, on many occasions have slightly different meanings than those used by non-IT individuals. For example, in everyday life you would not have any difficulty understanding what a Project is, or Issue, or Schemes. But you will be very surprised how those terms are defined in Jira. I find that I.T. folks, like any specialized work group, tend to speak their own unique language. While this specialized language is necessary, it doesn't translate well for the rest of us.

Additionally, I find the vast majority of the Jira documentation is written by I.T. professionals for I.T. professionals, which kinda leaves the rest of us in the dark. Finally, I find that Jira documentation, while quite good at describing individual steps, tends to lack an easy-to-understand overview of the Jira.

That's why I decided to write this book. I wanted to understand how Jira works and how all the Jira pieces fit together; and I wanted to describe it in a language for those of us who are NOT in I.T. can easily comprehend.

STRUCTURE OF THE BOOK

Earlier in the Introduction I discussed the different security levels within Jira. As stated, the book is meant for Novice Jira Administrators and Project Administrators. To make things easier, I will simply use the term Jira Admin and that will include the Project Admin unless specifically noted otherwise.

The goal of the Jira Administrator or Project Administrator is to make the Jira elements as simple as possible for the Users. If the Accounts Payable clerk (a User) only needs to see three fields on a task screen then don't show him eight. If the Salesperson (a User) only needs to see five fields on her specific task screen then there is no need to show her nine.

The Jira Admin needs to make the project and its screens as easy as possible for two reasons. First, you do it because there is no sense to buy software that makes life more difficult for the Users. Second, you do it to avoid resistance. Anything that makes life more difficult for a User is going to cause resistance. And continuous resistance results in failure. There are two main causes of resistance in software: the Users don't see how the product benefits them; or, they see the product as too difficult/confusing to use. So, while Jira can be used out of the box with its defaults, you probably will need to modify it (i.e. specialize and simplify) to make it succeed within your organization.

As just mentioned, you can start using JIRA Core as soon as you download it. Jira Core comes with enough default 'stuff' that you can create a project quite rapidly. As a matter of fact, I would recommend you do so. Try setting up a trial project just using the defaults, and invite a couple of volunteers to participate. As you work with your project you may find the defaults work fine for your situation. Which is fantastic, why create unnecessary work if you don't need to. However, after a while you will probably realize the defaults need to be modified slightly, or a lot, in order to meet your business requirements or to make it more efficient.

This ability to bespoke the software into just about any imaginable configuration and meet almost any situation, is the true value of Jira.

'The rest of us' usually like to focus on the software itself rather than installing it; so, we are going to assume that you have, or someone in your organization has, installed Jira Core on your computer. We are also going to assume that someone has set up the basic email requirements and things like that.

Jira Core 8 Basics: Beginner Guide for Novice Jira Administrators will:

- Walk you through the creation of a simple project using the Jira's Core defaults
- Explain the most common screens in Jira Core and how they work
- Describe the various Jira elements (what I call the 'puzzle pieces'), and show how they fit together
- Modify the project we have built by creating some specialized screens and fields.
- Provide a 'cheat sheets' section with scripts for most of the standard activities.

When finished you will have a good understanding of how Jira works, and having built your first 'Jira's Core business project you also will be able to move forward confidently on your own.

WHAT YOU WON'T FIND

Since this is a Beginner's Guide dedicated to the business user you will not find:

- I.T. terms and details
- Programming language
- Jira system set up and configuration
- Topics I consider to be of Intermediate or Advanced level

Assumptions

In writing this book we assume the following about you:

1. You are a beginner to Jira Core
2. You are a 'business' user, not an I.T. professional
3. You have a copy of Jira Core already installed on your computer
4. You have been given Jira Administrator or Project Administrator rights. These Administrator rights mean you can make some changes to the program. If not, make sure you get it right away, you will need it in order to make modifications to the program. If I.T. is resistant, tell them you are not asking for "Jira System Administrator" rights, you are asking for "Jira Administrator" rights. The System Administrator has access to all background I.T. stuff; you don't want and don't need that. Being a Jira Administrator allows you to make 'business arrangement' changes to projects.

Formatting

To try and make it easier for you to make sense of everything the following formats will be used in this book.

CAUTION: Indicates a warning or caution

Regular font (like this) will be used for normal text.

1. SMALL CAPITAL FONT WILL BE USED AS AN INSTRUCTION FOR YOU TO FOLLOW (E.G. CLICK **ADD**).

Bold Font will indicate an element in Jira such as a button, link, a field, screen, etc. Also, it will emphasize some important messages.

Italic font will specify a term used by Jira such as Step, Status, etc., or it will be the information that you might be asked to enter into a Jira field.

The word **'view'** will mean something the **User** will see when working with an Issue or Project. A **User** has very few rights and is typically limited to viewing only the screens necessary to complete his or her tasks.

NOTE or TIP: Indicates a Note or Helpful Tip.

Is it really so easy to work in Jira? No, it takes practice. But I would strongly argue that it is not the software that is difficult. The reality is that designing a process or project can be, by itself, a very difficult exercise, irrespective of the software used. If looked at from that perspective I believe Jira to be the easiest process/project software to work with. They have really worked hard over the years to translate a difficult topic into a software that is as intuitive as possible.

The good news is that within a fairly short time it does indeed become quite instinctive to use. I recommend you practice by creating a fiction project first, draw it on the paper and play with it in Jira to 'feel' how all Jira elements fit together. I did it, and so can you.

WHAT DOES JIRA MEAN?

In case you are wondering what Jira means, here is the explanation as quoted from the Atlassian Jira website.

"Like all good names in the software industry, it started as an in-house code name.

We originally used Bugzilla for bug tracking and the developers in the office started calling it by the Japanese name for Godzilla, Gojira (the original black-and-white Japanese Godzilla films are also office favorites). As we developed our own bug tracker, and then it became an issue tracker, the name stuck, but the Go got dropped - hence Jira!

Further investigation into the name has revealed that Gorira is Japanese for "gorilla", whilst Kujira is Japanese for "whale". So Gojira is roughly translated to mean "gorilla the size of a whale"! (Thanks to yusuke_arclamp — Oct 2002)"

Chapter 1- Create Your First Jira Project

Chapter Objectives

I suppose, logically, we should start this book by explaining the technical elements of Jira Core and how they all work together. However, if you are like most people, you probably want to get started as quickly as possible. So, **in this chapter you will create your first Project and first Issue within that project. Then we will take a quick tour of the Issue you just created.**

At the end of the Chapter you will have a high level of understanding of the Project, Create Issue, and Issue Details views.

NOTE: The chapters following this one will answer most of your questions as to 'how does it work', or, 'where can I find this'.

But first...

Let's start with a brief explanation of the Issues and Projects. A Jira Core Issue is something that needs to be done, fixed, or resolved. In other words, it is a 'packet of work'.

It may be more accurate to describe a Jira Core Project as a file folder containing Jira Issues. An Issue must reside within a Project. More importantly **Issues can only be created within a Project**.

Before you can create your first Issue, you must first create a Project. We will do that now.

Create a Project

Exercise: Create your First Project

To create your first project, follow these instructions:

1. On the Main Menu Bar, click **Projects**
2. In the Projects menu, click on **Create Project**:

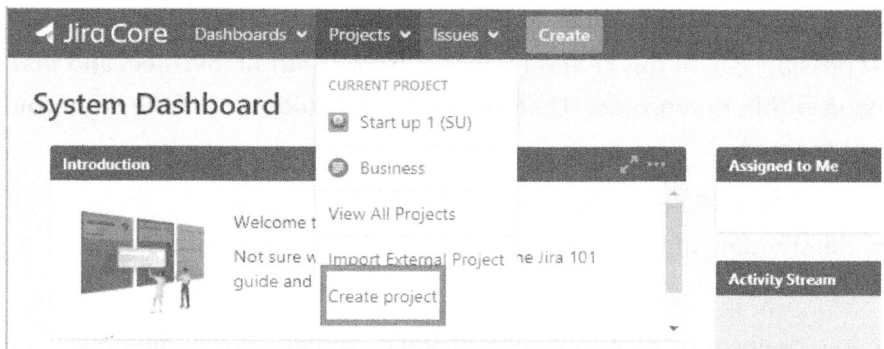

CAUTION: You may be asked to log in to the Administrator area with your Username and Password as only Jira Administrators or Jira System Administrators can create projects; Project Admins and Jira Users cannot create projects.

The **Create Project** wizard opens:

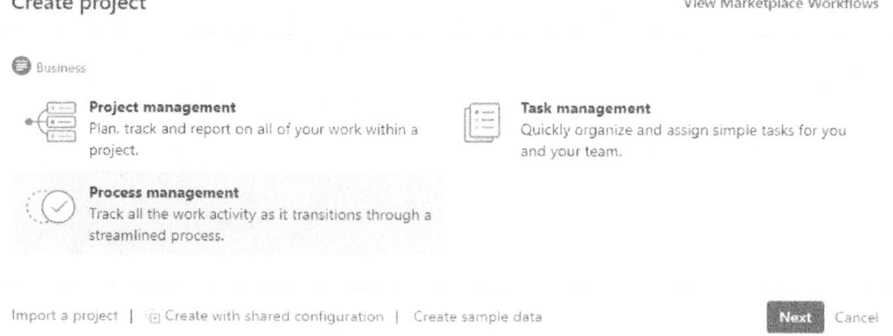

3. THERE ARE THREE **BUSINESS** PROJECT TYPES TO CHOOSE FROM: **PROJECT MANAGEMENT, PROCESS MANAGEMENT,** AND **TASK MANAGEMENT**. CLICK '*TASK MANAGEMENT*", THEN CLICK THE NEXT BUTTON

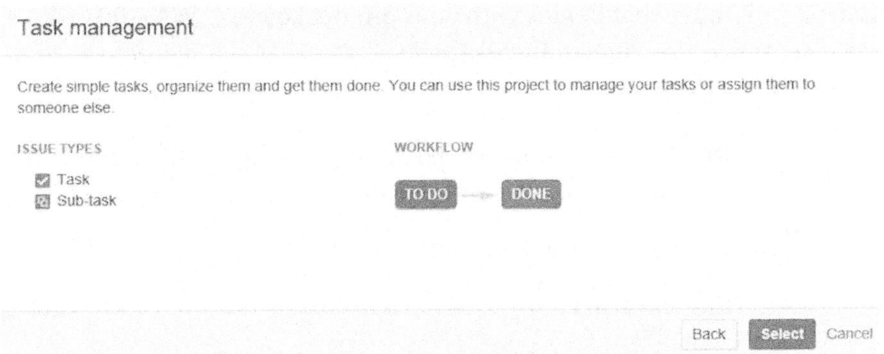

This pop-up provides an overview of the Task Management Project Type. It shows that two **Issue Types** are available to you, and it shows the **Workflow** that operates with this choice. We will discuss Issue Types and Workflows very soon, but for now

4. CLICK **SELECT**

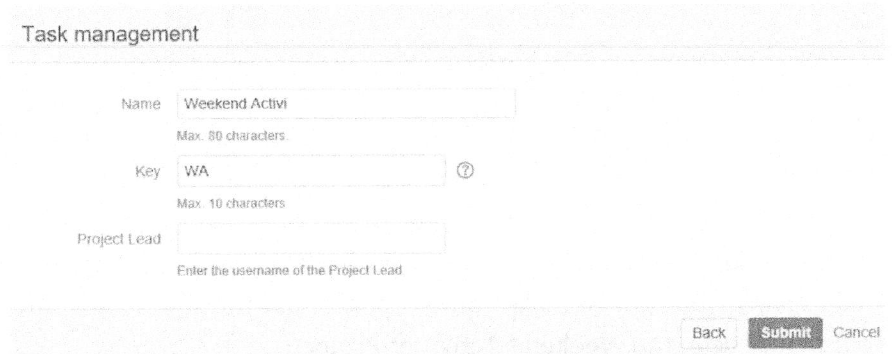

Here you name your project and assign a project lead.

5. IN THE **NAME** FIELD, TYPE "*WEEKEND ACTIVITIES*".

Notice that as you typed in the name of the project the **Key** field automatically filled with some Capital letters. The **Project Key** performs two functions. First, it is how Jira identifies your project in its internal database. This key field creates a unique combination of letters that will differentiate your current project from any other project. Second, anytime you create an Issue in this project, Jira will assign to that Issue an Issue key number that begins with your project key (e.g. WA – 001, WA – 002, etc.). You can change the project key but that is not a very easy or wise thing to do.

6. IN THE PROJECT LEAD FIELD, CONFIRM YOUR NAME HAS BEEN AUTOMATICALLY ENTERED, OR IF BLANK ENTER YOUR USERNAME

You are now the owner of the project.

7. CLICK **SUBMIT**

Congratulations, you have just created your first project in Jira Core and you should now be in the **Open Issues** view. This is where all your project's issues will be shown after you create them. But since you have not yet created any, the view looks like this:

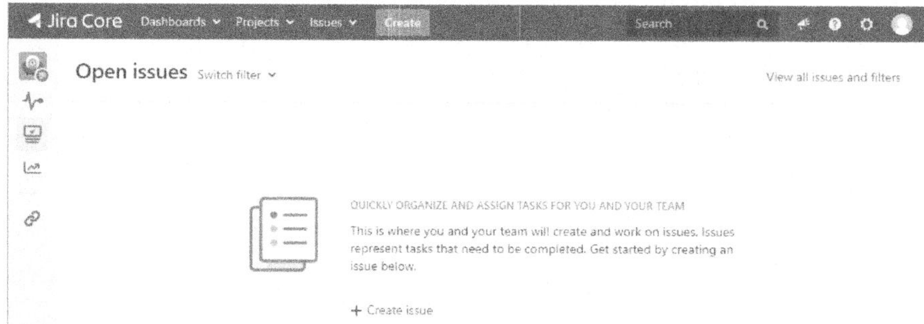

We will explore the Open Issues view in more *detail* in a later chapter as well as show you how to make some changes, but for now let's create your first Issue in the **Weekend Activities Project**.

Create an Issue

Exercise: Create your First Issue

We have created a project; now it is time to create our first Issue.

1. On the Main Menu Bar, click **Create**

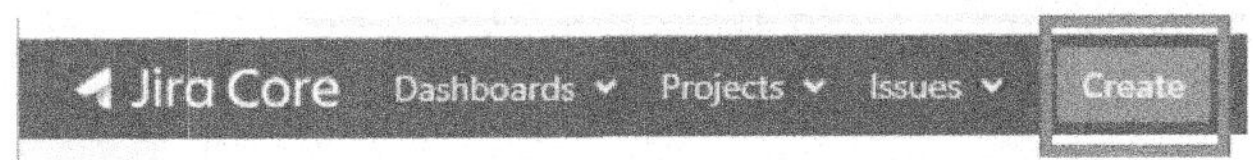

The **Create Issue** popup appears:

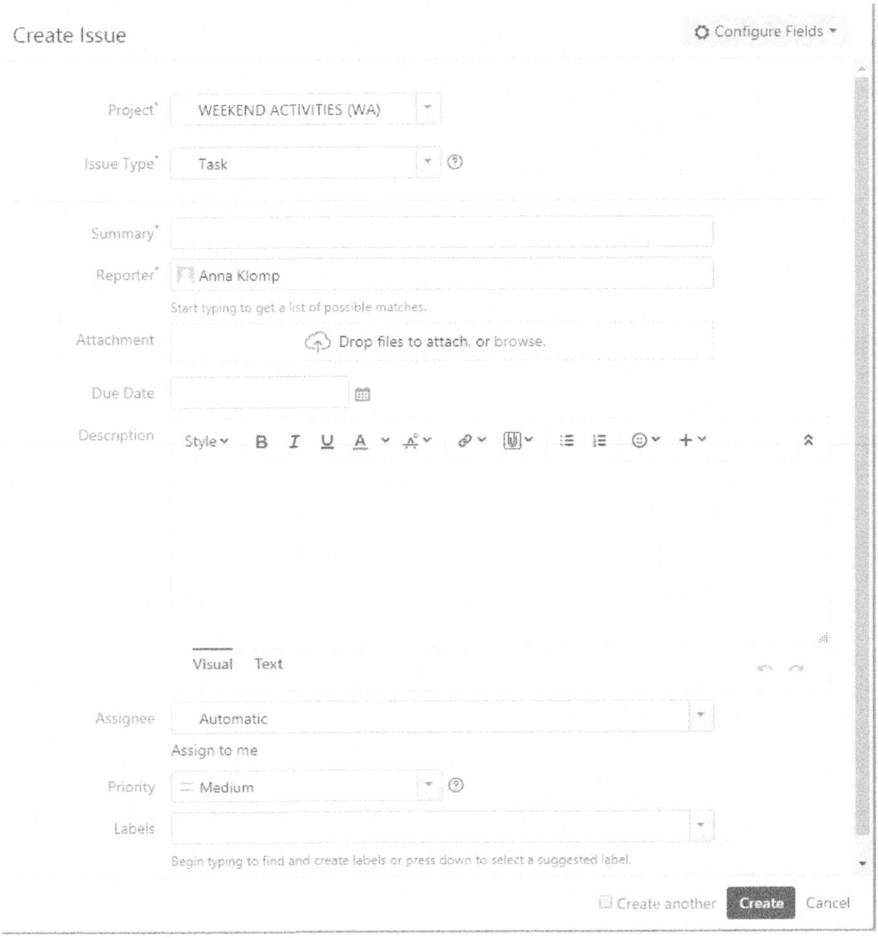

Create Issue

Configure Fields

Project* WEEKEND ACTIVITIES (WA)

Issue Type* Task

Summary*

Reporter* Anna Klomp

Start typing to get a list of possible matches.

Attachment Drop files to attach, or browse.

Due Date

Description Style B I U A

Visual Text

Assignee Automatic

Assign to me

Priority Medium

Labels

Begin typing to find and create labels or press down to select a suggested label.

Create another Create Cancel

2. In the **Project** field, select **Weekend Activities (WA)** project if it is not already selected
3. In the **Issue Type** field, select **Task** if it is not already selected
4. In the **Summary** field, Type '*New Weekend Chore*'
5. The **Reporter** field should already contain your name; if not, go ahead and enter your user name
6. In the **Due Date** field choose Friday of next week
7. In the **Description** field you can type a description of your newly created project and choose a style, font, size, insert link or/and attachment, etc. by selecting the relevant icon on the toolbar above your text
8. In the **Assignee** field click on the Assign to me link below the field
9. In the **Priority** field select **High** by clicking on the drop-down arrow
10. In the **Labels** field type in or select from the drop-down list an appropriate label (or key word) for the issue
11. Click **Create**

Woo Hoo! You have just created your first issue. Let's take a look at it in more detail.

The Issue Details View

*On the **Main Menu Bar**, click on **Issues** and select our just created **WA-1 New Weekend Chore**. Clicking on this issue will bring you to the **Issue Details View**:*

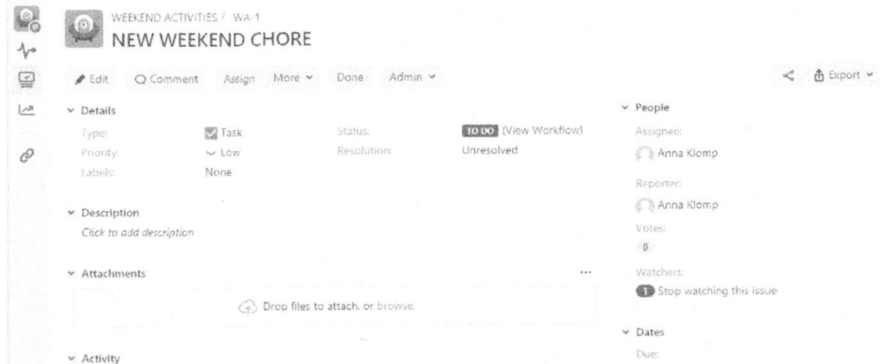

This view shows the details of your issue(s).

Wow, quite a busy view isn't it! If you want to know what's happening with your Issue, here is where you go. Don't worry, as it will probably be your most commonly used view, you will soon get quite used to it. Let's take a quick look at this view as it is so critical.

The name of that issue - **New Weekend Chore** - and the autogenerated issue key - **WA-1 -** are displayed automatically for you (the key is shown in the red circle in the image below):

The Issue Header Bar

The first thing you see in the Issue Details View is the Header Bar. It displays the name of the **Project**, the **Issue Key,** and the **Summary** of the Issue ("New Weekend Chore"):

Yes, a little bit confusing: what you or I might call a title or issue name, Jira calls an "Issue Summary":

WEEKEND ACTIVITIES / WA-1

NEW WEEKEND CHORE ⟸ Summary

Edit Comment Assign More Done Admin

When I first started working with Jira software, "Summary" was the one thing that confused me the most. I kept looking for a place to enter the name or title of the Issue, and I could not find it. I have no idea why they just don't call it Issue Name or something that we, regular folks, would understand. But it's their product and they can do as they wish, so let's live with it.

Issue Menu Bar

Below the header area is the Issue menu bar, which begins with the **Edit** (pencil) icon:

WEEKEND ACTIVITIES / WA-1

NEW WEEKEND CHORE

Exercise: Edit an Issue

1. Click on the **Edit button**:

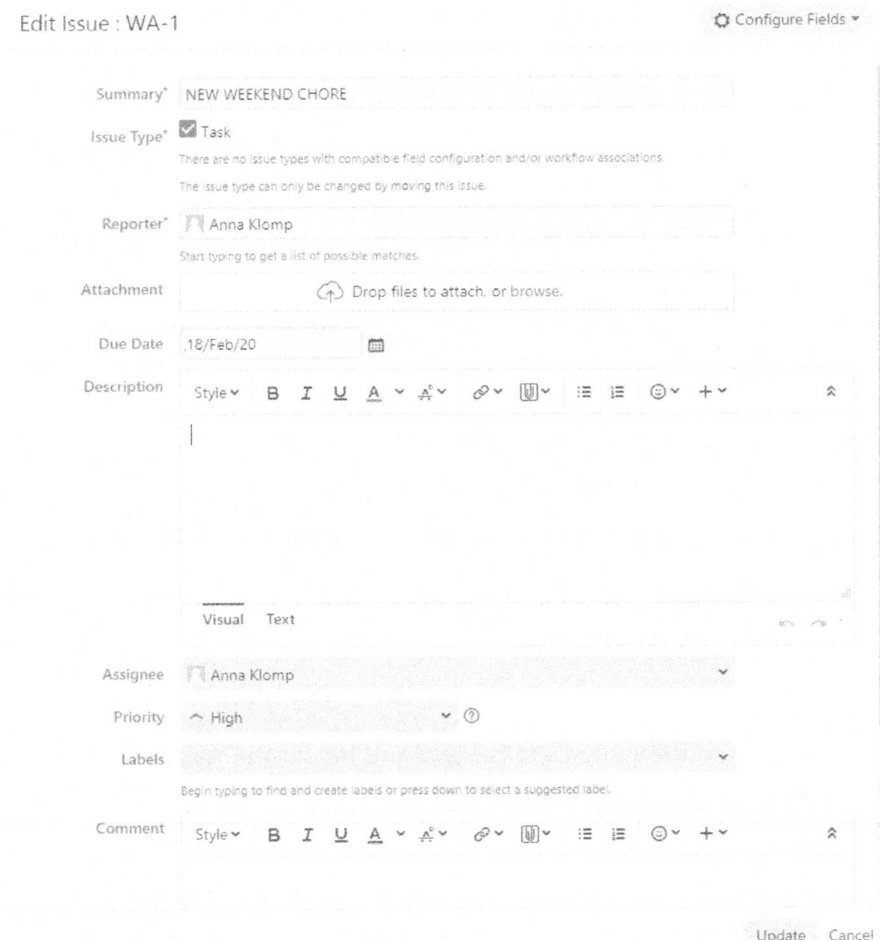

The **Edit Issue** view is usually identical to the **Create Issue** view, but here you can enter more information such as **Due Date, Assignee, Reporter** that we didn't enter when we created the issue. This is very useful if you need to add additional information or edit existing information after you create the issue. In this view you can also easily add (drag and drop) an **Attachment**, create a Label, and post a **Comment**. You can also limit who sees this issue by clicking on the **Viewable by All Users** drop down arrow at the very bottom of the view.

2. IN THE **DUE DATE** FIELD, CLICK ON THE **CALENDAR** ICON AND SELECT THIS UPCOMING SATURDAY
3. CONFIRM THAT YOUR **USERNAME** IS IN THE **ASSIGNEE** FIELD.

TIP: If your Username is not in the **Assignee** field, you can add it in one of three ways:

i. CLICK THE BLUE **ASSIGN TO ME** TEXT BELOW THE **ASSIGNEE** FIELD
ii. START TYPING YOUR **USERNAME** IN THE **ASSIGNEE** FIELD (THIS FIELD HAS SMART FILL: AS SOON AS YOU START TYPING, JIRA WILL SHOW YOU A LIST OF OPTIONS)
iii. CLICK THE **ASSIGNEE** FIELD DOWN ARROW AND SELECT YOUR **USERNAME** FROM THE LIST

When you are done do not forget to click the **Update** button.

Let's ignore the other menu items right now (don't worry, we will look at them later in the book).

ISSUE DETAILS

Back in the Issue Details View and below the Issue menu bar in the **Details** section you see the Issue Type is Task; Status: TO DO; Priority is High.

You may not notice it at first glance, but all the information you entered when you created and then edited the Issue are in this view somewhere.

In **Description** you will find the text you inserted when creating the Task.

Attachments will show images and/or files that you attached. If not, and you need to include them, simply drag and drop an image or file to any part of the Issue Detail View. You can also use your paste option (by using the keyboard or by right-clicking).

In the **People** section there is your name as the **assignee** of the issue.

Finally, in the **Dates** section below People, is the **Due** date of the Issue.

You also see other information that, you might think, has nothing to do with your issue. Don't worry. It is amazing how quickly you will learn to ignore the unnecessary stuff and zero in on only those fields important to you.

Now that our quick tour of the Issue is over, let's go back to the **Open Issues** view. Click on the **Weekend Activities** (Project Name) link:

To view the Issue Detail View in a larger view (in full screen, as we did recently by clicking on double arrow icon), you can also do so by clicking on the **Issue key link** above the Issue Summary:

Later on you will learn as well how to modify various Jira Core screens and fields; however, the **Issue Detail View** is the one view you cannot modify yourself. Changing this view requires developers who will need to dive deep into the bowels of the program in order to change it.

On the far left of the Open Issues view there is a **Project Navigation sidebar** which we will discuss soon in the “Projects” chapter.

Chapter 2- A Tour of Jira Core

Chapter Objectives

In this Chapter we will walk you through each item of the Jira Core Main Menu Bar.

At the end of this chapter you will have a good understanding of how the Jira Core elements fit together and be able to navigate the software.

> NOTE: The easiest way to work with this chapter is to have a copy of the software open and take a closer look at each element as we discuss them in the chapter.

Jira is an incredibly powerful tool that can help improve the efficiency of your organization while making life easier at the same time.

While most of the work in Jira occurs behind the scenes to make the user's job as simple as possible, it does take some time for the Jira Administrator or Project Administrator (that would be you) to learn the system and modify it to suit your organization's needs. Below are two examples of what I mean. This first image is the **Issue (task) Details View** that the Users will see when opening up their assigned issue:

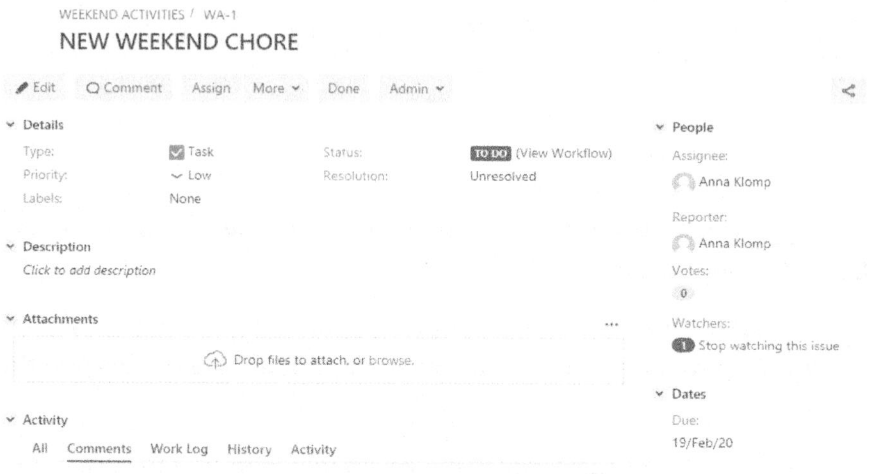

WEEKEND ACTIVITIES / WA-1

NEW WEEKEND CHORE

Edit Comment Assign More Done Admin

Details

Type: Task
Priority: Low
Labels: None
Status: TO DO (View Workflow)
Resolution: Unresolved

Description

Click to add description

Attachments

Drop files to attach, or browse.

Activity

All Comments Work Log History Activity

People

Assignee: Anna Klomp

Reporter: Anna Klomp

Votes: 0

Watchers: 1 Stop watching this issue

Dates

Due: 19/Feb/20

The image below is a diagram of the Jira Core elements and their relationship to one another:

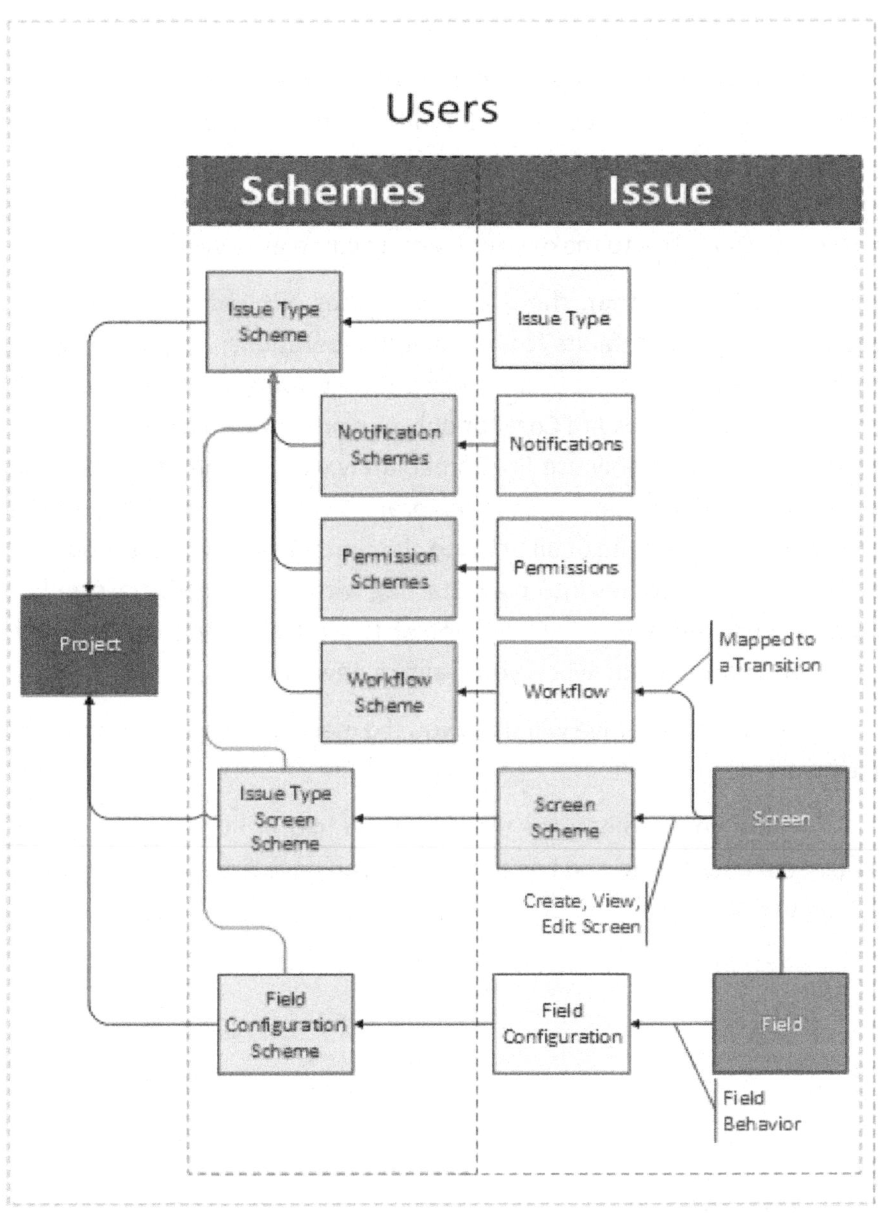
Users
Schemes
Issue
Issue Type Scheme
Issue Type
Notification Schemes
Notifications
Permission Schemes
Permissions
Project
Workflow Scheme
Workflow
Mapped to a Transition
Issue Type Screen Scheme
Screen Scheme
Screen
Create, View, Edit Screen
Field Configuration Scheme
Field Configuration
Field
Field Behavior

Jira Core 8 Basics

There is a saying that, "Skiing is easy to learn, but difficult to master. Snowboarding is difficult to learn, but easy to master." Jira is a little analogous to Snowboarding. It is difficult to learn, but relatively easy to master. The two images you just saw give you an idea that Jira is NOT intuitive like Word Processing Programs, or Spreadsheet software. But do not panic! Our job is to make your learning curve as easy as possible.

Having said that, there are two pieces of good news. First, Jira comes set up with defaults for many of its operations; and it is possible to start a task, a process, or a project without doing anything special. If your organization uses Jira Core for only one project with only one or two issues, you can probably use Jira immediately with its 'out of the box' set up. However, if you have a complex project with many issues, you will have to customize some or all of those elements. That's where the second bit of good news comes into play. Starting with Jira Core 7 Atlassian has done a great job at setting up a lot of those customizations that are triggered automatically when you create a new project.

In this chapter we will show you the main Jira Core views and how they work.

I am going to assume that you have had Jira Core installed and assigned a **User Name** and **Log In** and that you have Jira Admin or Project Admin permissions.

Log In to Jira Core using the following view:

Welcome to Toreno Jira Core 8.7

Username

Password

Remember my login on this computer

Not a member? To request an account, please contact your Jira administrators.

Log In Can't access your account?

Atlassian Jira Project Management Software (v8.7.1#807001-sha1:03e3702) · About Jira · Report a problem

ATLASSIAN

Once you have logged in, you will see the **System Dashboard:**

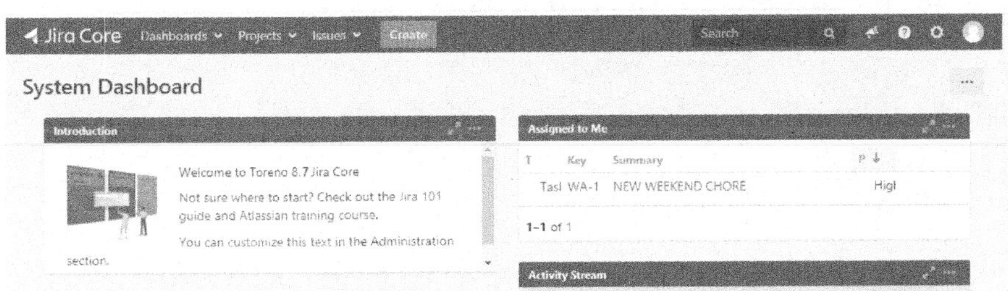

This view has two main sections: the Main **Menu Bar** and the **Main View**.

Main Menu Bar

The main menu bar navigates you throughout Jira and serves to perform actions.

Once you log in, you will always see this menu bar regardless of where you are in Jira Core.

Let's take a quick tour of the main menu bar items.

ORGANIZATION NAME

The first item you will probably see on the Main Men Bar is "Jira" and its icon (**Avatar**), or it may have already been changed to show your organization's logo and name. Jira is the default. Clicking on it brings you to the **System Dashboard**, which is helpful if you are somewhere deep in the Jira Core software and want to return to this main view quickly.

DASHBOARDS

A **Dashboard** is a collection of reports or tools usually arranged around a specific theme. Below, on the main view, you see the default system dashboard.

Click the down arrow on the Dashboard menu item and you see that the menu is divided into two parts:

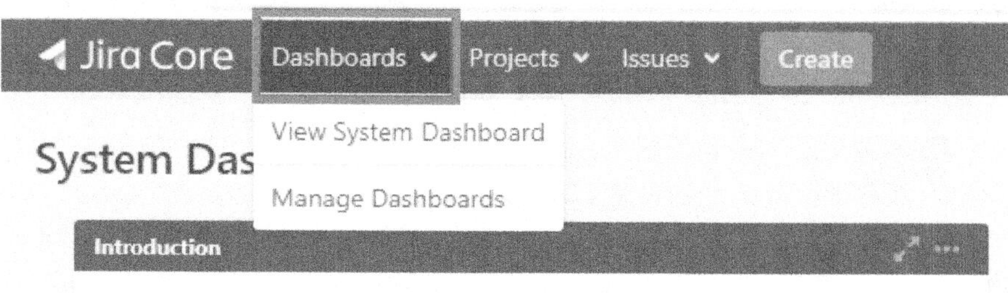

The first part, above the horizontal line, is **System** Dashboard (or you might see **View System Dashboard**; regardless, they are both the same) and clicking on it will open the **System Dashboard**. It will also list any custom dashboards your organization has already created and made available for you to use. Below the horizontal line it should say '**Manage Dashboards'**. Clicking on it will take you to the section in Jira Core where you can create new dashboards or alter current dashboards to suite your needs. Dashboards are covered in more detail in the Dashboards chapter.

Projects

The **Projects** menu is divided into five sections. The first (top) shows your most current project and typically displays the last project you have worked on, or are working on right now.

The second section shows recent projects you have worked on. Essentially, they are quick links.

In the third you will see 'Business'. Clicking on this link will bring up all your Business project types. If you have purchased Jira Software and Jira Service Desk licenses, then you will also see 'Software' and 'Service Desk' here as well. Clicking on any link will bring you to a list of projects matching the project type criteria selected.

The fourth section is a command that will list all projects with which you are involved or have permission to see.

The final section deals with the creation of projects. You can do nothing practical in Jira until you create a project. To be more specific, **you can only create and work on tasks/issues within a project.** You may create a project in two ways: by clicking the **Create Project** link, which brings you to a wizard where you will indeed create a project; or, by clicking **Import External Project**. I can already hear you thinking, "Hey, cool, I can *easily* import my Excel or Microsoft Project file and get started." While the import function is indeed straightforward it is certainly not "easy". To do so you must first convert them to a CSV file format. This option is definitely not for beginners.

Issues

Issues, in Jira, are not something you discuss with your psychiatrist or best friend. As you may recall, Jira started life as a way for programmers to track issues when designing and building software. As Jira has grown into project management software, it has kept that original term. An **Issue** can be best defined as something that needs to be done, fixed, or resolved. If you want Jira to capture issues, then Issue is a perfect description. If you want to use Jira for the creation of tasks, then maybe it isn't the best description, but you will quickly get used to the word. The Issues menu deals with Searching for Issues, Recent Issues, and Issue Filters:

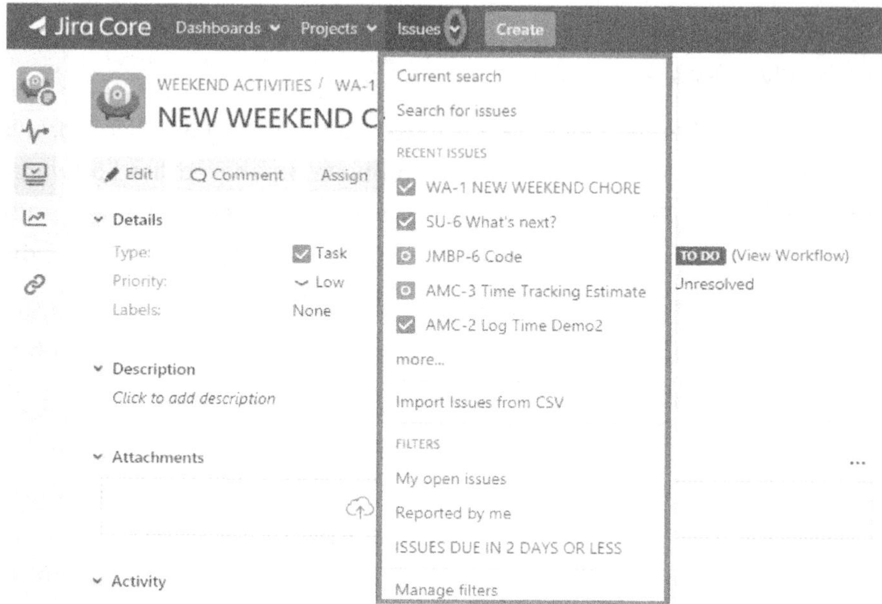

We will cover **Search, Search for Issues, and Issue Filters** in much more depth in the Filters chapter, but right now let's take a look at Recent Issues and Import Issue from CSV.

Recent Issues lists your five most **Recent Issues**. Clicking on any of them will open the **Issue Details View** for that particular issue. You can click on the **more...** link to see, well, more. Typically, clicking **more...** brings up a list of your 25 most recently viewed issues.

Next on the menu is a section called **Import Issues from CSV**. CSV means Comma Separated Values. Needless to say, that is I.T. terminology and is out of scope for this book. However, if you have imported CSV files in the past (usually with spreadsheet programs), you should be able to do so in Jira.

CREATE

We next come to **Create**, the heart of the program, which is probably why it is placed in a bright blue button. As you might guess, clicking **Create** begins the 'create a new Issue process'.

Click the Create button:

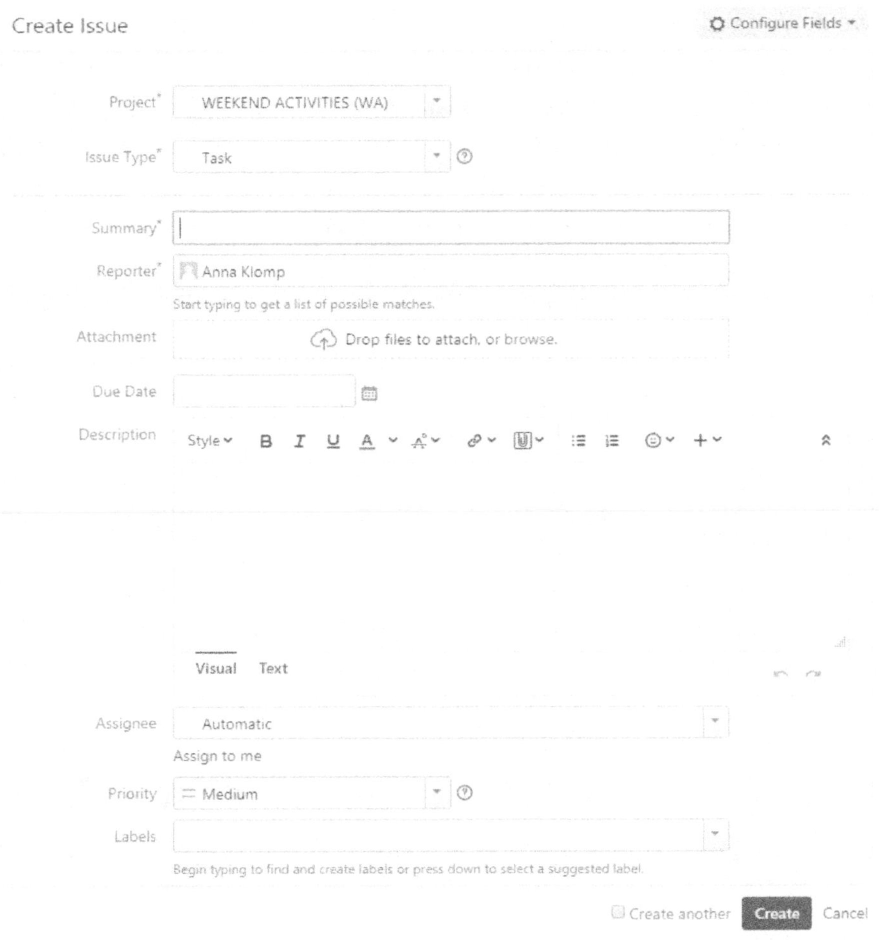

You will see a pop-up window appear with a number of fields. We covered creating an Issue in the previous chapter; so, there is no need to go further into the topic again. CLICK CANCEL in the lower right corner of the Create Issue pop-up to exit this view and let's move on to the next item on the menu bar.

QUICK SEARCH

You have undoubtedly seen Search boxes in other software; so, we don't need to spend a lot of time with this item. Just keep in mind that the quick search function in Jira works a little differently. If you are going to search for specific text be aware that Jira will only look in the Summary, Description, and Comments fields. No other fields will be checked. You can also preface your search with specific Jira query terms for specific fields (check Atlassian documentation for those terms).

I tend to use this search box rather than going to the Search view, as I find it a little faster. Which is probably why it is called 'Quick' Search.

FEEDBACK

Jira wants to hear from you as to how to improve their software. After opening the Feedback pop-up you can leave a message, concern, or recommendation.

JIRA HELP

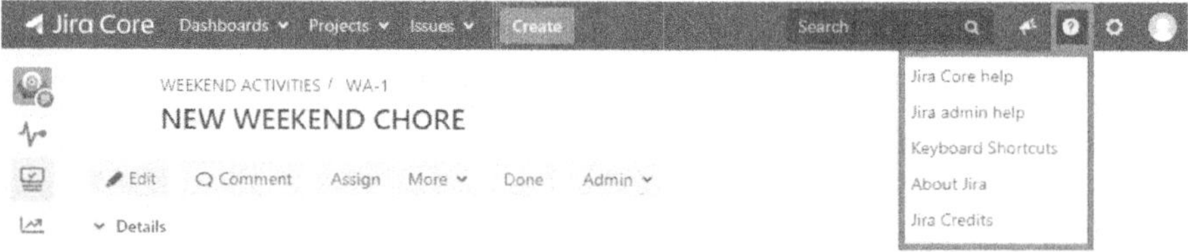

Here we have the Jira Help menu which contains a number of links such as Jira Core help, Jira admin help, Keyboard Shortcuts, About Jira, and Jira Credits.

Cog Wheel

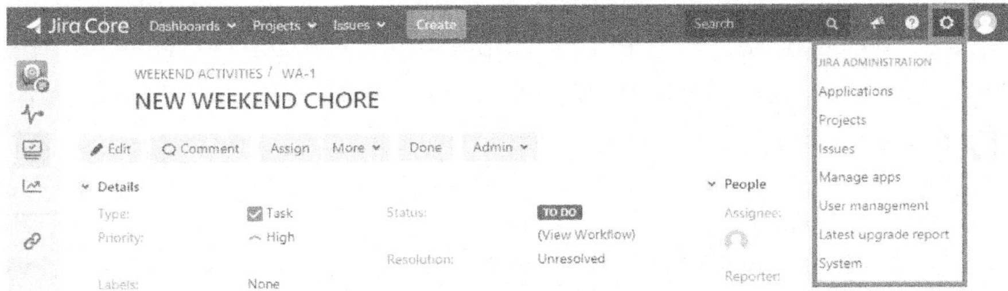

Next, you should see a **Cog** wheel. This is the **Jira Administration** menu, and it is only available to Jira Administrators (i.e. NOT available to Jira Project Admins). If you are going to create projects or issues types you will need to be granted Administrator access, so get in touch with the System Administrator and make sure that happens.

The **Jira Administration** menu has seven links: **Applications, Projects, Issues, Manage apps, User management, Latest upgrade report, and System.** Be aware that after clicking one of these links you will probably have to enter your password again in order to gain access to these areas.

Applications

Clicking on **Applications** will open the **Administration** view:

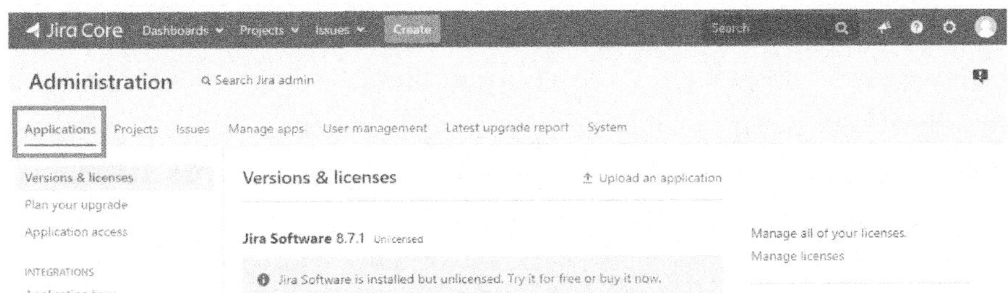

This is where you manage your Jira applications. This is where you can also **upload** a Jira application such as Jira Service Desk or Jira Software. It is also where you can find Jira's messages regarding versions' updates and licenses.

The other options of the Application's view such as **Application Access, Integrations (including Application Navigator)** will not be discussed in this book; these are all topics for the System Administrator and not we humble Jira Administrators or Project Administrators.

PROJECTS

Clicking on **Projects** will land you on the same **Administration** view, but now you will be in the Projects tab. This is where you can change many aspects of your project. It will list your projects and allow you to **Create project, Edit**, and **Delete.** It also gives you a view of some high-level details about the project such as Project Lead, the URL for the project, Assignee, etc.

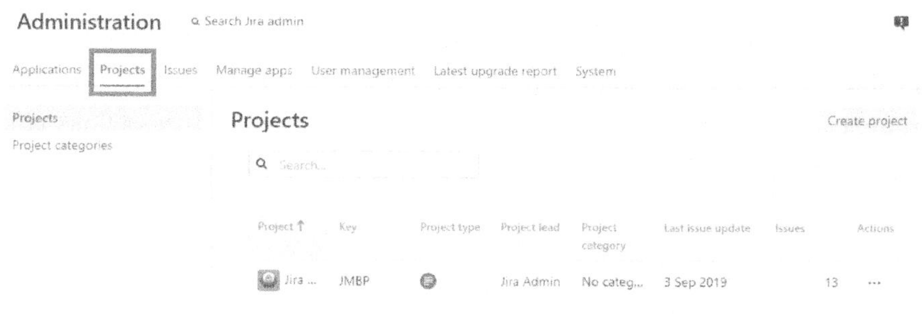

ISSUES

This will become your most important view when you start to bespoke your project. It is the coordination point for all defaults and modifications done in Jira. Here you make changes to **Issue Types, Workflows, Screens, Fields, Priorities, Issue Features, Issue Attributes, Security, Notifications,** and **Permissions**.

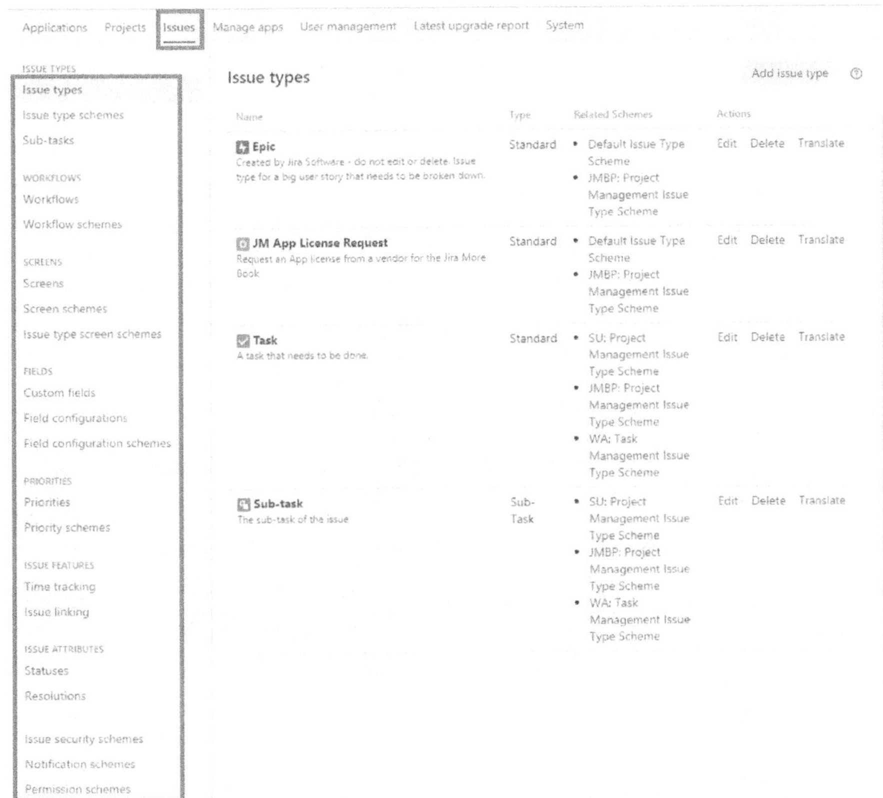

We will cover most of these items in following chapters, so, for now let's move on to our next COG menu item.

CAUTION: Just one word of caution! You may be tempted to start making changes on your own. I strongly discourage doing it until you have read the remainder of the book. **Changing any of the defaults will affect the entire program and is often difficult to reverse. If you are going to change anything, first, copy one of the Jira's existing defaults (e.g. Issue Type, Screen Scheme, etc.), rename it, and then edit it.** You can always delete your copy with no damage to the Jira defaults.

Manage Apps

Jira has a great number of applications (apps) available, and they focus on specific issues such as exporting reports or importing projects, workflow enhancements, forms and custom fields, creating charts and diagrams, roadmaps, planners, etc. These are all managed through the Atlassian Marketplace, which is where the manage apps link sends you.

Some applications are free and others are very reasonably priced. Atlassian makes sure that all apps work with Jira, but that's not the same as saying they provide good value. That's why there is also a four-star rating system where customers can rate the product.

If your business team is looking for Jira Apps that don't need I.T. involvement, then look for my book "Jira More: Apps to make your Jira Core, Service Desk, and Workflows more productive!" (available Summer 2020 at Amazon). It includes the most popular, business team oriented, Jira Apps. In this book we explain the what the App does, how it benefits the business, provides a high level tour of the App, and a quick start guide to get you up and running immediately.

User Management

Next in the Jira Administration menu is the **User management** link that brings you to the **Users** page:

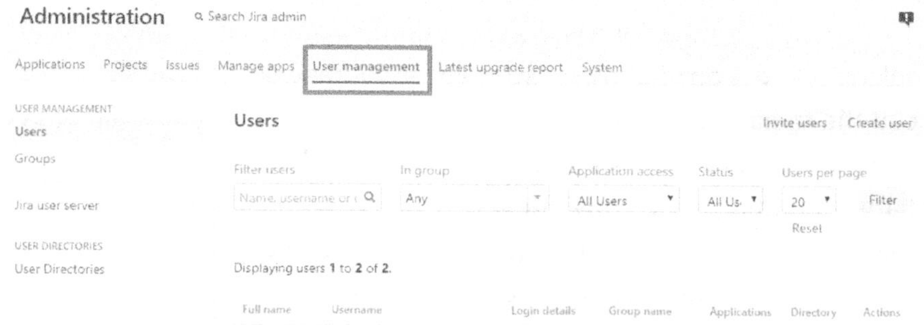

The **Users** page shows you a list of all your licensed users. It displays a number of things such as **Username**, the full name of the individual and his/her email addresses, login details of the user, the groups the user belongs to, applications the user uses, in which directory the user details can be found, and the actions you can perform such as Edit, Edit user groups, View project roles, and Delete user.

Click on the **Edit link**, and you can **Edit** the user's profile such as username, full name, and email. You can also change the user's status from active to non-active and vice-versa.

To **Edit user groups, View project roles, or Delete user**, click on the More button in the Actions column and choose one of those options:

Full name	Username	Login details	Group name	Applications	Directory	Actions
Jira Admin	admin igc@nullgrip.com	**Count:** 19 **Last:** 30/Nov/17 4:08 PM	jira-administrators jira-core-users	JIRA Core	JIRA Internal Directo	Edit ••• Edit user groups View project roles Delete user
		Count: 61	jira-	JIRA Core	JIRA In	

In this Users page you can **Invite Users** and **Create User** as well.

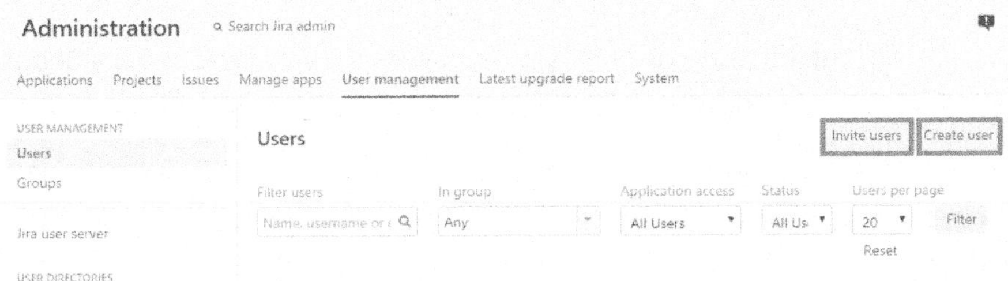

Create User is straight forward; you simply type a Username for the individual along with his/her Full name and Email address. You can include a temporary password for them, and if you don't, Jira will automatically create one. Finally, you can check the option to send them a notification email, and access to an application other than Jira Core (Jira Core is a default).

Alternatively, you may invite users to join Jira Core. This is done by clicking the **Invite Users button** and entering their email address. But you must have, or set up, an outgoing mail server.

Two notes of caution. First, when you send an email to a user with a password, the password is only good for 24 hours. Second, when inviting users, make sure you a) are authorized to invite, and b) have enough Jira Core licenses. There are 10, 25, 50, 100, 500, 1,000, and 3,000+ license packages available. Needless to say, if your company purchases a package on the smaller end of the scale you will need to be careful with your allocation of licenses.

If you have a great many users, you may **Filter** them using the Filter boxes near the top of the page.

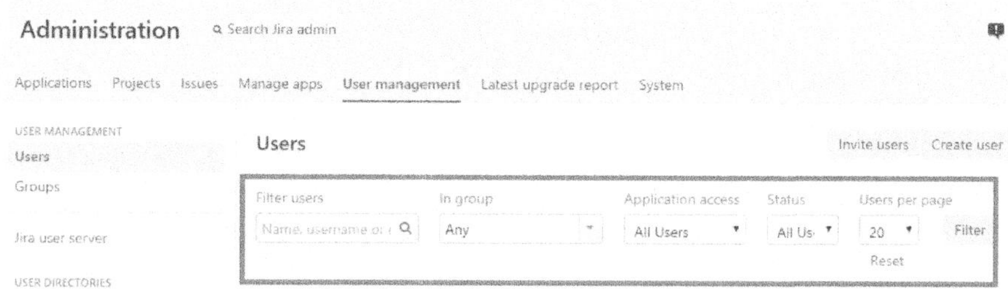

On the left side of the User management view you see a sidebar providing more options in addition to the current User page.

The User Management sidebar menu also contains a link to the **Groups** page, where you will be able to Add or Edit groups (among other things).

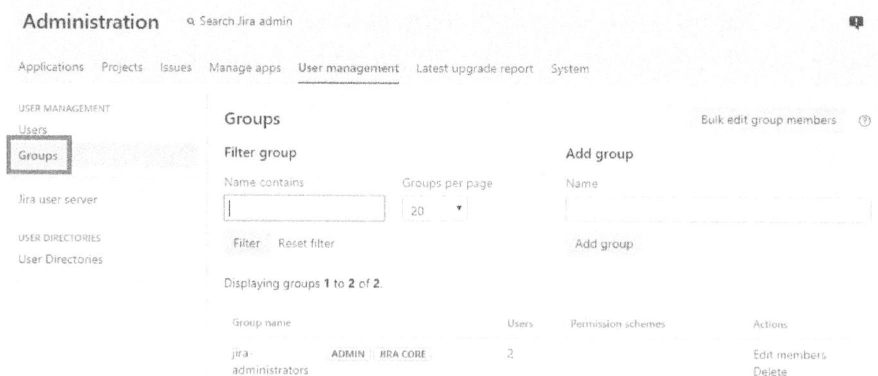

Jira sorts people into three categories: **Users, Roles, and Groups.**

A **User** is someone licensed to use Jira. For example, Jane Doe is a User.

A **Role** is a project specific assignment. Users are typically assigned to these project Roles. Quality Control Analyst in the ACME Project is an example of a Role. And Jane Doe can also be assigned to the QC Analyst role. Roles have security permissions only for the project(s) designated.

A **Group** in Jira might be best defined as a number of users performing a similar function or task: a Financial Analyst Group may be a good example. Unlike Project Roles (found in the System page in the Security section sidebar), Groups are global in nature; meaning they are not bound to any one project. **It is easier to assign permissions and security rights to the group than to individuals.** If the individual leaves the organization or changes job position, you just delete him/her from the group and they no longer have permissions. Otherwise, you need to manually delete all the permissions from the user and manually add those same permissions to the new user. You can add a User to as many groups as you wish, with each Group having different permissions.

When an Invited User accepts the invitation, s/he is automatically added as a Jira-Core-User, unless you have already placed them in the Jira-administrator group.

The Users, Roles, and Groups chapter provides more information on these topics.

The next two items in the sidebar are **Jira User Server** and **User Directories,** and are meant for the Jira **System Administrator.**

Latest Upgrade report

Click on the **Latest upgrade report** tab to see, well, the Latest upgrade report for Jira 8.7.1. The opened page shows what was upgraded and when the upgrade took place. If you need to know more details, click on the Show details links.

System

Click on **System**, and the **Jira General Configuration** page will be open:

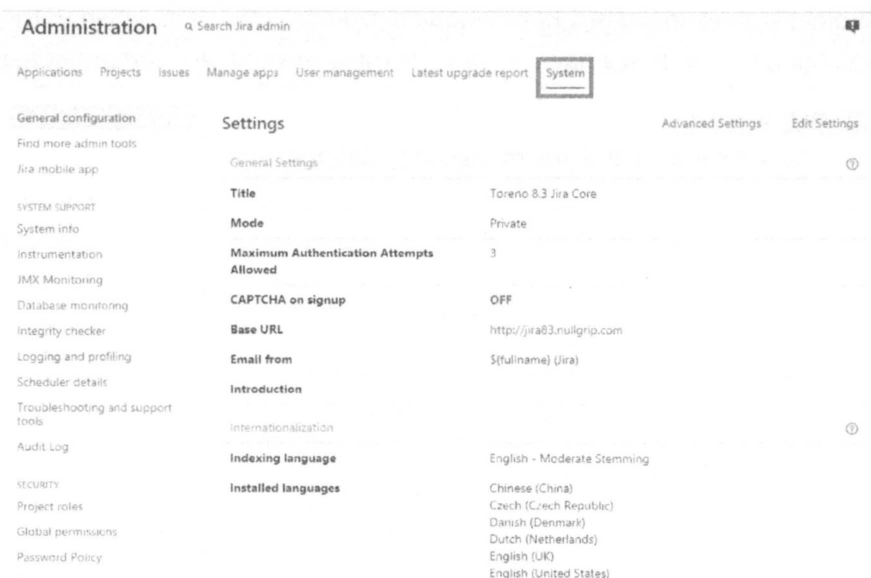

Much of this page deals with stuff needed to make Jira work as a program, interact with other programs, databases, and email systems. These things will be administered by the Jira System Administrator, so don't touch them. However, as you become more experienced with Jira, you, as a Jira Administrator, will use this page to alter the look and feel of Jira Core (color schemes, page layouts, etc.), as well as set security levels for your project roles and groups.

Profile

The last item on the menu bar is all about you. This is your **Profile** menu. You should see a small 'photo' image with a grey head outline. If you hover the mouse arrow over the image you should see your User name show up.

The **Profile** menu has four sections.

Profile

The first item on the Profile menu is, appropriately enough, the **Profile** link. Clicking on it will bring you to the **User's Profile.**

The right side of the view contains your Activity Stream. This area lists the Jira issues and projects with which you are involved. You can filter your activity by choosing from the options in the **Filter** drop-down button in the upper right up corner. This is a helpful feature if you are dealing with many issues and/or projects.

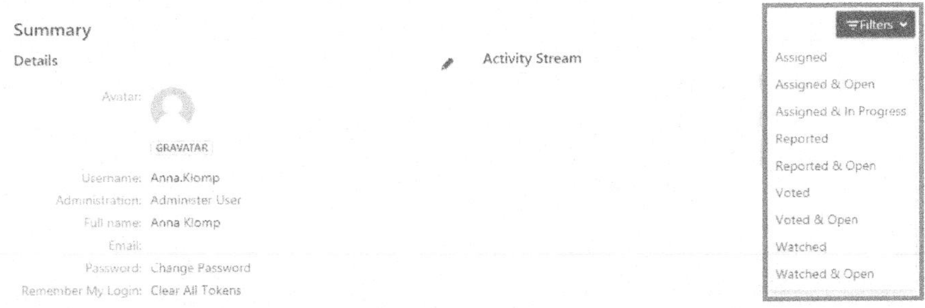

The left side of the view contains a **Summary** of your Personal **Profile Details** and **Preferences**. You can edit your Profile Details and Preferences by clicking on the little pencil icon located to the right of each heading.

Atlassian Marketplace

If you recall, Atlassian is the parent company of Jira. This link takes you to the Manage apps section. Applications are just that, smaller products that perform specific Jira functions you can add to Jira. Jira has created a marketplace that provides one location for Jira third party vendors. Some apps are free, and most of the others are very reasonably priced.

In most cases Atlassian verifies that the product works with Jira Safely. This is not the same thing as saying the product has value. However, Atlassian does have a four-star rating system, where those who have downloaded the product can rate it for usefulness.

My Jira Home

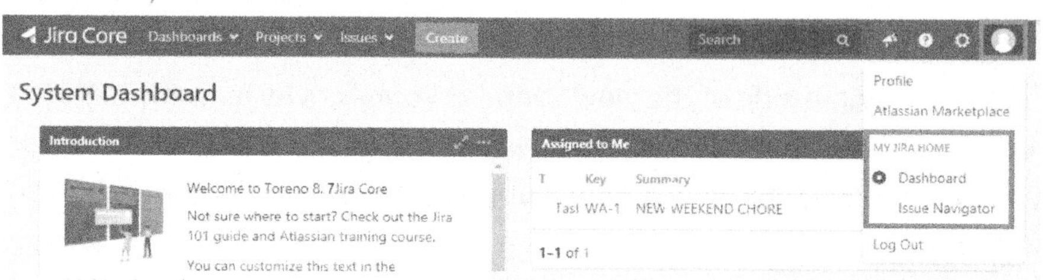

Under My Jira HOME you will typically see two items: **Dashboard** and **Issue Navigator**. Clicking on these links will bring you to the same Dashboard and Issue Navigator views we saw earlier when we used the Main menu bar > Dashboards and Main menu bar > Issues approaches.

The **System Dashboard** is the default **main view** you will see when you first log on.

On the System Dashboard you see the issues **Assigned** to you; or, you could be a very lucky and find a kindly message that you do not have any. You can also skim the **Your Company** activity stream there.

Instead of opening the Dashboard you can get “straight to the point” by clicking on the **Issue Navigator** to see all issues you are permitted to see. You can then filter them to narrow your search and to work with your issues. We have already covered this topic a little earlier; so, we won’t repeat ourselves here.

Log Out

This is the final menu item and appropriately enough you use it to Log Out of the program.

Chapter 3 – Jira Core Projects

CHAPTER OBJECTIVES

By the end of this chapter you will be able to navigate the various Project views, understand their parts, and make some minor changes.

Additionally, you will understand the differences between the Jira Core Project types.

THE PROJECT NAVIGATION VIEW

Jira has a number of views dedicated to managing a project or projects. In this section we will take a closer look at the Project Navigation view and its constituents. Why don't we start with a project we already know.

As you recall, in Chapter 1 you created a Task management project called Weekend Activities. Let's use that project as the basis for our tour.

On the main Menu Bar Select Projects > Weekend Activities (WA):

You should now be seeing the **Project Navigation** view. The view has two parts: Project Navigation Sidebar and Main View (the Open Issues you see in the image above).

PROJECT NAVIGATION SIDEBAR

The Project Navigation Sidebar is located on the left side of the Project Navigation view:

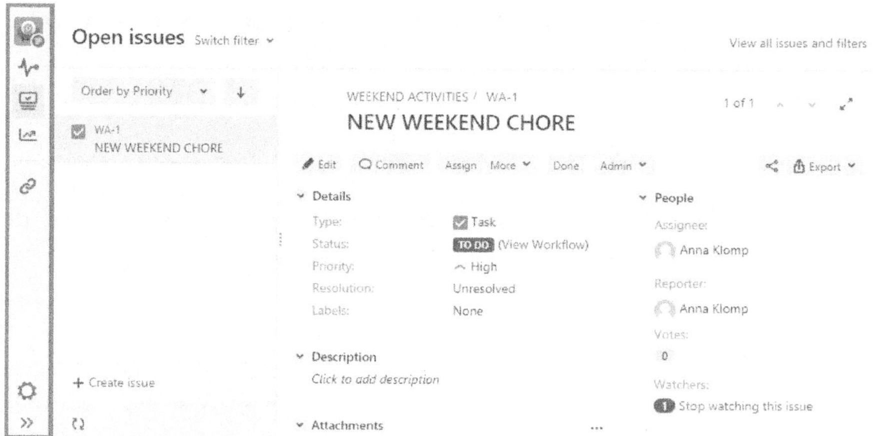

On the bottom right of the sidebar you will see two right facing chevrons (arrows). That is **Expand/Collapse sidebar** button:

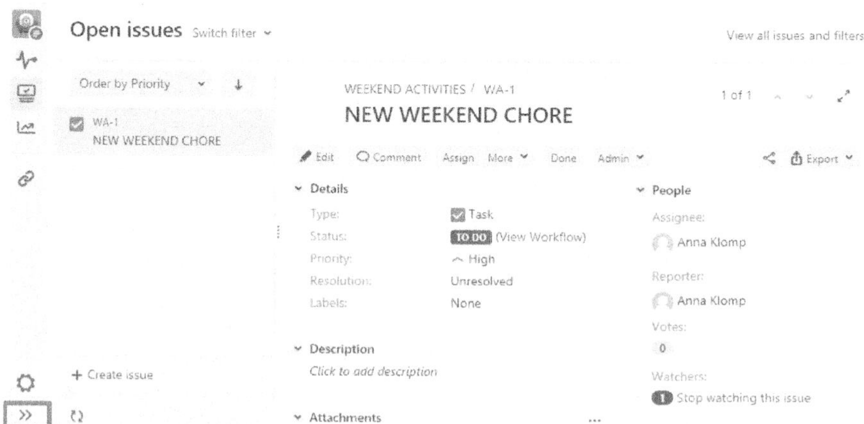

Click on this chevrons button to expand the sidebar:

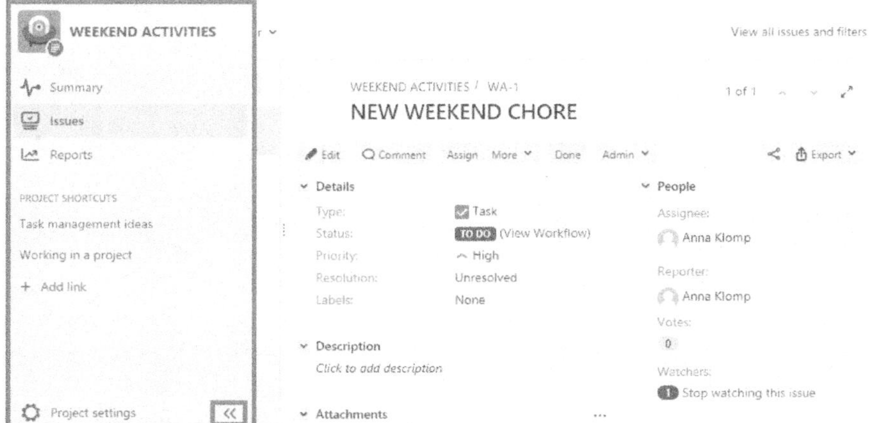

To hide the sidebar, click again on this arrow - button. When collapsed, it occupies a very small space and the chevrons change from left facing to right facing (Expand sidebar).

If you have a lot of detail on the Project Navigation view, it is sometimes convenient to hide the sidebar.

The Project Navigation sidebar has at least five options: **Summary, Issues, Reports, Project Shortcuts,** and **Project settings.**

SUMMARY

Clicking the **Summary** link in the Project Navigation sidebar will open the Project Activity view, which lists the most recent things done with the project by the project lead or authorized users. The first item on the list is the most recent.

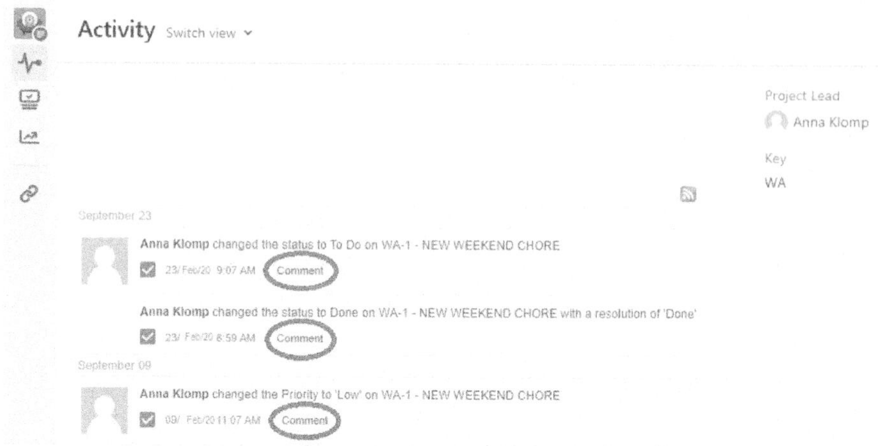

A nice helpful feature to these activity listings is the **Comment** link. Clicking on this link will open a Comment field where you may add your own comment. For example, let's say a project lead assigns you to a new task, starting this Monday. You can, politely, comment that you will be on vacation starting Monday for three weeks and will not be able to accept this kind invitation. Be aware that comments added are visible to everyone on the project; so, tact and diplomacy are always recommended when using the comments field.

On the right side of the Activity view you will find the **Project Lead** name, people who were **most active last week**, and the **KEY** of the project.

If you want to see detailed **Statistics** about your project, click on the **Switch view** down arrow and select, well, Statistics:

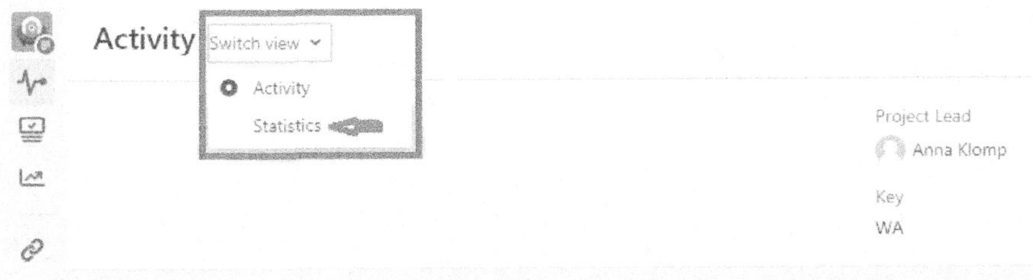

The **Statistics** view shows you how many issues are **unresolved by Priority** and **by Assignee, Status Summary, etc.**

You can drill-down into those issues for further investigation by clicking on the **View Issues** link under each issue's category.

There are also a number of additional filter links below the Statistic title:

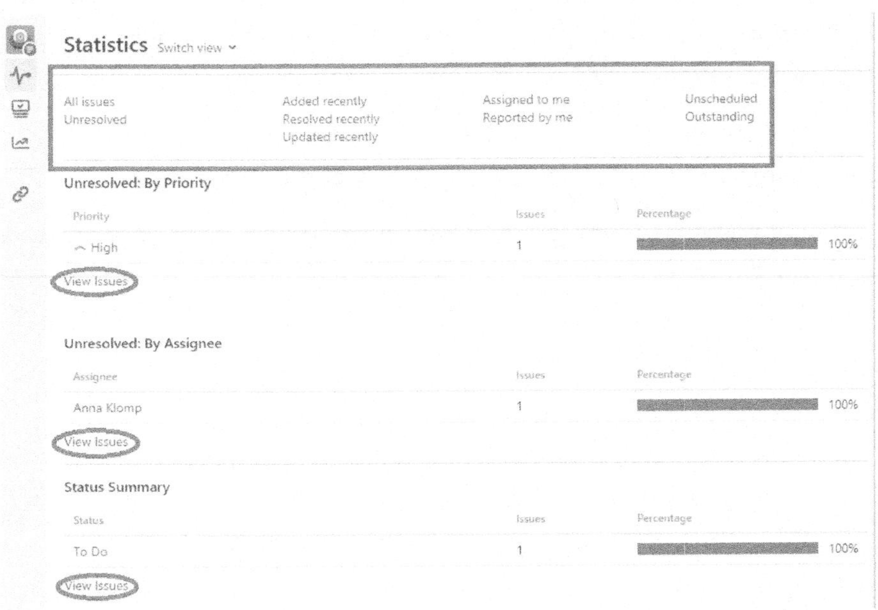

ISSUES

On the Project Navigation Sidebar Select **Issues:**

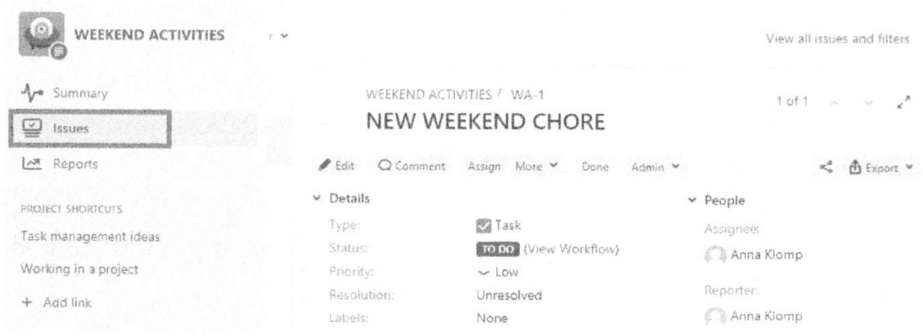

The **Issues** view looks similar to the **Search for Issue** view, but instead of listing **all** issues it shows only those issues associated with the project. For example, since we opened *Weekend Activities* project, we will see only *Weekend Activities* issues. Right now, we have only one issue, and it is *New Weekend Chore WA-1* (see image above).

While there are a number of ways of seeing issues, I like this particular view as it allows me to focus on a **particular project**.

If you have many issues in your project the **Switch filter** link can help you sort them:

To view All issues and filters in any projects click on **View all issues and filters** link:

If you wish to open an issue in the full screen, click the expand issue button:

Reports

Reports gives you access to a number of predefined reports.

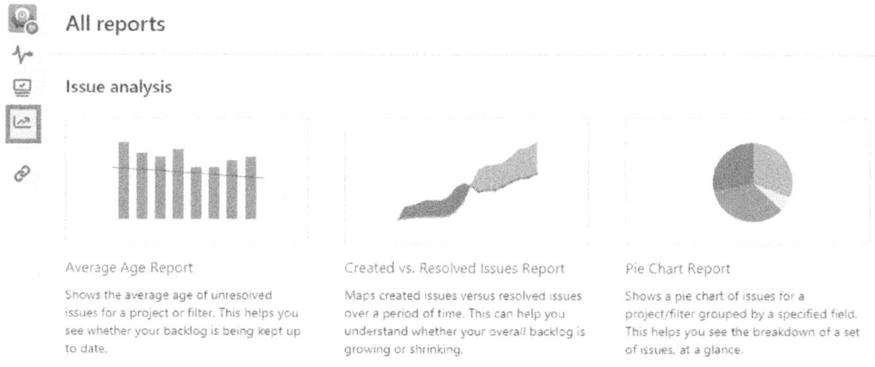

Clicking on any of these reports sends you to a 'Configure' page where you can modify the design of that report to some degree. For example, the Average Age Report shows the average age of your project's unresolved issues. You can specify the period (Hourly, Daily, Weekly, Monthly, Quarterly, Yearly) as well as the number of days to be shown in the graph.

To answer your next question, Jira does give you the ability to create your own reports based on Jira elements (issues, projects, users, issue types, etc.). However, if you want to create reports based on custom fields you have created, that is more challenging. Here is where I will insert a shameless promotion and ask you to contact us at Toreno

Information Solutions where we can help you with your customized reporting.

Additional Links

You may have additional links in this section of the sidebar depending on your software set up, installed Jira Apps, and some other conditions. For example, if your project has gone through a number of Versions (i.e. enhancements or changes), then you will also see a link to a Versions view.

Project Shortcuts

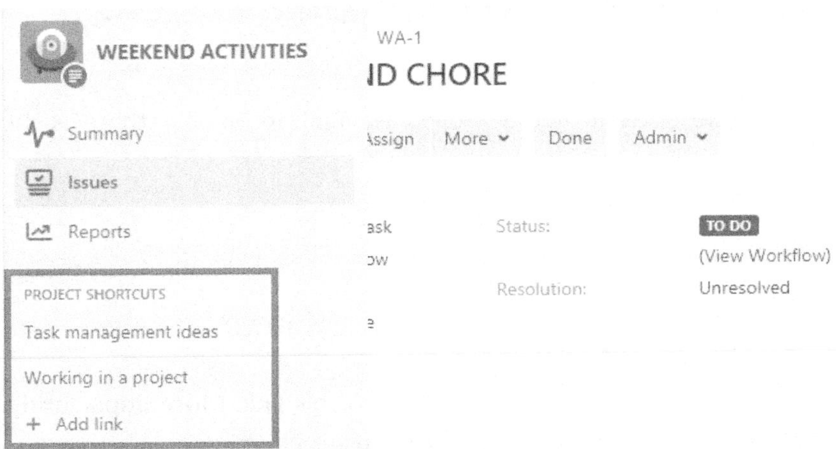

Next item on the Project Navigation sidebar is **Project Shortcuts**. As a default, two links are shown: **Task management ideas** and **Working in a project**. Both of them will send you to the **Atlassian Documentation** area.

Task management ideas

This link will open the Jira Core Support Documentation page where you can read more about a task management project template: how to work with and customize it.

Working in a project

On clicking the "Working in a project" link you will land on the eponymous Jira Core Support Documentation page. Here you will find Atlassian's definition of a **project**, learn more about how to view a project, work with issues, search for issues, manage your user profile, do reporting, add and customize gadgets, and configure dashboards. The link Using Jira on a mobile device is also provided on this page.

+ Add link

You can add a link to useful information for your team. For example, if your project is associated with another project, you can add the link to the other project in the Add Link pop up. Or, you might want to add a link to a training document for the project.

Project Settings

On the bottom of the Project Navigation Sidebar there is the Project settings link:

As a Jira Admin you have access to this link. More importantly, this is the link the Jira Project Admins will use to manage their project.

Clicking Project settings carries you to a view displaying the various puzzle pieces that make your project work and that you can modify or configure.

Project Settings View

Click On The Project settings Link To Open that Project Settings view:

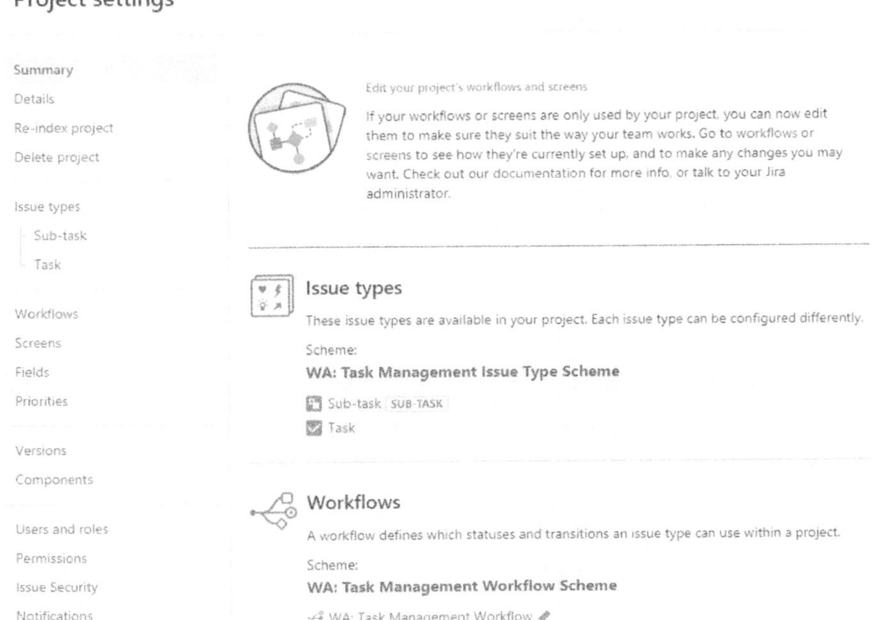

When creating a project, I cannot think of any single area in Jira more important than the **Project Settings Summary**. I must admit, when I started to build my first project in Jira it took me a while to realize the essential role this view plays. It should be the number one view you constantly visit when developing your project.

Why? First, it provides the necessary information about the Jira elements (issue types, workflows, screens, fields, priorities, project's components, users and roles, permissions and notifications, etc.) you are using in this particular project; and second, it acts as a portal to each of those elements in the event you want to make changes.

These various Jira elements, which I call the puzzle pieces, are described in more detail in the next Chapters.

The Project Settings view is divided into two segments: Project Settings sidebar and Main area.

Project Settings sidebar

The Project Settings sidebar lists all the elements that make up your project, including: Issue Types, Workflows, Screens, Fields, Priorities, Users and Roles, Permissions, Notifications, etc. Clicking on any of these links brings you to a related view containing more details about that element and gives you the ability to make changes.

Project Settings: Summary

The main view of the Project Settings **Summary** is similar to the sidebar, but provides, well, a short summary of each element listed on the Summary sidebar:

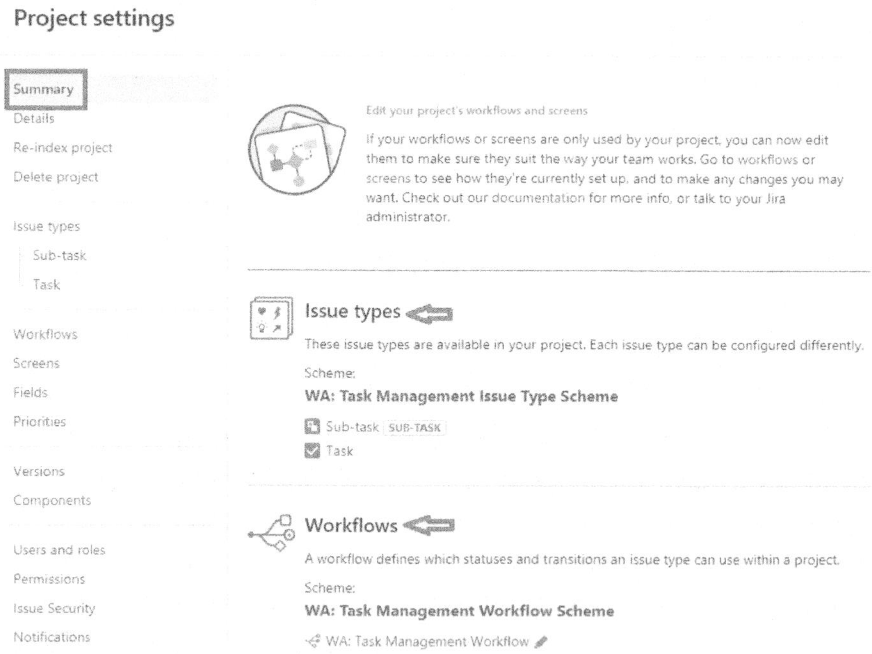

For example, instead of a simple Workflows link it shows the Workflow scheme and workflows associated with the project. Again, clicking on any of the links brings you to the related view where you can make changes.

Project Settings: Details

Exercise: View Project's Details

1. Click on **Details** on the Project settings sidebar:

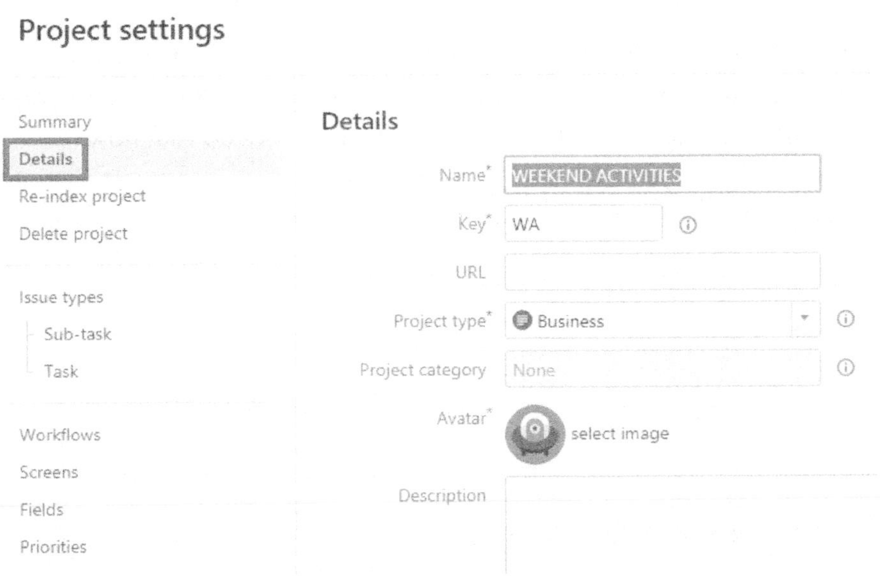

Project settings

Summary
Details
Re-index project
Delete project
Issue types
Sub-task
Task
Workflows
Screens
Fields
Priorities

Details

Name* WEEKEND ACTIVITIES
Key* WA
URL
Project type* Business
Project category None
Avatar* select image
Description

Here you can edit the project. For example, you can change the name of the project. Changing the **Project name** will NOT change the **Key**. If you really want to change the project key (**not recommended**), click on the Information icon right beside the Key field and press the "Learn more about project keys" link.

You can change your **URL** if you are so inclined.

You can change **Project type** to a *Software project* type or *Service Desk project* type, assuming you have the license to do so. Why would you want to change project type? Well, first, there may be workflows available in these other project types that are not available in the

Business project type. Second, it will give you access to other functions not possible in Business. For example, you can manage Agile and Epics in a Software project type, or the Service Desk shell in a Service Desk project type (don't worry if you don't know what I am referring to (Agile or Service Desk), as it's not important for this book).

You can also change the **Project category**. If you have not created yet any, click on the Information icon right beside the Project category field and click the "Add a new project category" link.

You can also change your Project **Avatar**. I personally like to use unique avatars for each project, as this makes it a little easier to keep track of them and their related issues. Why don't we do that now.

2. CLICK ON **SELECT IMAGE** LINK:

Click to edit this avatar

Upload a new avatar

Choose File No file chosen

Close

You have a couple of options: you can select from a predefined set of icons, or you can browse your files for an image you like. As Weekend Activities is generally a repeating set of activities, let's select the circular arrows icon. As soon as you click on the icon you are brought back to the **Details** area and your new icon should be showing.

The final area is the **Description** field.

3. TYPE IN SOMETHING LIKE "WELCOME TO WEEKEND ACTIVITIES. THIS PROJECT LISTS THE CHORES AND RECREATIONAL ACTIVITIES FOR THIS UPCOMING WEEKEND."

The description area will take wiki markup (notice the two little icons below the description text field). It allows you to make font and formatting changes in the description area (such as adding hyperlinks), but let's stay away from that right now.

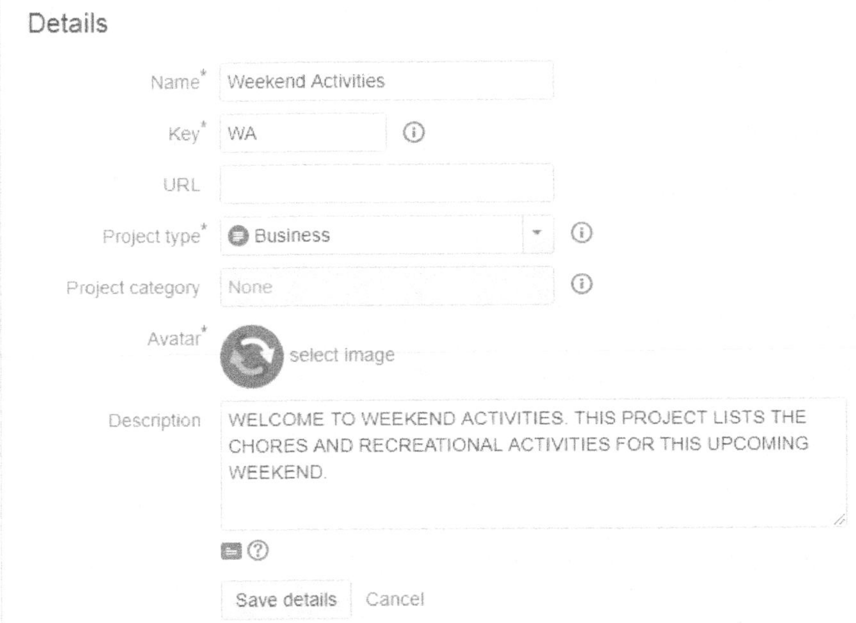

4. IF YOU LIKE THE CHANGES, CLICK **SAVE DETAILS**.

Project Settings: Re-index project

The **Re-index Project** option is used to "clean up", or up-date the software database, the project, and its collaboration with other Jira elements after you make any major changes in the Project, for example after editing the KEY of the project.

Project Settings: Delete project

To Delete a Project, choose the **Delete Project** option.

View All Projects

There are two ways of viewing your list of projects depending on what you want to do and what **Permissions** you have.

User View of Projects

On the menu bar select **Projects > View All Projects**:

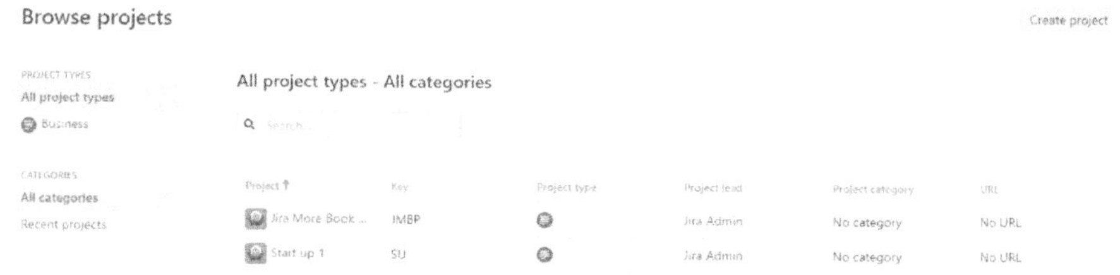

This is the **Browse Projects** view. If you are a Jira licensed User, you will see a list of **All Project Types – All Categories** projects with which you have permission to see and browse. Clicking on any of the project names will open up that particular project.

Jira Administrators' View of Projects

Exercise: View Projects

1. On the Main Menu Bar select **Jira Administration** (the Cog Wheel) > **Projects**

This **Administration Project List** is similar to the **Browse Projects** view but with one major difference. Because it is meant for those with Administrator access, it includes an **Actions** (the last) column where the Jira Administrator or Project Administrator can **Edit** or **Delete** the project.

The **Create Project** button on the upper right corner of the Project List works the same as **Create Project** from the Browse Projects view.

2. WHILE STILL IN THE ADMINISTRATION PROJECT LIST, CLICK ON THE **PROJECT CATEGORIES** LINK IN THE SIDEBAR:

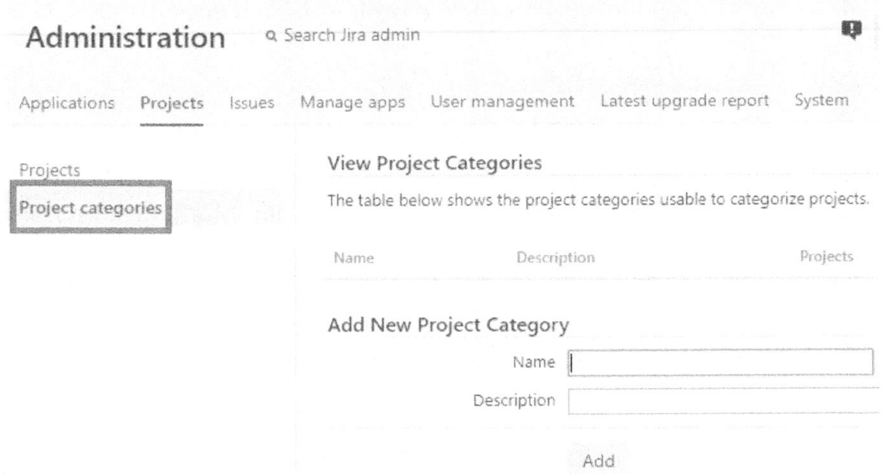

The **Project Categories** view allows you to create new project categories. Why do you need it? In some cases, you may have hundreds of projects within your organization, each one representing some sort of issue or group of issues. Many of these projects may belong to particular departments or may belong to cross functional process such as Supply Chain or Marketing. Categorizing makes it easier to associate and keep track of your projects.

Which Project Type to Select

As you remember, when you clicked on the **Create Project** from the Projects on the main menu bar, you were taken to the **Create project** wizard pop-up, where you were asked to select from one of three Business project type options: **Project management, Process management**, or **Task management.** Your choice will depend on the complexity of the tasks within your project. The more complex the tasks, the more complex is the 'workflow' associated with the project. A workflow is simply a representation of the steps a user goes through to complete a task.

Let's take a look at these three options more closely.

Task Management

Let's say you want to create a project that deals with simple action items or simple To Do activities such as: Send file to Barry, Sign approval form, Check with Dave on Option B, Phone Mom, Pick up Milk on the Way Home.

Each of these activities are 'checklist' items. They tend to be completed very quickly. In these cases, all you need is a workflow that has two steps or statuses: To Do and Done.

Project Management

Next is the Project Management option. Where the Task Management project type works well with simple, quick checklist tasks, Project Management works best with straightforward tasks that need a significant amount of time to complete. Examples might be: ship product from China to USA, grow a crop of corn, pour concrete for a building foundation. If you have tasks where a supervisor or customer may phone you up a few times and ask, "Is it done yet?", then those are eligible to be project management type tasks. To manage these types of tasks, the Project Management project type has a three-status workflow: To Do, In Progress, and Done.

Process Management

The Process Management project type is designed for tasks or processes that have an approval step. As seen in the image below, the steps have a number of options available for the user to select, based on conditions within the task or process. For example, while a task is 'In Progress' it can either be sent to a review status or the task can be cancelled.

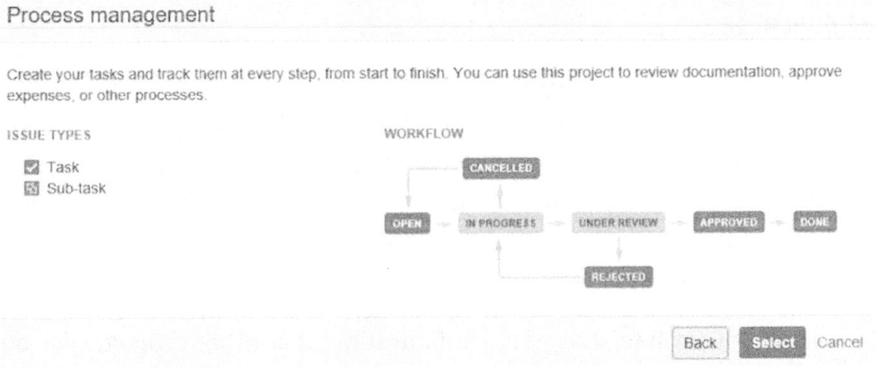

A COUPLE MORE THINGS

Any business project type you select (Task, Project, or Process management) requires a workflow. Atlassian supplies you with additional workflow templates. You can look at them by clicking on **View Marketplace Workflows** link. Or, you can create your own. But for right now, experimenting with Workflows is not recommended.

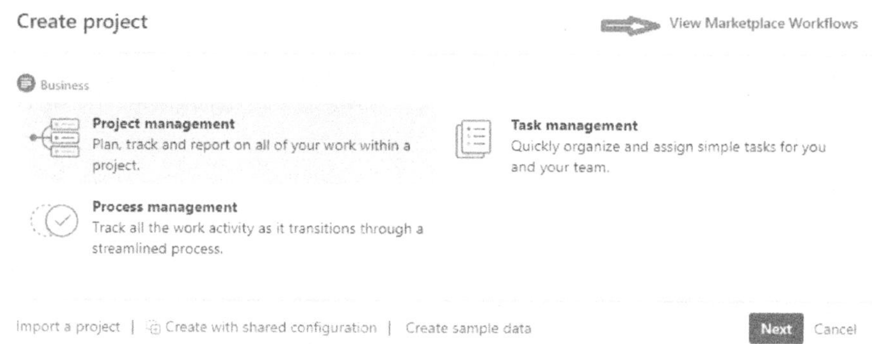

On the bottom of the Create project pop-up there are three more links: **Import a project, Create with shared configuration**, and **Create sample data**.

Clicking on the **Import a project** link will bring you to the Jira import wizard allowing you to import your project from CSV, or Microsoft Excel, or other products. It is the same option as the **Import External Project** from Projects item on the main menu bar. However, as we mentioned earlier, to "import project" sounds easy, in reality you need some special technical skills to do it.

If you wish to share the configuration of another project, click on "Create with shared configuration" link and select a project. Atlassian notifies "**When a configuration is shared with several projects, it means that any changes made to the configuration will affect all the projects**".

What this really means is "Don't touch this unless you are an expert, and even then be careful." Enough said.

Create sample data link will open **Create project with sample data** pop up. This is really an example project and is quite helpful if you are starting out. Just follow the instructions.

Chapter 4 – The Jira Core Puzzle Pieces

CHAPTER OBJECTIVE

In this Chapter you will gain an understanding of the Jira Core elements (puzzle pieces) and their interaction.

THE NEED FOR CHANGE

In the previous chapters we demonstrated how to work with Jira Core Projects and Issues using the default settings. Indeed, it is recommended you continue to work with default settings until you develop a good working knowledge of the program and gain experience. As the saying goes, 'practice makes perfect'.

In this chapter we want to take a high-level overview of the various elements of Jira. They are **Issue Types, Workflows, Screens, Fields, Schemes, Roles, Permissions, Notifications**, etc. These elements (I call them the 'Puzzle Pieces') form the structure that makes Jira work. An understanding of these elements is necessary for the customization of any Jira project.

Like most of you, I started with the basic assumption that all I needed to do was create an Issue or Task and everything would be fine. And indeed, in many cases the default settings are good enough. Jira has done a really great job at making a 'Swiss Army Knife' that meets most requirements right out of the box. If you want to build a simple project where all you ask of a User is to mark an Issue as complete when it is done, then the Jira Core program with its prebuilt defaults will work fine for you. And often, that is all you need. Why over complicate things?

Yet, in today's business world where employees are asked to do more, in less time, there is a need to 'automate' and simplify wherever possible. For example, what happens if a User has a question related to her Issue? How can we help improve the Issue process if there is an approval step? What can we do to make the User's screen as simple and as useful as possible? How do we manage things if we need to reopen the Issue because of a quality control problem?

Sooner or later you will undoubtedly find that you need to modify your project, issues, screens, the fields on those screens, workflows, etc. These modifications can be categorized in two ways: Customization and Simplification.

Customization

Users will often ask for the creation of bespoke fields or screens tailored towards specific business requirements. For example, someone may need a custom field where a user can select from a list of options. This field needs to be created AND it needs to be placed on a specific screen. Additionally, users may ask for explicit project roles to be created. These roles will be given precise permissions as to what the user assigned to that new role can and cannot see and what s/he can and cannot change or edit. These are just a few examples of customization requests.

Simplification

When creating a standard, default Task Issue, Jira may include fields you don't need in your specific Jira project. Users often become confused as they are unsure what to do with those fields. As a Jira Administrator, or Project Administrator, one of your responsibilities is to create screens focused on a single type of user and include on that screen only those fields absolutely necessary for the user to complete his or her issue. That may mean simplifying a project by removing fields.

Customization and Simplification both have the same goal: to build explicit screens and fields for specific user roles based on the work that is to be performed. This is not a simple undertaking, and it explains why there are so many complex elements in Jira that must be addressed when bespoking the software.

Overview of The Jira Puzzle Pieces

If you have ever designed a process, you know that in addition to the *process* itself you must consider the *people* who will be involved, as well as the *technology* to be used (technology can be something as simple as a pencil or as complex as a Heavy Rocket). The interaction with People and Technology is essential to the successful implementation of any Process; and I believe Jira Core is the best software for managing this People, Process, Technology (PPT) interaction. We will cover these People, Process, Technology components: **Issue Types, Workflows, Screens, Fields, Permissions and Notifications, Users, Roles, and Groups** in more detail in the next five chapters.

The collaboration of customized screens, fields in the screens, workflows, and User roles (I collectively call them a 'process') is what makes Jira such a strong product.

The challenge is that a Jira process with all its puzzle piece elements is complex. And that's because it's very complicated to build a process in the first place, regardless of whether you are using Jira or not. You will immediately relate to this if you have ever sat in a meeting (or many meetings) trying to design, or improve, a work process. Like I said, it's very complicated, but we do it because the benefits are substantial.

Jira recommends, and I whole heartedly agree, that you design your process on paper and then build it in Jira. (If you need help in project and/or process design, don't hesitate to give our company – Toreno Information Solutions – a call.)

The diagram below indicates, to some degree, the complexity of a Jira Project:

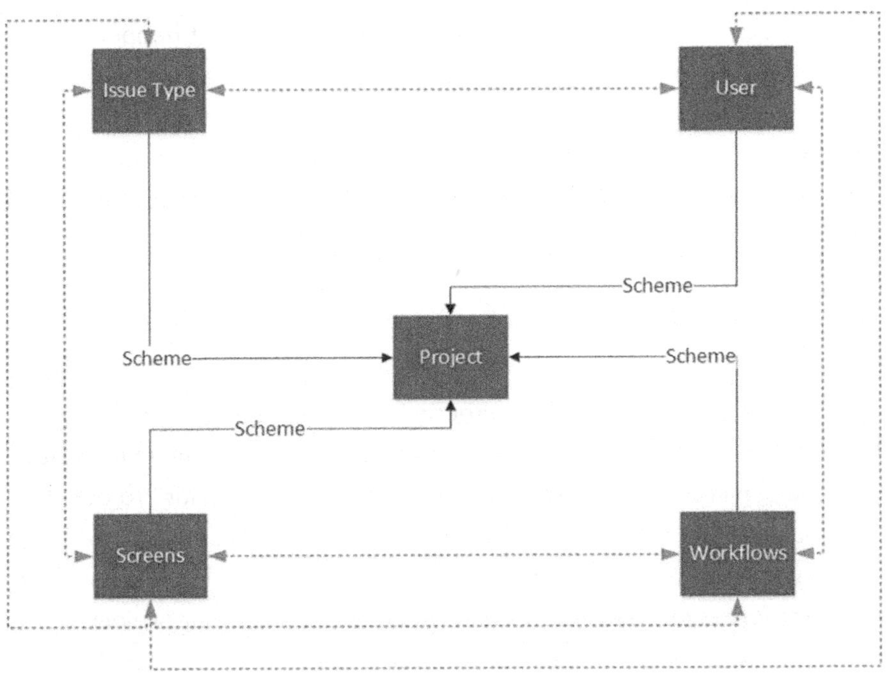

If you are going to modify a project, you need to consider things such as:

- what type of work (Issue Type) will be done, and what User's security permissions and job rules will you need to first put in place
- what Screens and Fields will the User need for the type of work to be done
- how will the work progress (Workflow) be presented in the Issue life cycle

When you customize any of these three things you also make significant changes to the program. For example, if you are going to modify one of the screens (**a screen is a group of fields**), you don't just change the default, you create a new screen with a new name. You do this because the default screen may still be in use on another project, or you may need that default screen somewhere else. What happens if you decide you need six screens for your project? You need to create six unique screens with unique names. All these modifications must to be recorded somewhere so the software knows *What* screens to use with *Which* Projects and *Where* in the process to make a specific screen available to a designated User.

SCHEMES

Once you create your screens how will Jira know that screen X belongs to project Y? That is the role of **Schemes**. To use an analogy, let's pretend San Francisco is a Screen, and Reno, Nevada, is your Project. How are you going to link San Francisco with Reno? You do so with Interstate 80, the highway that connects the two cities. A scheme is the connecting road. If there is no road, your screen won't work with your project; it's as simple as that. And notice, it is Interstate 80 that takes you from San Francisco to Reno. Not M1, which takes you to from London to Nottingham. Certainly not E26, which runs from Berlin to Hamburg. Just like you need to know the specific road to take to go from city to city, Jira also needs to know the same thing. This is why you are required to build roads (schemes) with unique names.

Often you must take more than one road to go from city A to City B. Such is occasionally the case with Jira. If I want to drive from Toronto, Canada to Miami, USA, I will take Highway 401 to the U.S. Border at Detroit Michigan. There I need to clear Customs, and then get on Interstate 75 which will take me to Miami. There are occasions in Jira where you need to take similar multiple roads, and these routes and actions (such as clearing the border) must all be rigorously defined and recorded, otherwise you end up in Fargo, North Dakota, or you don't get out of Toronto at all.

Schemes let Jira know which **Issue Types, Workflows, Screens, Fields, Permissions,** and **Notifications** work with your **Project**. Without schemes how would the software know to open your "Select my Weekend Activities" screen, or your "Make a Peanut Butter and Jam Sandwich" workflow?

There are a number of different schemes in a Jira Project. These are Issue Type Scheme, Screen Scheme, Issue Type Screen Scheme, Workflow Scheme, Field Configuration Scheme, Permissions Scheme, and Notification Scheme. Each tie an element to your project.

So far, we have been talking in theory about our roadmap. Let's look at it in reality. The diagram below shows a typical project structure. We have the elements (the cities) and the schemes (the connecting roads). While this diagram certainly isn't complete, it will give you very good idea of how all the Jira elements, the puzzle pieces, fit together.

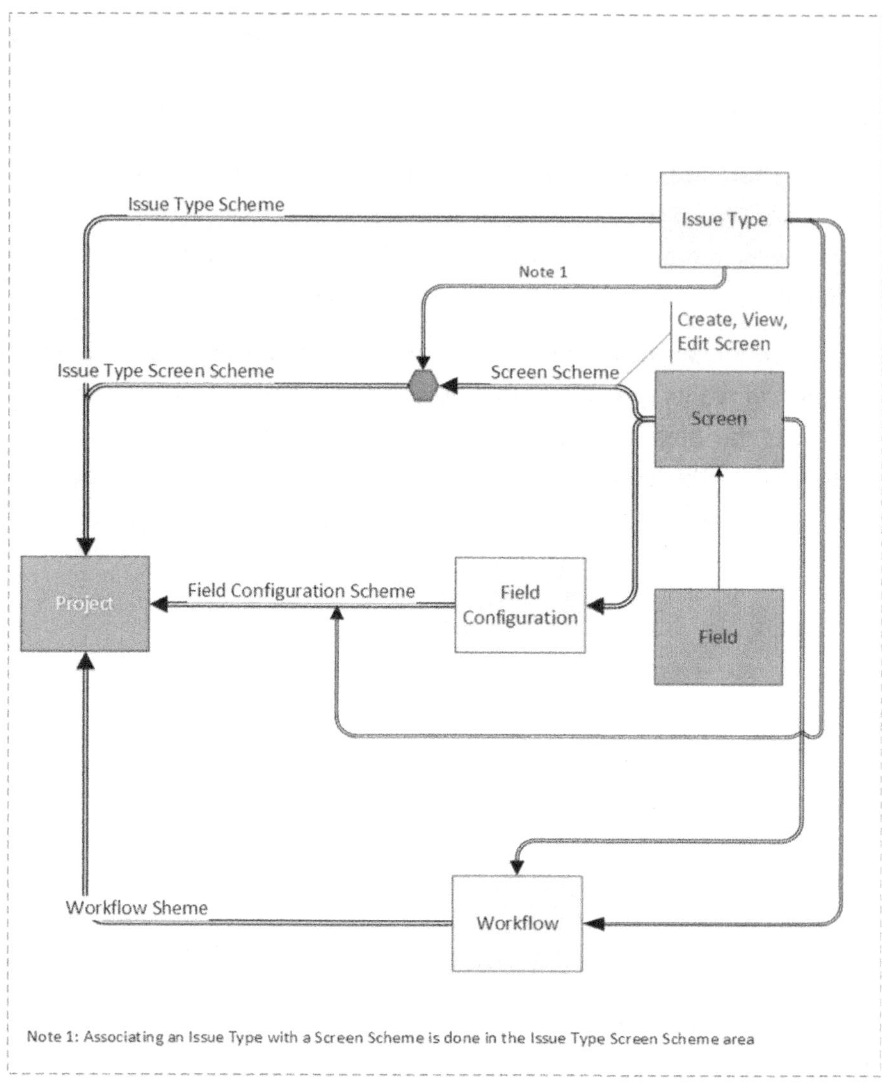

Before going into the details of all of these pieces let's take a brief detour and look one more time at the two major Jira components: **Project and Issues,** as they both play a fundamental role in the software.

Project, Issues, and Issue Types

Projects

Jira works first with **Projects**. Without a project you cannot create an Issue.

We typically think of a project as a unique 'something' that must be completed by a certain date. In many instances this is also true of a Jira Project. However, it is probably more accurate to think of a Jira Project as a file folder which contains a number of files (the Issues) needing completion. While I suppose it is technically possible to create one big project called, "Stuff We Need To Do", most people create Jira Projects based upon work themes or similar activities.

You can create projects manually, or you can import projects from other sources.

Issues

In Jira, an Issue is a piece of work to be completed. It may be easier to think of an Issue as a task. It's as simple and as complex as that. An Issue can stand alone, or it can have Sub-tasks associated with it. Sub-tasks cannot have their own Sub-tasks. In other words, Issues can only contain two levels: Task and Sub-tasks.

Issues can also be linked or associated with other Issues, either in the existing project or with other projects.

Just as a Process requires People, and Technology, Issues require the same People-Process-Technology components in order to work. These can be categorized as: **Issue Types** and **Workflows** (the Process), **Screens** and **Fields** (the Technology), and **Users** (the People).

Issue Types

Most of us tend to categorize work. We may have Action Items, To Do lists, Approval tasks, or process tasks such as Marketing, Accounts

Payable, Receiving, Repair, Delivery, etc. We categorize them because the work process, or effort required, in each of these categories is similar.

Jira calls each of these categories an **Issue Type**. An Issue Type may represent a very simple single-operation 30-second task, or a complicated work type that can require a number of steps and take a month or more to complete. Regardless, an Issue Type is something most of us would recognize as a single deliverable.

Previous versions of Jira had up to 20 different Issue Types including: Issue, Action Item, Task, Sub-task, Bug, Improvement, etc. Many of these are so similar that Administrators were often confused as to which to pick. Jira Core has simplified things by making only two default Issue Types: Task and Sub-task. This was done with the assumption that most business teams will want to build custom Issue Types that match the team's existing work processes and terminology. You may however see three additional Issue Types in your Jira Core package: Epic, Story, and Bug. These are designed for use with the Jira Software program: so, just ignore them.

How the Three Work Together

When you first create an issue, you will notice the two fields at the top of the Create Issue pop up. These two fields ask you to select the Project and Issue Type for this issue. Many folks skip over these two fields rather quickly and don't understand the full importance of them. Here's **why they are important**: when you select the Project and Issue Type, you also (behind the scenes) select ALL the following:

- Users who are authorized to view, edit, and work with the issue
- Screens and Fields the Users will see and use
- Workflow steps the process will take
- Rules the Issue will follow

If, when creating an Issue, you didn't select a Project or Issue Type, the software wouldn't know what to provide you for that Issue. It's as simple and as complicated as that.

Chapter 5 – Jira Core Issue Types

CHAPTER OBJECTIVES

In this Chapter you will:

- **gain a deeper understanding of Issue Types, Issue Type Schemes, and Sub-Task Issue Types**
- **create your first Issue Type and Issue Type Scheme**
- **Learn about the default Priority flags, creating your own flags, and creating Priority schemes.**

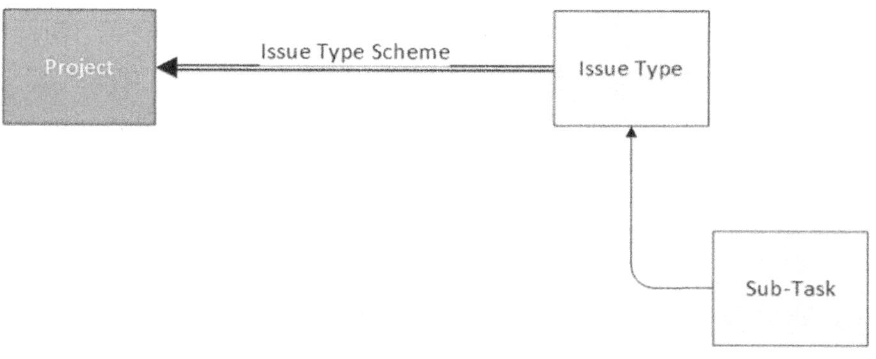

ISSUE TYPES AND SCHEMES

ISSUE TYPES

An **Issue Type** is the category of work to be performed. It acts as a linchpin to directly or indirectly connect all the Jira elements (users, workflows, screens, fields, etc.) required to complete an Issue. When you create an Issue within a Jira Core Project, regardless of Project Type you choose (Task Management project, Project Management, or Process Management), the default for the Issue Type is **Task**.

You can add (or create) your own Issue Type. You might want to make a "Design Package" Issue Type, or you might want to build a "Peanut Butter and Jam Sandwich" Issue Type. If you believe you are going to work with a specific Issue repeatedly, it is recommended you add your own Issue Type (if the defaults aren't exactly what you want).

Let's see how to add an Issue Type.

In the COG Administration drop-down list, click on Issues to open the Administration Issues view:

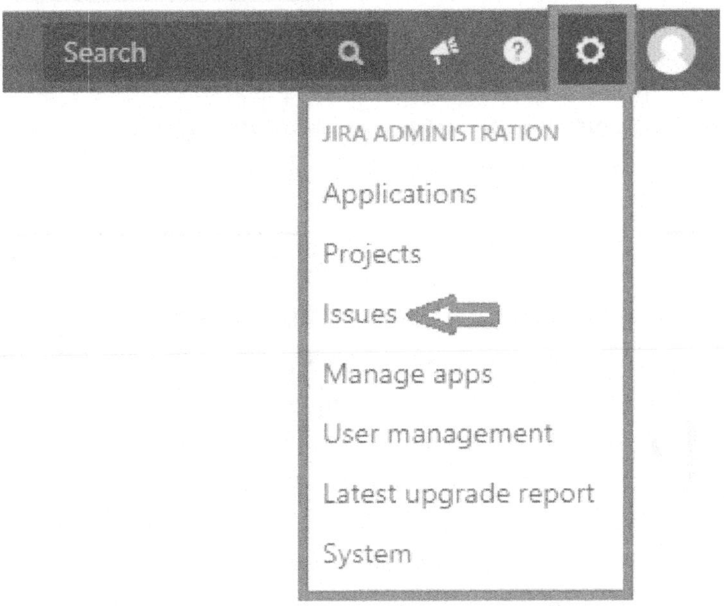

The Administration – Issues – Issue Types view contains four columns: **Name, Type, Related Scheme,** and **Actions:**

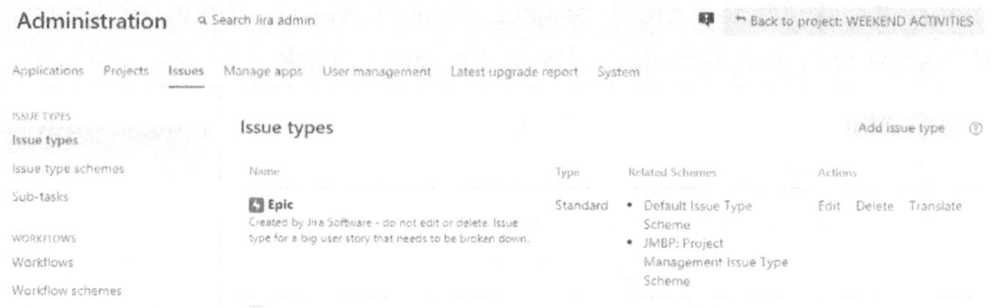

NAME

This column lists, in alphabetical order, the **Names** of the **Issue Types within your version of Jira Core**. It includes the Jira supplied Issue Types as well as any you added. The column also contains the Icon of the Issue type and the description.

TYPE

The next column indicates if it is a **Standard** or **Sub-task** Issue Type. This is very simple, if an Issue Type is not a Sub-task, then it is a Standard Issue Type.

RELATED (ISSUE TYPE) SCHEME

An **Issue Type Scheme** connects the **Issue Type** to your Project. Put another way, it controls which Issue Types a Project is permitted to use. Let's say you have 13 Issue Types available to you in your Jira Core program (the three default Issue Types supplied by Jira and 10 Issue Types created by your organization), but you want only four of these Issue Types associated with your project. You do this using the Issue Type Scheme. Basically, when you create an Issue Type Scheme, it asks you the name of the project and which Issue Types are permitted to be used in your project.

You associate an Issue Type to an Issue Type Scheme in the Issue Type Scheme screen. Issue Type Schemes is discussed in more detail later in this chapter.

Actions

The Actions column allows you to **Edit**, **Delete**, or **Translate** the Issue Type.

Edit

In the Edit Issue Type page, you can:

- Change the name of the **Issue Type**
- Change the **Description**
- Change the **Avatar**

Delete

An Issue Type can be deleted. But be aware, Jira may not allow you to delete an Issue Type if there are Issues, Workflows, Schemes, etc. associated with your Issue Type. You will need to delete or modify them first.

> CAUTION: It is highly recommended you NOT delete an Issue Type if it is associated with Workflow Scheme(s), Field Configuration Scheme(s), or Screen Scheme(s), as doing so will really, really, *really* mess up your project(s). If the Issue Type is associated with any of these schemes you will need to move them to a new Issue Type.

Translate

In the Issue Type Translation page, you can add a translation of your Issue Type Name and Description. Note that Jira will NOT do the translation for you. To use the translation function, you first select the language you are going to use from the drop-down list. At this point Jira supports 23 languages (or language dialects). Next, you enter the translated Name and Description in the translation fields.

What's the point, you may ask, if Jira doesn't actually translate the language for you? It's very simple. You may build a project where Users are located in different countries, thereby requiring you to work with multiple languages. That is why Jira provides the Translation function.

Exercise: Add new Issue Type

1. Navigate Main Menu Bar > [gear icon] > **Issues**
2. The **Administration Issue Types** view should be open. If not, on the Sidebar click on Issue Types
3. In the upper right corner of the Issue types view, click on the **Add Issue Type** button
4. In the Add Issue Type pop-up:
5. Enter a **Name** for the Issue Type (Required)
6. Enter a **Description** for the Issue Type
7. When asked to select the **Type** of Issue, choose *Standard Issue Type*
8. Click **Add**

Add Issue Type

Name*

Description

Type ◉ Standard Issue Type
○ Sub-Task Issue Type

Add Cancel

As you can see it is very easy to add an Issue Type. You simply fill in the name of your new Issue Type, add a Description and select whether it is a Standard or Sub-Task Issue Type.

Please note, if you are going to add an **Issue Type, think carefully about the Name**, especially if you believe you will need a lot of custom Issue Types. It is very easy to get lost in a sea of Issue Types. The majority Issue Types belong to specific projects; so, when I create Issue Types for my projects, I first type the title, or initials, of the Project and then a unique Issue Type name. After that I try to find a unique Icon I can easily mentally associate with an Issue Type and Project. In this approach, all the Issue Types for a particular Project are kept together in the list of Issue Type names (remember they are shown in alphabetical order). For example, if I create Issue Types for a specific retail project, I add a shopping cart icon for all my Issue Types relating to that project, and I start the name of the Issue Type with the initials of the Project. I strongly recommend you develop your own method for organizing your Issue Types.

Try to do it by yourself in the exercise below.

Exercise: Create new Project and Issue Type

In this exercise you will:

- Create a new **Project**
- Create a new **Issue Type** for the new project

1. Navigate to Main Menu Bar > **Projects**
2. Select **Create Project** from the **Projects** Menu
3. In the Create Project pop-up, click on **Task management**
4. Click on **Next**
5. In the **Task management** Diagram pop-up, click on **Select**
6. In the **Task management** pop-up, enter '*Shopping List*' in the **Name** field
7. Enter your Name in the **Project Lead** Field (if it is not already there)

8. CLICK ON **SUBMIT**

You have now created a new project named *SHOPPING LIST*. Let us now add a new Issue Type.

9. NAVIGATE MAIN MENU BAR > ⚙ > **ISSUES**
10. THE **ADMINISTRATION ISSUE TYPES** VIEW SHOULD BE OPEN. IF NOT, ON THE SIDEBAR CLICK ON ISSUE TYPES
11. CLICK ON **ADD ISSUE TYPE** BUTTON IN THE UPPER RIGHT CORNER OF THE ADMINISTRATION - ISSUE TYPES VIEW
12. IN THE **ADD ISSUE TYPE** POP-UP ENTER '*GROCERY SHOPPING LIST* ' IN THE **NAME** FIELD
13. ENTER 'ISSUE TYPE FOR THE GROCERY SHOPPING ACTIVITY' IN THE **DESCRIPTION** FIELD
14. ENSURE **STANDARD ISSUE TYPE** IS SELECTED IN THE **TYPE** FIELD
15. CLICK **ADD**

You should see your new Issue Type appear in the list of Issue Types.

ISSUE TYPE SCHEMES

The **Issue Type Scheme** defines a relationship between the Issue Type and a Project; in other words, it is used to link the **Issue Type(s)** to your **Project**. Just as importantly, it prevents all the other unnecessary Issue Types from interfering with your Project and causing confusion. If you are creating a project about weekend household tasks, why would you want an Issue Type that is meant for software **Bugs**?

Issue Type Schemes can be reused with different projects.

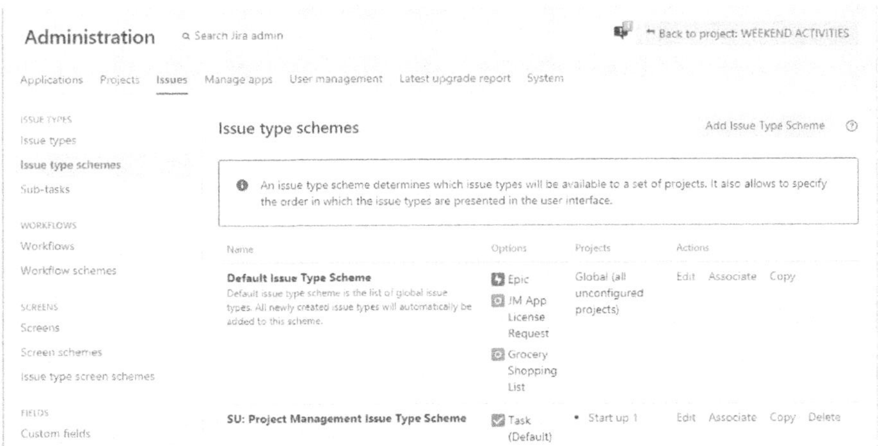

The Issue Type Schemes view contains four columns: **Name, Options**, **Projects**, and **Actions**.

Name

Here is the listing of all of your Issue Type Schemes. Unlike Issue Types, they are *not* listed alphabetically. The Default Issue Type Scheme is always first. After that all the other Issue Type Schemes are listed in no particular order.

Options

The Options column contains Issue Types (and their related Icon) associated with each Issue Type Scheme.

Projects

This column shows all Projects associated with an Issue Type Scheme.

You associate a Project to an Issue Type Scheme in the **Actions** column. You will learn how to do this a little later.

Actions

Finally, in the Actions column you can **Edit, Associate, Copy,** and **Delete** an Issue Type Screen Scheme.

Edit

CLICK ON THE EDIT LINK OF ANY ISSUE TYPE SCHEME (EXCEPT THE DEFAULT SCHEME) TO OPEN THE MODIFY ISSUE TYPE SCHEME VIEW:

Modify Issue Type Scheme — SL: Task Management Issue Type Scheme
+ Add issue type
USED BY 1 PROJECT

Scheme Name* SL: Task Management Issue Type Sch
Description
Default Issue Type Task

Change the order of the options by **dragging and dropping** the option into the desired order. Similarly, **drag and drop** the option from one list to the other to add or remove them.

Issue Types for Current Scheme
Remove all
Task
Sub-task (sub-task)

Available Issue Types
Add all
Epic
QA - Consumer Prod Production Run
QA - Non-commercial Prod Production Run
QA - Custom Order production run
USER Training - Time Tracking Issue Type
GROCERY SHOPPING LIST

Save Reset Cancel

In the **Modify Issue Type Scheme** view you can change the

- **Name** of your Issue Type Scheme
- **Description**
- **Default Issue Type** (i.e. the Issue Type which is shown first in the Issue Type drop down list when you create an Issue in a Project)
- **Issue Types for Current Scheme or Available Issues Types** by dragging and dropping or removing them from one column to the other.

CAUTION: It is highly, highly, and even more highly recommended you NOT edit the Default Scheme.

In addition, you can – except with the Default Scheme – add a new Issue Type through this page by clicking on the **Add Issue Type** button at the upper right corner.

Associate

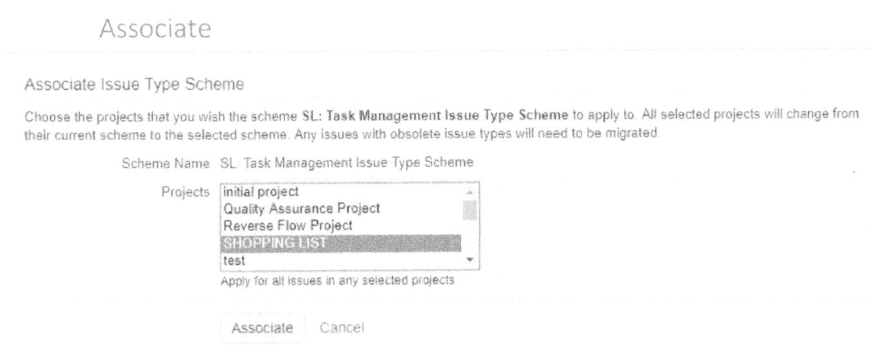

The **Associate Issue Type Scheme** page is where you link your **Issue Type Scheme** to your **Project**(s). You can associate an Issue Type Scheme with more than one project by holding down the **Control** button on your keyboard and selecting the projects you want to associate with your Issue Type.

Copy

Let's say you want to create a new Issue Type Scheme. It is often better to copy and rename an existing Issue Type Scheme if it has most of the features and Issue Types you are looking for in your new Scheme. You can then modify the copied scheme to meet your new needs, which is much easier than building a complete new Scheme.

Delete

Lastly, you can delete an Issue Type scheme (except the Default Scheme) by accessing the **Delete Issue Type Scheme** page. Before you can delete a scheme, you must first remove any Projects associated with the Issue Type scheme. You do so through the **Project(s)' Administration Issue Types** view by changing the current Issue Type Scheme to a different one.

Exercise: Create new Issue Type Scheme

In this exercise you will:

- create a new **Issue Type Scheme**
- associate an **Issue Type to** the **Issue Type Scheme**, and
- associate the **Issue Type Scheme to** the *Shopping List* **Project**

1. Navigate Main Menu Bar > ⚙ > **Issues**
2. In the Administration view, Select **Issue Type Schemes** on the sidebar
3. In the Issue Type Schemes view, click on **Add Issue Type Scheme** button
4. In the Add Issue Type Scheme view:
   i. Enter 'Grocery Shopping List Issue Type Scheme' in the **Scheme Name** Field
   ii. Enter 'Issue Type Scheme for the Shopping List Project' in the **Description** field
   iii. Skip Default Issue Type for now
   iv. If there are any Issue types in the **Issue Types for Current Scheme** field, click **Remove All** link
   v. Find *Grocery Shopping List* in the **Available Issue Types** list
   vi. Select and Drag *Grocery Shopping List* to the **Issue Types for Current Scheme** Field
   vii. In the **Default Issue Type** Field, Select *Grocery Shopping List* (It should be your only option)
5. Click on **Save** at the bottom of the view

You will be brought back to the **Issue type schemes** view. DO NOT navigate away from this view.

Now you will associate the Issue Type Scheme to your *Shopping List* project.

6. In the Issue Type schemes view, Scroll down to find your newly created Grocery Shopping List Issue Type Scheme

Notice there are **No projects** associated with this Issue Type Scheme

7. CLICK THE **ASSOCIATE** LINK IN THE ACTIONS COLUMN FOR THE GROCERY SHOPPING LIST ISSUE TYPE SCHEME
8. IN THE **ASSOCIATE ISSUE TYPE SCHEME** VIEW, GO TO THE **PROJECTS** DROP DOWN LIST AND SELECT THE *SHOPPING LIST* PROJECT YOU WISH TO ASSOCIATE WITH THE SCHEME
9. CLICK THE **ASSOCIATE** BUTTON:

Associate Issue Type Scheme

Choose the projects that you wish the scheme **GROCERY SHOPPING LIST ISSUE TYPE SCHEME** to apply to. All selected projects will change from their current scheme to the selected scheme. Any issues with obsolete issue types will need to be migrated.

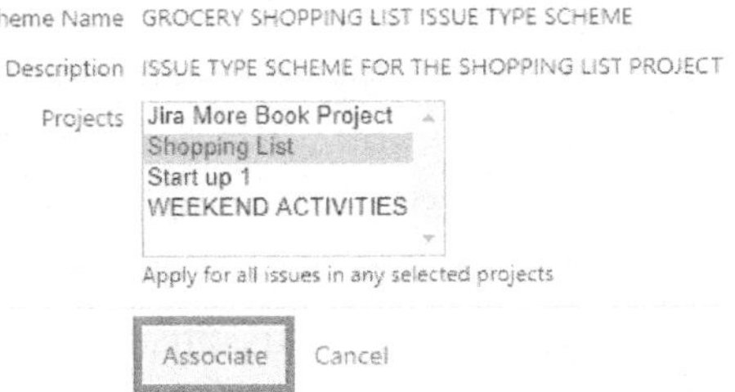

10. BACK ON **THE ISSUE TYPE SCHEMES** VIEW SCROLL DOWN TO MAKE SURE THAT THE *GROCERY SHOPPING LIST ISSUE TYPE SCHEME* IS NOW ASSOCIATED WITH THE *SHOPPING LIST* PROJECT:

GROCERY SHOPPING LIST ISSUE TYPE SCHEME'
ISSUE TYPE SCHEME FOR THE SHOPPING LIST PROJECT

GROCERY SHOPPING LIST (Default)

11. SELECT MAIN MENU BAR > **PROJECTS > SHOPPING LIST > PROJECT SETTINGS > ISSUE TYPES**, AND THERE YOU WILL ALSO SEE THE GROCERY SHOPPING LIST ISSUE TYPE SCHEME:

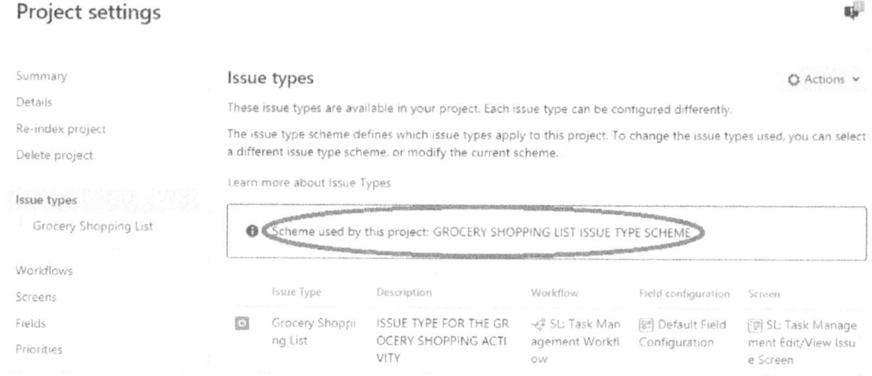

SUB-TASKS

Finally, Issue Types also allows you to create unique **Sub-task Issue Types**. If your Issue is complicated, you can sub-divide the Issue into a number of sub-tasks (but they will still be connected with the main Issue). One of the major benefits of sub-tasks is that you can assign different default Users, workflows, screens/fields, etc. to each of the sub-tasks. This is very helpful if your work process has a number of steps and involves a number of Users. On the other hand, you may find that using a workflow with built-in handoffs to different Users is a better solution. Jira has the flexibility to help you create a solution that works best for you.

Sub-tasks cannot have their own sub-tasks. But you can convert (promote) a Sub-task to an Issue, and then create additional sub-tasks.

Any Standard (i.e. not a Sub-task) Issue Type can have Sub-tasks.

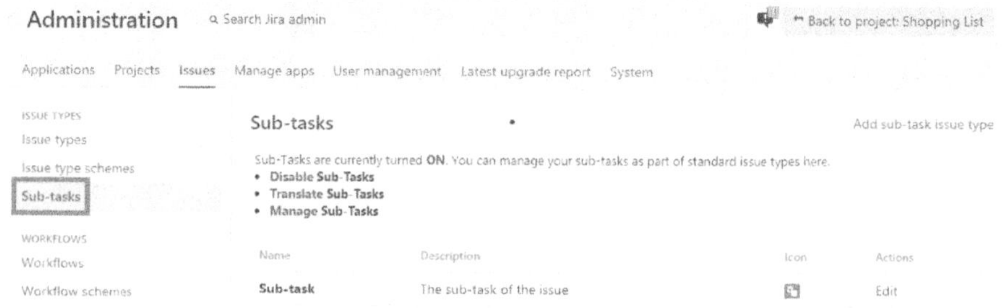

The Sub-tasks screen has four columns: **Name Description, Icon,** and **Actions**.

Name

Here is a list of your Sub-task types, listed in the order they were created.

You can add a new Sub-task by clicking the **Add Sub-Task Issue Type** button and entering a **Sub-task Name** and **Description**.

Description

As the name of this column states, here you will find the purpose of the Sub-task. I would recommend you be very specific when entering the reason for any newly created Sub-task. Often a Sub-task is created for very narrow business needs, and it is often easy to forget just why exactly it was created.

Icon

This column shows the Icon associated with the Sub-task. By now you know I am a big fan of using Icons to easily identify related elements in a project. I recommend you do the same with Sub-tasks.

Actions

In the Actions column you can Edit or Delete a Sub-task.

Edit

In the **Edit Sub-Task Issue Type** pop-up you may change the **Name**, **Description**, and **Avatar** of the Sub-task:

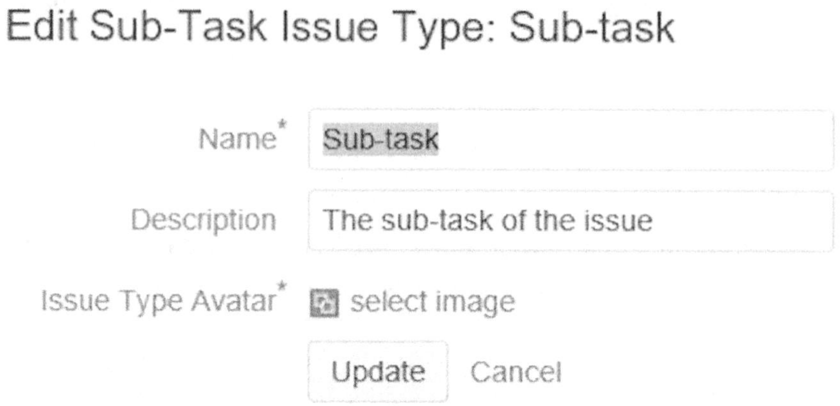

Edit Sub-Task Issue Type: Sub-task

Name* Sub-task

Description The sub-task of the issue

Issue Type Avatar* select image

Update Cancel

Delete

You may **Delete** any Sub-task Issue Types **not currently associated** with an Issue. The easiest way to Delete a Sub-task Issue Type **associated** with an active issue is to open the specific **Issue Details View** and delete the Issue from the **More** menu:

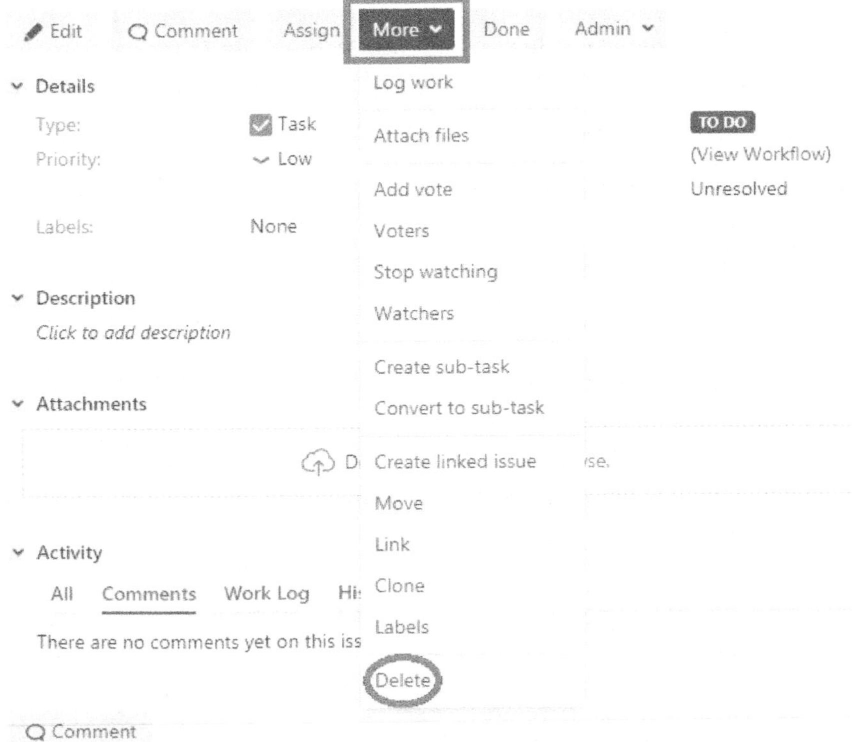

Other Sub-task functions

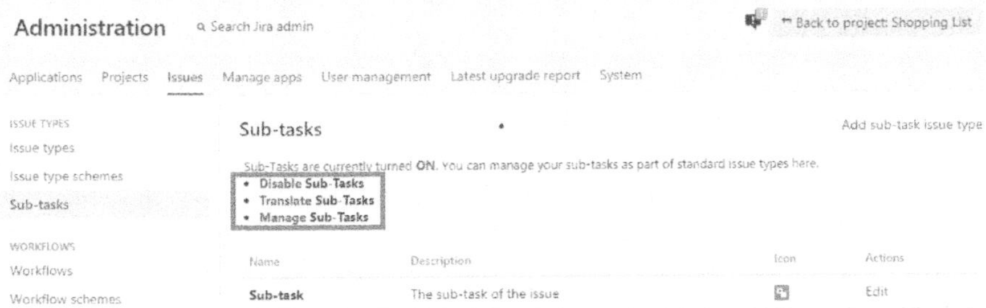

If you wish, you can also **Disable** all Sub-tasks. This function might be used to avoid confusion as it is sometimes difficult for beginners to differentiate between Tasks and Sub-tasks.

One of the great things I like about Jira is its **Translation** ability. Right now there are 23 languages/dialects supported. We covered translation earlier; so, let's move on.

You can also **Manage Sub-tasks.** Clicking on this link will bring you to the Administration – Issues – Issue Types view. Here you would manage the Sub-task in the same manner as managing Task Issue Types.

Issue Priorities

Priorities

You may, when creating an **Issue,** want to associate a **Priority** to that Issue. It's actually quite easy: when creating an Issue simply click on the **Priority field** and select the priority you want. The Priority Field is included in the standard Task Issue Type, and you can also add it to any custom screen you build. You can also change a priority in the **Issues Detail View** after an issue has been created.

If you don't like the default priority method, you can also change it.

Exercise: View Priorities

1. Navigate Main Menu Bar > > **Issues**
2. On the Administration - Issues View, select **Priorities** in the sidebar:

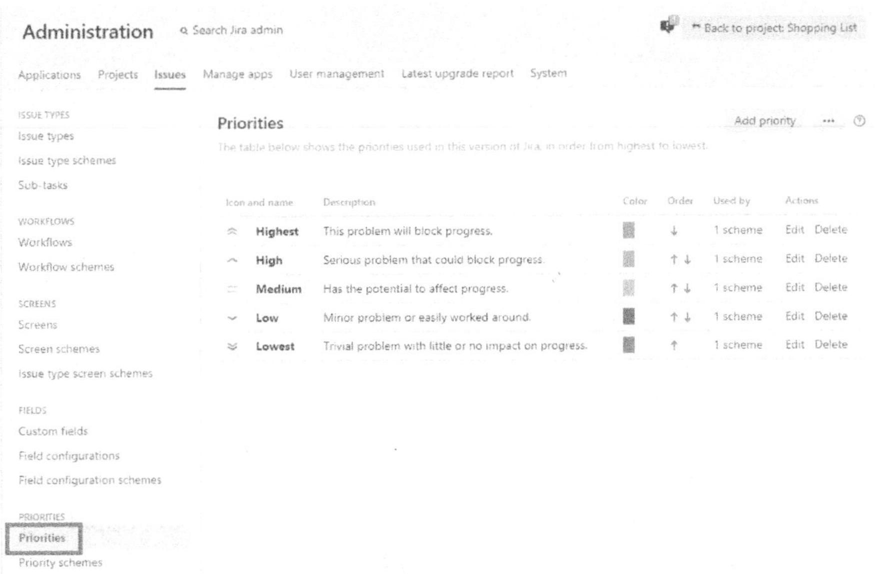

The **Priorities** view shows you all current **Priorities**. On this view you can edit, delete, **Add Priority** (the button at the upper right corner), translate priority, change its color and icon, etc. This is helpful if you have a specific **Priority** structure in your organization (as many do).

CAUTION: You can only assign a priority to the entire issue, not to a specific field in an issue.

PRIORITY SCHEMES

Jira Core gives you the ability to build and assign unique priority schemes to different projects.

EXERCISE: VIEW PRIORITY SCHEMES

1. NAVIGATE MAIN MENU BAR > ⚙ > ISSUES
2. ON THE ADMINISTRATION - ISSUES VIEW, SELECT **PRIORITY SCHEMES** IN THE SIDEBAR:

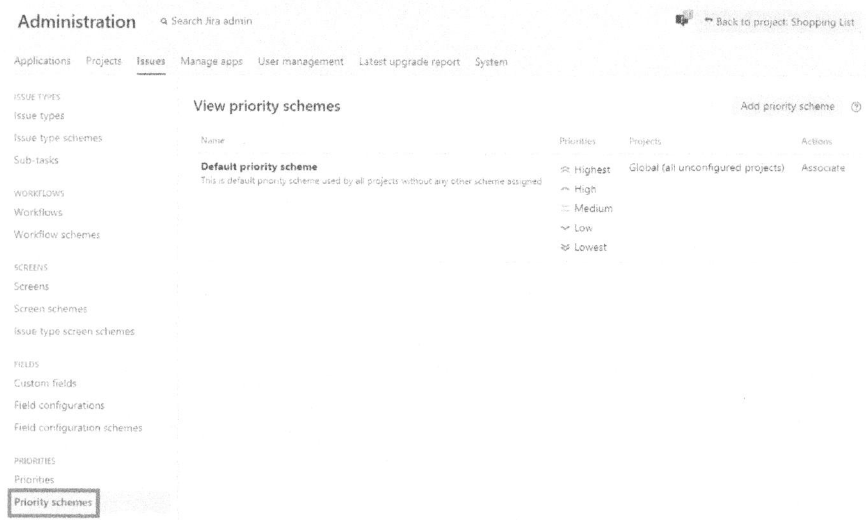

If you click on the **Add Priority Scheme** button in the upper right corner, the Add Priority Scheme view appears.

Here you can name a Scheme and determine which priorities you want in your new scheme. Of course, if you want new, different priorities, you first need to create them in the Priorities view.

Once you **add** the new scheme you can, back in the **Priority Schemes** view, associate the scheme to one or more Projects.

Chapter 6 – Workflows

Chapter Objective

In this chapter you will develop a good understanding of Workflows, Workflow schemes, and their interactions with other elements.

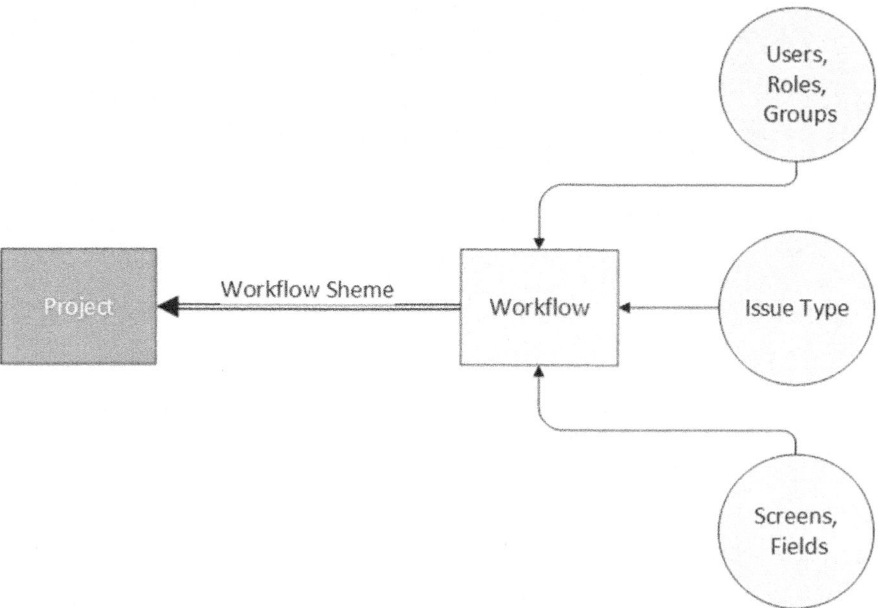

Understanding Workflows

To me, Jira workflows are probably the best reason to purchase Jira Core. It allows you to develop and manage work processes without involving your I.T. department. A well-trained Jira business user can easily design and implement a time saving workflow that can improve work efficiencies and collaboration.

Workflows

Atlassian Documentation states that "A Jira workflow is the set of *statuses* and *transitions* that an issue goes through during its lifecycle. *Workflows typically represent business processes.*" I would alter that last statement slightly and say, 'a *Workflow represents an Issue's process*'.

At this point it is essential to understand the difference between **Process** and **Procedure**. Many people confuse the two definitions because they often overlap each other. According to my trusty Oxford dictionary, a **Process is**, "*a continuous and regular action, or succession of actions, taking place or carried on in a definite manner, and leading to the accomplishment of some result;* ***a continuous operation or series of operations***", while a **Procedure is** a "***course of action***, *method, system, strategy, way, approach, formula, mechanism, technique, routine, drill, practice*". To be clearer, I would say that Process is a set, or series, of Procedures (or steps) with the purpose of accomplishing a goal. A Procedure is a step that also includes the instructions for completing that step.

In I.T. terminology a procedure is a set of actions (or steps) *in a specific order.* We, business people, need more details and explanations on HOW to achieve, or accomplish, those steps. Let's take the example of making a turkey dinner. The Issue is 'make a turkey dinner', which is also the description of the process. The workflow *describes the steps involved* in making the turkey dinner (e.g. prepare the turkey, cook the turkey, carve and plate the turkey, etc.). However, notice that none of these workflow steps describes *how* to do the step. For example, it doesn't tell you what temperature to set the oven or how long it should take to preheat the oven, it doesn't tell you how long the turkey should sit in the oven, or how long it should rest afterwards.

So, please remember, **in Jira a workflow includes the steps necessary to complete an Issue, it doesn't describe *how* to do the steps**. Keeping this in mind avoids a lot of confusion later on.

To repeat, I do like Jira's definition of a Workflow, *"Jira workflow is a set of **statuses** and **transitions** that an issue goes through during its lifecycle."* A **status** is the state, condition, or situation at a particular time in the the process. The default Jira workflow has five statuses: **Open** (not yet started), **In Progress, Resolved, Closed,** and **Reopened**. An issue **transitions** (the arrows in the diagram below) from one status to another based on business rules set by the user (or the program defaults). One business rule might be: an issue transitions from In Progress to Resolved by *completing the issue.* Another business rule might be: an Issue transitions from Resolved to Closed if the Project Lead *authorizes it as Closed.*

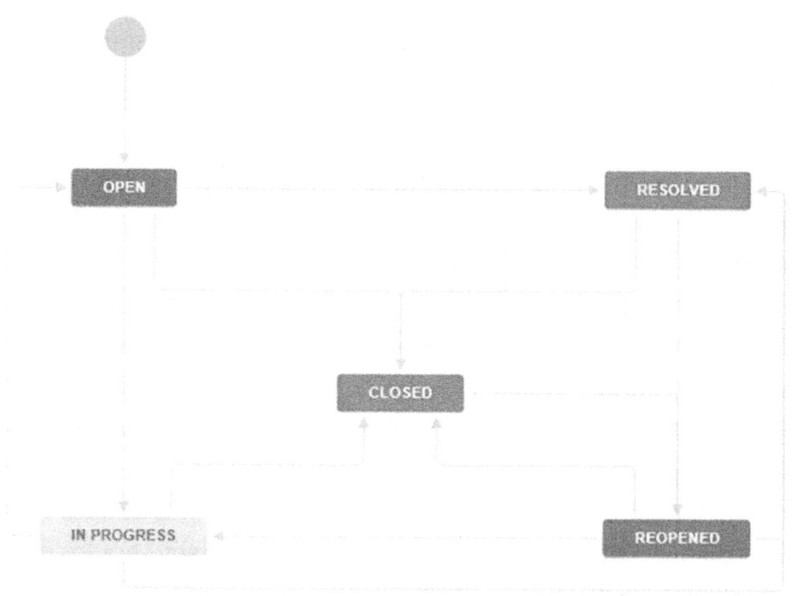

To avoid confusion between statuses and transitions, think of **a status as your current position in a workflow process, and a transition as the action that moves you to a new status.** I personally believe one of the main reasons for this status/transition confusion is that Jira uses a mix or tenses when describing statuses. For example, Open and In Progress each describe a current tense, while Resolved, Closed, and Reopened describe past tenses. Well, which is it? Is a status current or past? Jira should be consistent. I apply the past tense when naming a status; for example, I use *Issue Created* in place of Open, I use *Work Started* instead of In Progress. I find it easier to understand and work with, and more importantly, I find it easier to explain to the Users. You may prefer another method, but regardless, I recommend you be consistent with your naming format.

You may read or hear about a workflow **Step**. Very simply, a status along with **all** of its **outgoing** transitions is called a **Step**. Steps were more important in earlier versions of Jira, when building a workflow could only be done using text and defining a Step name was required. With Jira's 'new', easier to use, graphical design the Step is automatically created in the background; so, you don't need to worry about it.

While Jira Statuses are big and bold, they really don't do much. They simply tell you, and others, where you are in the Workflow process. All the power and activities in a Jira Workflow take place within the Transitions. Users usually do specific tasks during a transition. Therefore, it should be no surprise that transitions can have their own screens, called **Transition Views**. For example, if a User is required to approve an Issue, the **Approval Transition View** might contain two fields: an Approved/Not Approved checkbox field, and a Description Field meant for the User to enter details as to why the Issue was not approved. Jira has a few standard Transition Screens, but typically most are built by administrators to meet the specific requirements of the organization.

As you know by now, a new Issue can be created from a number of places in the program; and when you do so, a **Create Issue Screen** appears where you select the project name, issue type, etc. One thing not well understood or documented is that while this screen is technically an Issue Type 'Create' Screen it is also the first **Transition** in the workflow associated with your issue type. In the Jira workflow diagram notice the line (the transition) that connects the grey circle (workflow start) and Open (the first status). If you were to click on that line it would read "Create Issue" as the name of the transition, which includes the Create Issue Screen.

Users typically have the permission to change a workflow status for the part of the workflow with which they are associated. For example, a business analyst may have the authority to change an Issue's status from **Open** to **In Progress** and change In **Progress** to **Resolved**. However, they may not have the authority to change **Resolved** to **Closed**, as only the Project Lead may have the authority to do so (in this example).

Users change an Issue's status by clicking on the appropriate Transition Button on the **Issue Details View** (as shown below). In this example there are two transition buttons available: Stop Progress and Done. If I click the Done transition button, my status will change to Done, as you can see in the second image.

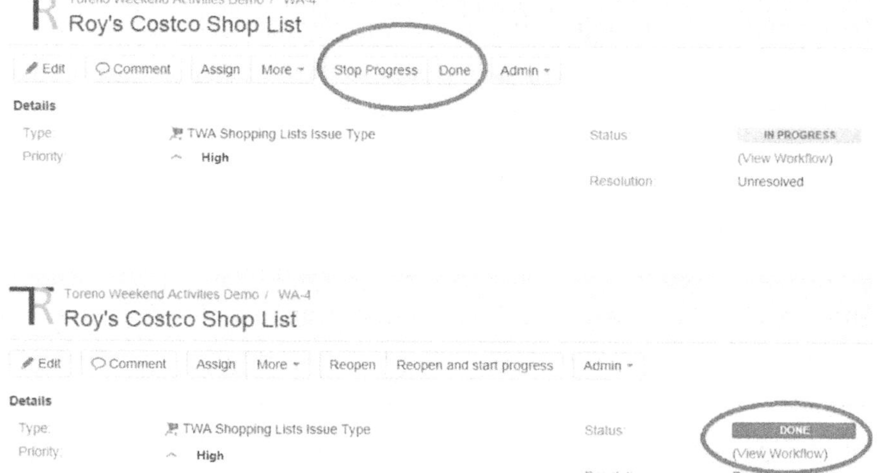

Remember, the Transition buttons a User sees in the Issue Details View will vary depending on the workflow associated with the Issue Type, where the User is in the workflow, and the permissions the User has.

You can also create your own statuses and transitions. This is where the incredible power of Jira workflows comes into play.

I recommend that when you first start using Jira Core, find a default workflow that is 'good enough' to work with and practice with it until you are ready to move to a customized workflow.

> CAUTION: When practicing, make sure the first thing you do is rename the workflow to something unique such as "TEST Workflow". I know of at least one company where an Administrator changed the workflow for his project, not fully realizing that the change affected every project in the organization using the same workflow. It was a nightmare to straighten out. I always recommend a best practice of **giving project specific workflow and scheme names to each project** to avoid these sorts of problems.

WORKFLOW SCHEMES

After you create a Workflow, you will need to associate it with a specific Project and a specific Issue Type in order for the workflow to work. That's the purpose of Workflow Schemes.

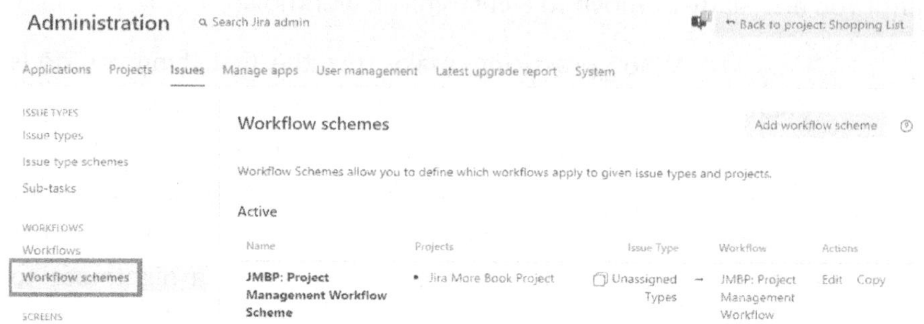

Adding a workflow scheme is as simple as clicking on the **Add Workflow Scheme** button at the top right corner of the Workflow Schemes view and then entering a Workflow Scheme **Name** and **Description**. The Workflow Schemes view contains five columns: **Name, Projects, Issue Type, Workflow,** and **Actions.**

NAME

Here is a list of your Workflow Schemes. They are sorted into two categories: **Active** and **Inactive**. A Workflow Scheme is Active if it is associated with a Project. Workflow Scheme names are listed alphabetically within each category.

When you open the Workflow Schemes' view you first see Active workflow schemes:

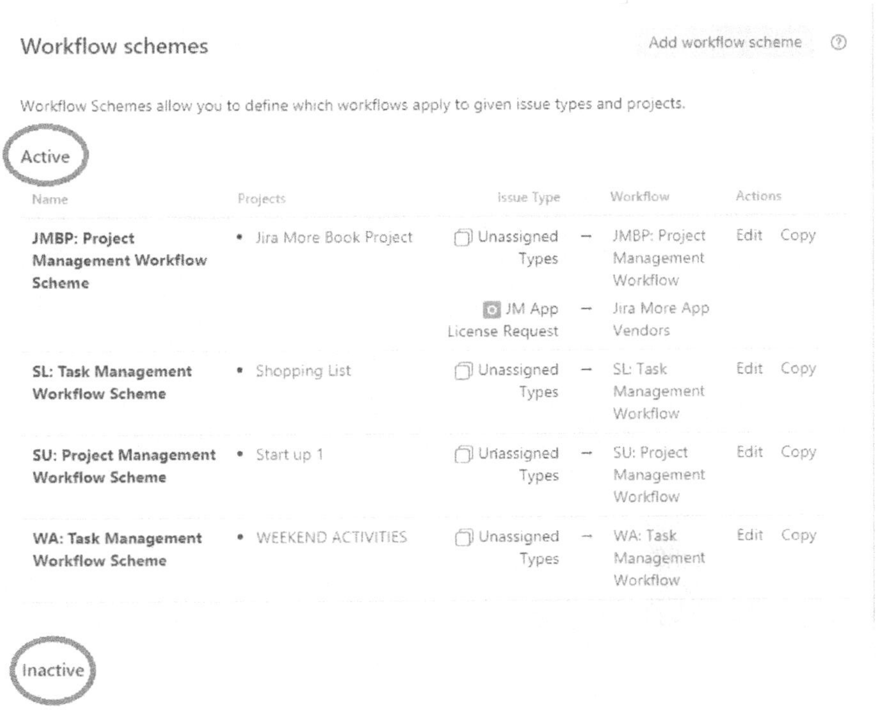

Workflow schemes

Add workflow scheme

Workflow Schemes allow you to define which workflows apply to given issue types and projects.

Active

Name	Projects	Issue Type		Workflow	Actions
JMBP: Project Management Workflow Scheme	• Jira More Book Project	Unassigned Types	–	JMBP: Project Management Workflow	Edit Copy
		JM App License Request	–	Jira More App Vendors	
SL: Task Management Workflow Scheme	• Shopping List	Unassigned Types	–	SL: Task Management Workflow	Edit Copy
SU: Project Management Workflow Scheme	• Start up 1	Unassigned Types	–	SU: Project Management Workflow	Edit Copy
WA: Task Management Workflow Scheme	• WEEKEND ACTIVITIES	Unassigned Types	–	WA: Task Management Workflow	Edit Copy

Inactive

Projects

In this column the projects associated with your Workflow schemes are displayed. You can have only one Workflow Scheme associated with a Project. However, the reverse is not true: you can have multiple projects associated with a workflow scheme. This allows you to reuse existing schemes; so, you don't need to recreate them in new projects. Just remember, if you have two or more projects sharing a workflow scheme, then any time you make a change to the shared scheme in one project you will affect all the other projects sharing that scheme.

Note: To switch a Project's Workflow scheme, click on the **Back to Project** button on the upper right corner, or go to the **Project Settings view** (Main menu bar > Projects (select your project) > Project settings (at the bottom of the Project's sidebar)), find the **Workflows** section and click on the workflow shown:

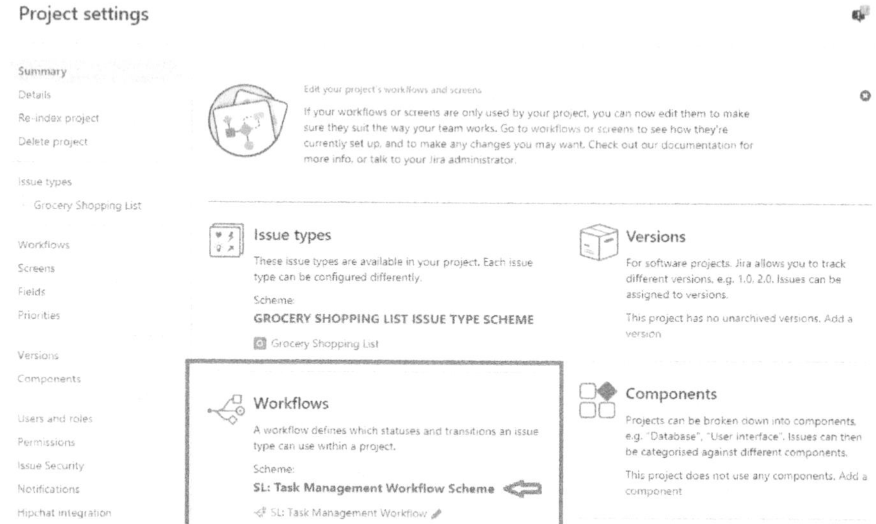

The **Workflows** view will open, where you will find the **Switch Scheme** button.

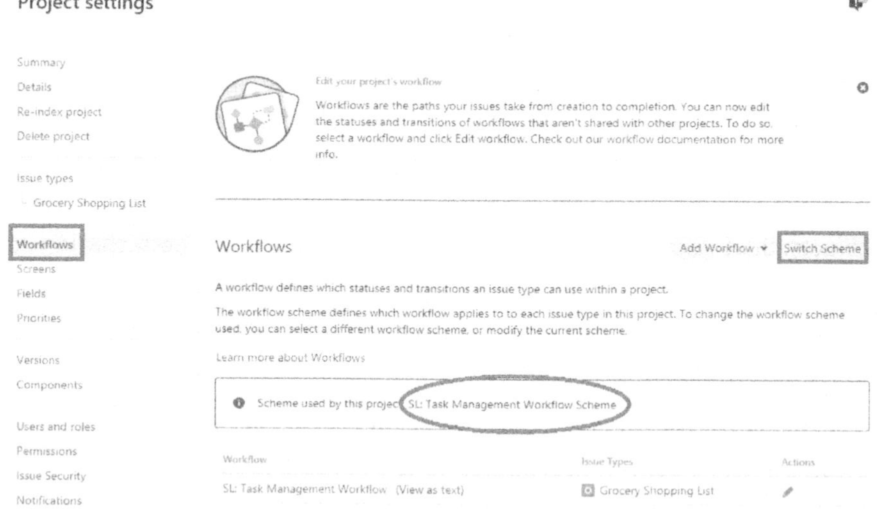

In the opened **Associate Workflow Scheme to Project** wizard select the **Workflow** scheme you want from the drop-down list and follow the wizard steps to associate the new scheme with your project.

Issue Type

Back in the Main menu bar > > Issues > **Workflows scheme** view we next see the Issue Type column:

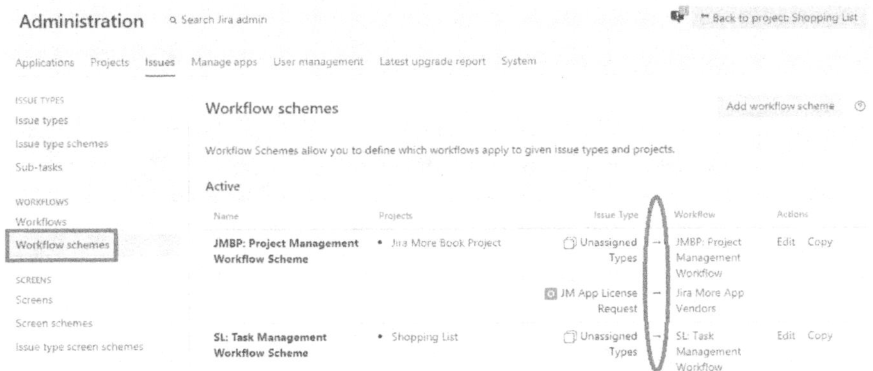

This column lists the Issue Types associated with the Workflow Scheme. As we have just seen, while you may have more than one Issue Type in a Workflow Scheme, each Issue Type can only be associated with a single Workflow within the Scheme. That's why you see **the arrow**. Each arrow is pointing at the only workflow it will work with in the Workflow Scheme/Project combination.

Workflow

The Workflow column shows you the Workflow(s) associated with the Issue Type(s) in your Workflow Scheme. Please note that an **Issue Type can be associated with only one Workflow in a particular Workflow Scheme**. However, again, the reverse is not true. **A workflow can be associated with more than one Issue Type within a Workflow scheme.** Sounds confusing? Here is the bottom line: if an Issue Type were to be associated with more than one workflow within a project the software wouldn't know which one to use, causing the program to have a nervous breakdown. So, Jira put in a rule preventing this from happening. As simple as that.

OUTSIDE of a Workflow scheme an Issue Type can be associated with a different workflow, as long as the Issue Type is associated with different workflow schemes. For example, in Project A, the Task Issue Type may be associated with Workflow X in Workflow scheme Alpha, while in Project B the Task Issue Type may be associated with Workflow Z in workflow scheme Beta:

Allowed:

Issue Type	Workflow	Workflow Scheme	Project
Task	Workflow X	Alpha	Project A
Sub-task	Workflow Y	Alpha	Project A
Task	Workflow Z	Beta	Project B

Not Allowed:

Issue Type	Workflow	Workflow Scheme	Project
Task	Workflow X	Alpha	Project A
Task	Workflow Z	Alpha	Project A

ACTIONS

In our final, **Actions,** column you can **Edit, Copy,** or **Delete** a workflow.

Edit

The **Edit** link will take you to the **Workflow Scheme** view where you:

- may see the workflows associated with the scheme in more detail
- can add a new workflow to the scheme
- associate new Issue Types to a Workflow by clicking the **Assign** link.

CAUTION: It is highly recommended you NOT experiment with **Workflow Schemes** until you have a good understanding of the program.

Copy

It is often easier to copy an existing Workflow scheme and use it as a starting base for a new scheme than it is to build one from scratch. Just be aware that, unlike most of the other copy functions in Jira, a pop-up will NOT appear asking you to rename the Workflow Scheme when you click the copy link. Instead a new copy is immediately created and placed in your list of Inactive Workflow Schemes.

Delete

You can only delete Inactive Workflow schemes. First, you must disassociate any projects from your screen, which is done through the Switch Schemes operation we discussed in the Project section earlier in this chapter.

Exercise: Confirm Default Workflow

In this exercise you will:

- simply confirm that the Shopping List project uses the default workflow.

1. NAVIGATE TO MAIN MENU > PROJECTS > SHOPPING LIST > **PROJECT SETTINGS** VIEW

2. In the **Workflows** section find **Scheme**:

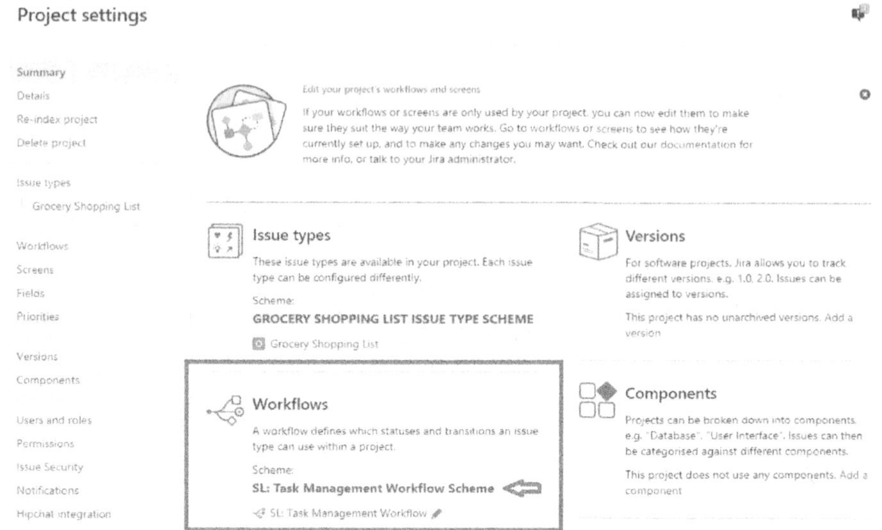

- If the **Scheme** is **'Default Workflow Scheme'** then the exercise is complete
- If the **scheme** does NOT say *'default'* click on the scheme shown

3. In the opened **Workflows** view click on the **Switch Scheme** button:

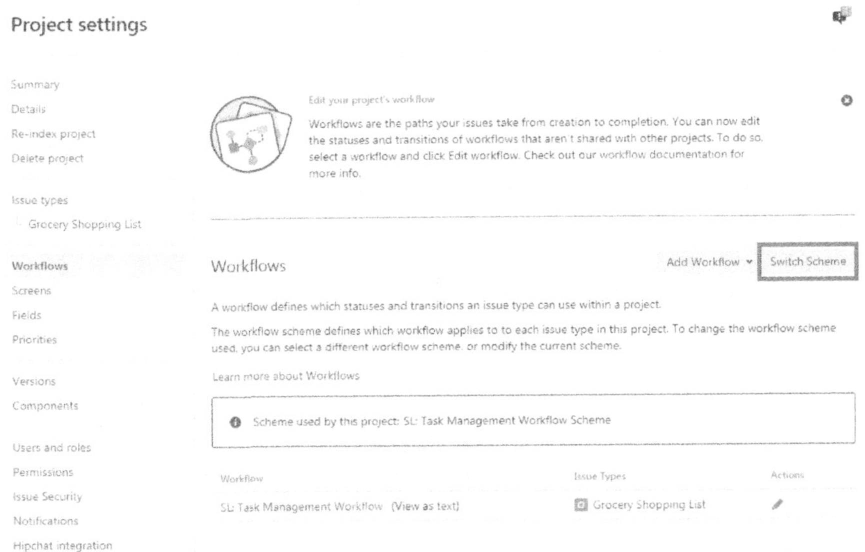

4. In the **Associate Workflow Scheme to Project** view select Default from the options in the Scheme list:

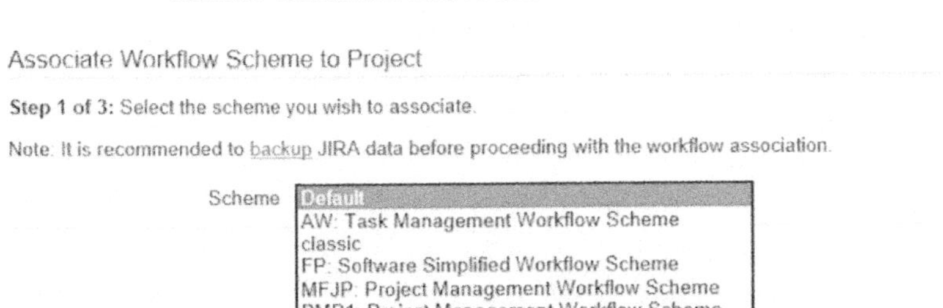

5. Click Associate

Back in the **Shopping List Project Settings Summary Workflows** section the Scheme will have changed to "Default Workflow Scheme":

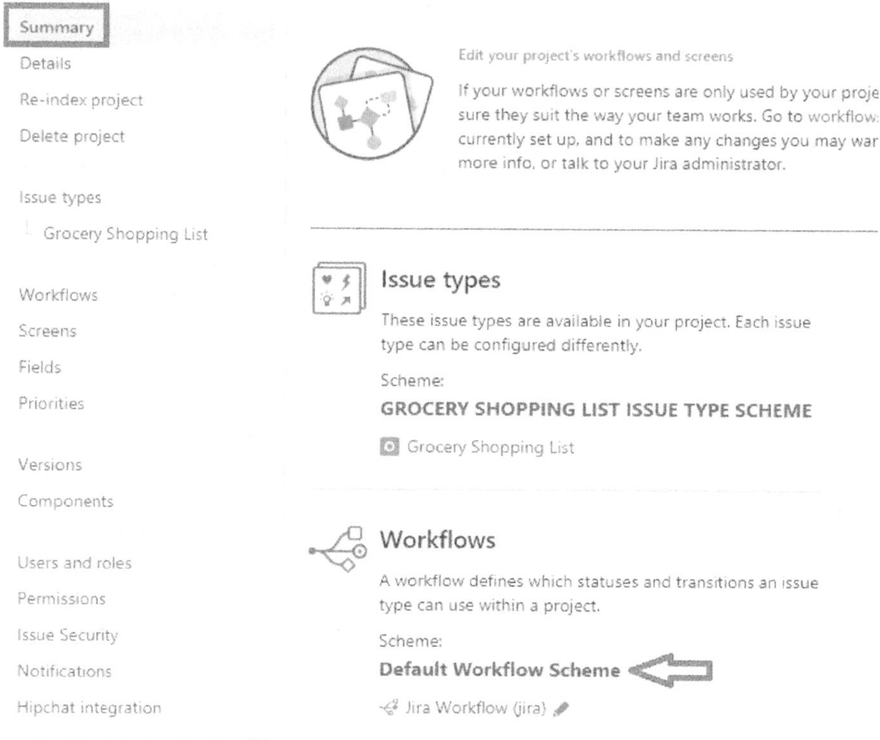

One thing to be aware of is that if you change the workflows significantly, the program may require you to go through a number of steps to complete the workflow transition. Don't worry about it, just go with the flow.

Issue Resolution

So, you have completed your Issue and then clicked a transition button that changes your status to Closed (or Done). You would logically assume that your Issue is Closed. And you would be very, very, wrong!

Clicking a transition button to change your status to Closed, or Resolved, or any other "Closed" type status does nothing more than indicate to you, and others interested in your Issue, that you have completed the Issue. But, and this is a big 'but', it means nothing to Jira. The software still thinks your Issue is 'open', and it will continue to think your Issue is open until you specifically tell Jira that it is closed, and that is called "Resolving" an Issue.

When you resolve an Issue, you do two things: you formally close the Issue in the software, and you state the reason for resolving the Issue. Jira has a number of default resolution reasons:

- Done
- Won't Do
- Duplicate
- Cannot Reproduce
- Issue Cancelled by Client

There are two ways of Resolving an Issue: Automatically or Manually.

Automatically

With an Automatic resolution, you can program a transition button to automatically resolve the issue when the User clicks that transition button. For example, you may have a transition button called "Close Issue" or "Done". When you click that button, your workflow status changes to Done (or whatever you are using for the final status), and the Resolution field also changes from Unresolved to Done, or whatever you have selected to indicate that your Issue is formally resolved (Done is an example of a resolution option):

Automatic resolutions are built using a workflow transition **post-function**.

Automatic resolutions are used when you want to use only one resolution reason.

Manually

With a Manual resolution, when you click that transition button a pop-up appears (actually called a "workflow transition screen") containing a resolution field. This resolution field will contain a list of resolution options (Fixed, Done, Cannot Fix, Customer Canceled, etc.):

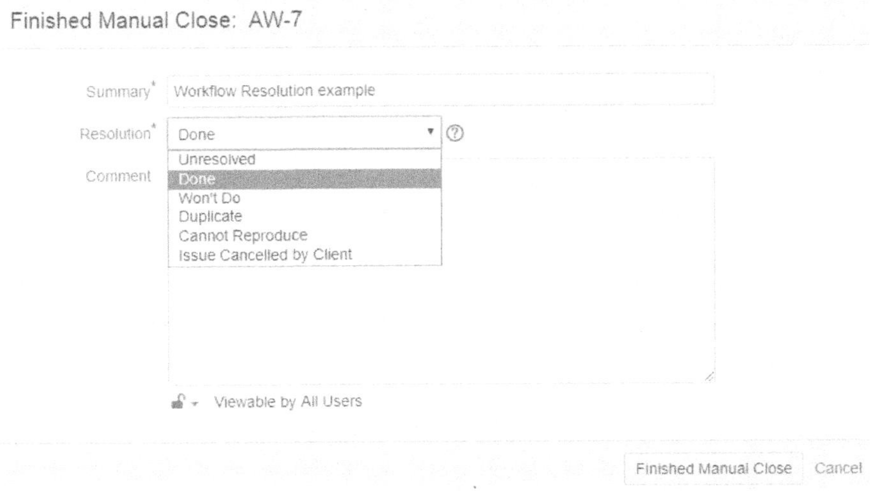

Finished Manual Close: AW-7

Summary* Workflow Resolution example

Resolution* Done

Unresolved
Done
Won't Do
Duplicate
Cannot Reproduce
Issue Cancelled by Client

Comment

Viewable by All Users

Finished Manual Close Cancel

The user selects one of the options and exits the pop up. The status has now changed to Closed (or whatever you are using as the final status), and the resolution field will show the value (option) you selected from the resolution field drop down list. Manual resolutions are also set up using a workflow transition post-function.

Automatic works fine if you have only one resolution option to choose from: you will need the manual option if you want to give your user a number of resolution options.

Once you have resolved an Issue, Jira will formally close it out in its database. In other words, it will no longer show in your Open Issues list.

More about Workflows

Configuring resolutions as well as workflows can be quite complex; so, if you want to learn more, I recommend you purchase my book **"Jira Core Workflows"**. It contains about 190 pages dedicated to helping you design, build, and configure Jira workflows. Available at Amazon.

Chapter 7 - Screens

Chapter Objectives

In this Chapter you will gain a working knowledge of Jira Core Issue Operations and Workflow Transition views

You will learn of Screen Schemes, Issue Type Screen Schemes, and the differences between the two

You will create a custom screen for your project along with a related Screen Scheme and Issue Type Screen Scheme

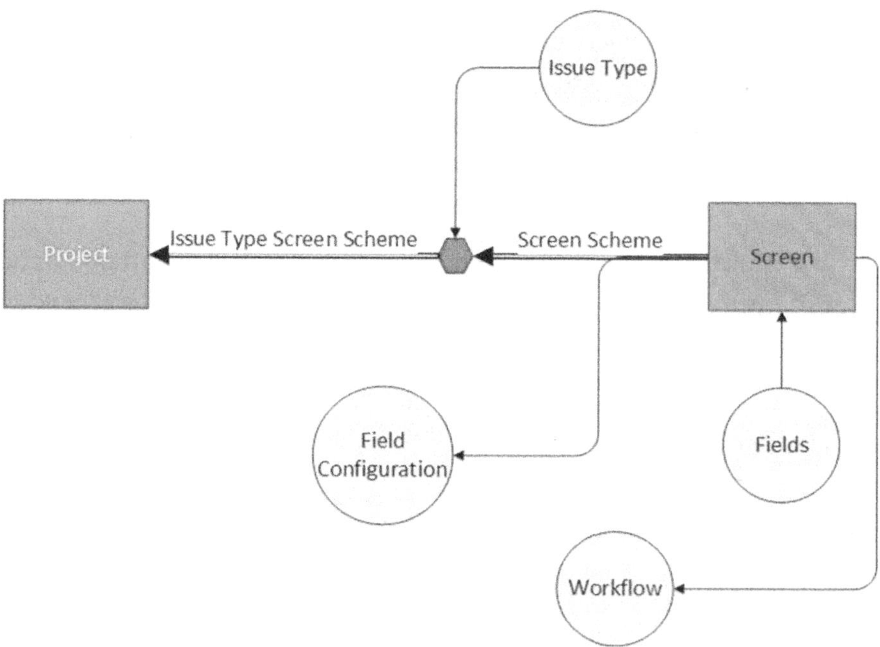

Screens and Schemes

Screens

A **Screen** is a unique User view, containing fields for a specific purpose.

A Screen can:

- Provide information
- Enable an action (clicking a button for example)
- Receive information (filling in a field, or selecting an item from a list of options, etc.)

Screens are generally designed to support the type of work associated with an Issue. For example, if you have an 'Order New Railroad Car' Issue Type you don't need to see a 'Pina Colada Recipe' Screen. You want to see a **Screen** showing the necessary fields (and **only** the required fields) for that particular step in the 'Order a New Railroad Car' process.

What Users will be able to see on a screen is based on their project **User Role**, type of **Permissions** (security) they have, and the type of work needing to be done at that moment.

There is another concept we should become comfortable with. Sooner or later, you will probably think to yourself, "I would like to add a couple of customized fields to a screen. Do I add this to a **Screen** or do I create a special **Form**?" Most of us naturally tend to think of a **Screen** and a **Form** as separate things. The reality is that in Jira **a Screen *is* a Form**; they are one and the same.

When adding new fields, you can add them to an existing standard Jira Issue Screen, to a Workflow Transition Screen (View), or to a custom-made Screen.

Jira uses its screens in two distinct ways: for Issue Operations and for Workflow Transition Views.

Issue Operations Screens

When working with an Issue the User is typically doing one of three things:

- creating the issue
- adding, deleting, or changing the data in the fields of the Issue
- looking at the issue.

Jira calls each of these activities an **'Issue Operation'**. The three Issue Operations are called **Create Issue Operation, Edit Issue Operation, and View Issue Operation.**

Each of these Operations **must** have their own screen: a Create Issue Operation screen, an Edit Issue Operation screen, and a View Issue Operation screen. Many times you will want the three screens to be the same; so, if you wish, you can reuse the same screen in each operation. However, there are also instances where - for a particular Issue Type - you may want the three screens to be a little, or a lot, different. Having the three Issue Operation types allows you to have these different screens. We will discuss Issue Operations in more detail later in the chapter.

Workflow Transition Screens (Views)

When working with an Issue you may only need the Issue Operation screens. For example, if you have a simple Action Item Issue Type, you may only need a few fields. However, you may also have Issue Types used for complex processes such as Accounts Payable, Marketing, or Human Resources. In these complex processes one option is to include all the required fields in an Issue Operation screen. Everyone involved in the process can then add or change data whenever they wish. That can work, but it tends to be messy and confusing for all the participants, and on the top of that there are security concerns as well (you probably don't want Sam in Marketing to change a price in an Accounts Payable field). A better solution is to create screens to be used at specific steps in the process. Each screen would contain only the fields necessary for that step, and could only be edited by a specific User. That is where Workflow Transition Screens (also called the Workflow Transition View) come in. To summarize, **a Workflow Transition Screen (View) is the screen a User will see at a particular step in the Issue lifecycle.**

A **Workflow Transition Screen (View)** is meant to support the original Issue information or the Issue's process or both, and may involve:

- Editing the original data
- Entering additional data or attaching of files
- Approving, or quality controlling, previously entered data or attached files
- Approving a request
- Requesting additional information
- Diverting or escalating based on business rules (e.g. if field xyz is greater than $10,000 it must be approved by a Vice President)
- Assigning a new Assignee for the next workflow step
- Entering a due date for the next step

A Workflow Transition Screen (View) only becomes visible when the User clicks a **Status Transition** button on the Issue Menu bar:

Issue Operation and Workflow Transition Screen (View) Example

Let's look at an example of how Issue Operation and Workflow Transition Screens (Views) may be used in an Issue.

The diagram above shows a typical process involving the three Issue Operation screens (Create Issue, Edit Issue, and View Issue) and one Workflow Transition Screen (View).

First, the User creates an issue using the Create Issue screen. While working on the issue she may edit the data or add additional data using the Edit Issue screen. When her work is complete, she sends the Issue to her supervisor by changing the status (using the transition button) in the View Issue screen. The Supervisor uses a Transition screen to either approve or reject the work. If the Supervisor rejects the work, there are a number of specialized fields to complete explaining the reason for the rejection. Assuming the work is approved; the User closes out the issue by changing the status in the Issue Detail View Screen.

This is a good, and typical, example of how all the various screens work in Issue process.

Let's move on and look at how Jira manages screens.

View Screens Page

Navigate to ⚙ *> Issues >Screens*

The View Screens page has four main columns: **Name, Screen Schemes, Workflows,** and **Actions.**

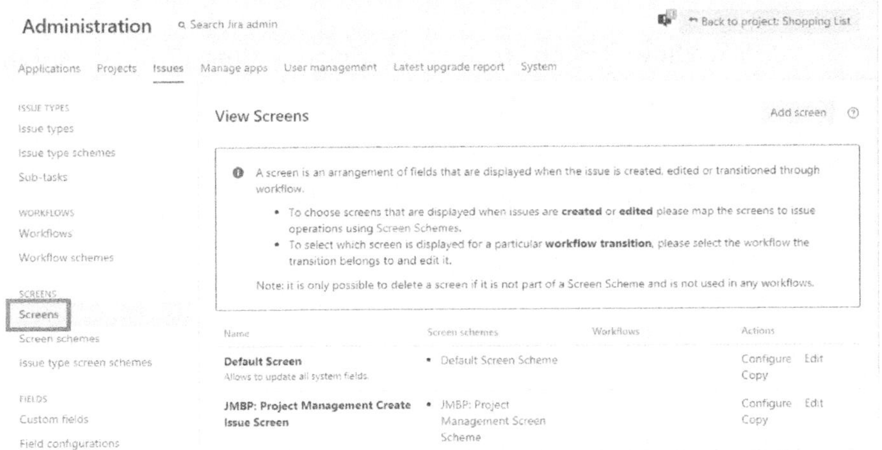

Name

Here, to no one's surprise, the names of the **Screens** are displayed in alphabetical order.

CAUTION: As always, do NOT mess with the **Default Screen**. If you want to make changes, copy the default, rename the copy, and make the changes in the new version.

Screen Schemes

One of the more confusing and technically challenging things about Jira is its Screens Schemes and how they work.

Screen Scheme, like Issue Type Scheme and Workflow Scheme, serves as a connection. It connects a Screen with a specific **Issue Operation**. There are three Issue Operations you can perform in Jira: **Create an Issue, Edit an Issue, or View an Issue.** These are discussed in more detail later in the Screen Schemes section.

The Screen Schemes column in the **View Screens** page indicates which **Screen Schemes** are associated with the Screen listed in the Name column.

Workflows

A **Workflow Screen** (technically called a **Workflow Transition View**) is the screen a User may see at a particular step in the Issue lifecycle.

The Workflow column shows what Transition Views are associated with the Screen listed in the Name column.

Actions

The Actions column allows you to **Configure**, **Edit**, **Copy**, or **Delete** your Screen.

Configure

On the Configure Screen page you design or edit your Screen layout.

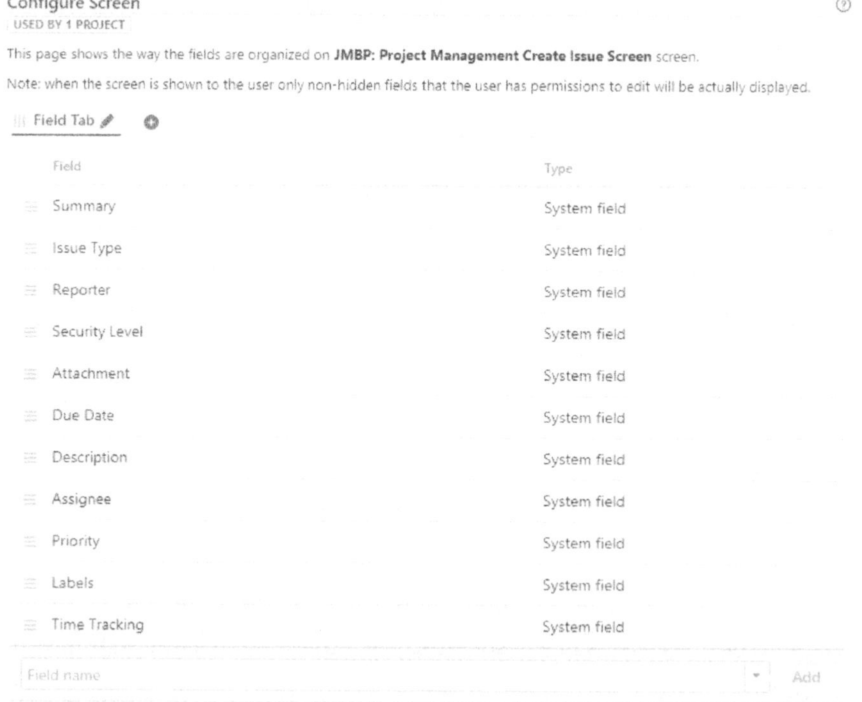

You can do a remarkable number of things with the Configure Screen page. You can:

- Remove unnecessary fields by hovering your mouse over the field and clicking the round **Delete** button that appears.
- Add standard Jira fields, or Custom Fields you have already created, to the Screen by using the **Add** area at the bottom of the page.
- Reorder the field layout by hovering your mouse over the hatch field (see image below) to the left of the field name. When your mouse arrow turns into a four-direction arrow, drag the field up or down to its desired position:

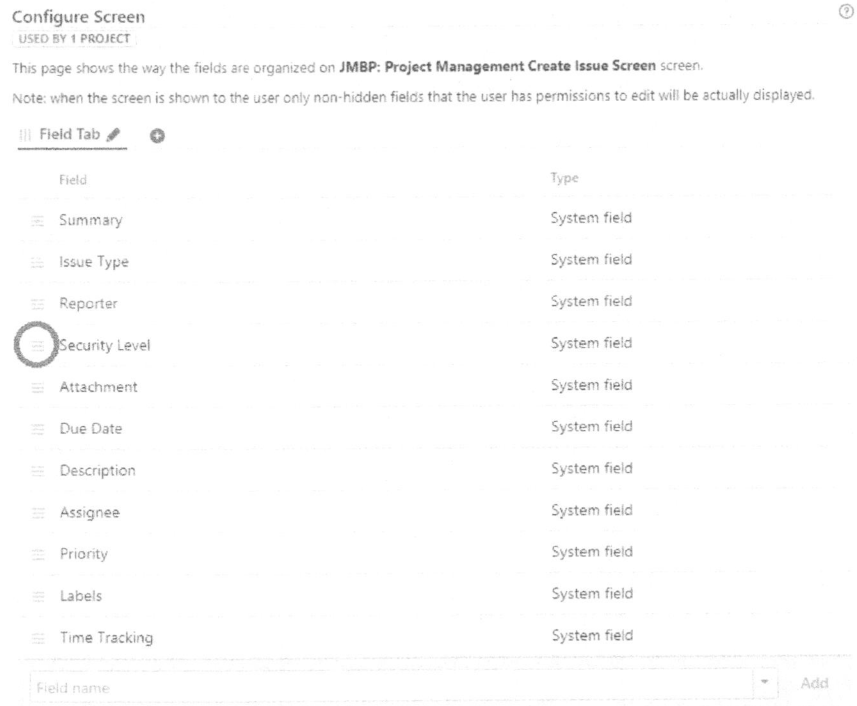

- Name the tab by editing the **Field Tab** at the top of the list of Fields. When working with the screen, the user will see that tab name. The User will NOT see the tab title if you don't change the Field Tab name AND there is only one tab in the Screen.
- Add new 'tabs' on the Screen and include additional fields by clicking on **Add Tab** (round plus button) at the top of the list of fields. Tabs are a helpful in two ways. First, it is great for squeezing a lot of information in a small space, and it is recommended if you believe your Screen will commonly be seen on a mobile device. Second, it is excellent for organizing your data fields into logical groupings. If you believe the screen will be edited often during a workflow process you may consider sorting the fields into logical work groups with each tab representing a distinct function or step in the process.

Edit

The Edit function allows you to change the **Name** of the Screen and to change its **Description**.

Edit Screen

Use the form below to change properties of the **JMBP: Project Management Create Issue Screen** screen.

Name: JMBP: Project Management Create Issu

Description:

Update Cancel

Copy

Copy does just that, it allows you to copy an existing Screen and rename it. This is helpful if you have an existing Screen you want to use in a new project and want a unique name for project management purposes. It is also helpful if an existing Screen has almost, but not everything, you want for a new Screen. You can make a copy and use that as the starting point for building your new Screen.

Delete

You can delete a Screen if there are no **Screen Schemes** and no **Workflows** associated with it. If there *are* existing **Screen Schemes** or **Workflows**, you must delete those first before you can delete the Screen.

Add Screen

You create a new Screen by clicking the **Add Screen** button on the upper right corner of the **View Screens** page. A pop-up appears asking for the Name and Description of the new Screen and that's it. A new Screen is created.

Of course, you need then to configure it using the configure link in the Actions column.

Exercise: Create and Add Screen to Project

We will now add a Screen to our *SHOPPING LIST* project. This Screen will, later, be used for our bespoke shopping list fields.

In this exercise we will:

- Create a Shopping List Screen
- Configure the Screen by eliminating unnecessary fields

1. Navigate to ⚙ > Issues > **Screens**
2. In the opened **View Screens** page click on **Add Screen**
3. In the **Add Screen** pop-up, enter '*Shopping List Screen*' in the **Name** field
4. Enter '*Screen for Shopping List*' in the **Description** field
5. Click **Add**

The **Configure Screen** page should appear. In this page you will add the fields for creating a shopping list to the newly created Shopping List Screen.

6. In the **Configure Screen** page, select the following from the **Field Name** drop down list:
    i. Assignee (and click **Add** button)

ii. DUE DATE (AND CLICK **ADD** BUTTON)
iii. PRIORITY (AND CLICK **ADD** BUTTON)

7. CLICK ON **SCREENS** ON THE SIDEBAR TO GET BACK TO THE **VIEW SCREENS** PAGE

You have now set up a basic Shopping List Screen:

Shopping List Screen Configure Edit
Screen for Shopping List Copy Delete

In many cases, Jira provides enough standard fields for you to complete your Issue. However, in this instance, we still need some additional fields (a list of products, for example), which we will create a little later in the Custom Fields section.

Since you only have one tab, you don't need to edit its name.

TIP: If you want to add or delete fields later on, simply go to the View Screens page, find your Screen and click on Configure link in the Actions column. After that it is straight forward: you can add, remove, and move fields up or down.

SCREEN SCHEMES

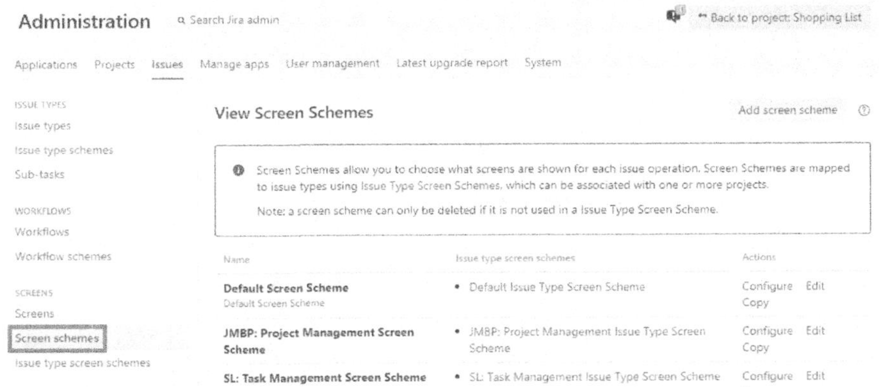

In my opinion, the Screen Scheme is probably the most complex and confusing of the puzzle pieces because to build it correctly you must do three things:

1. Associate a **Screen to a Screen Scheme**
2. Associate the **Screen Scheme to an Issue Operation**
3. Link a **Screen to an Issue Type by associating** the **Screen Scheme to an Issue Type Screen Scheme**

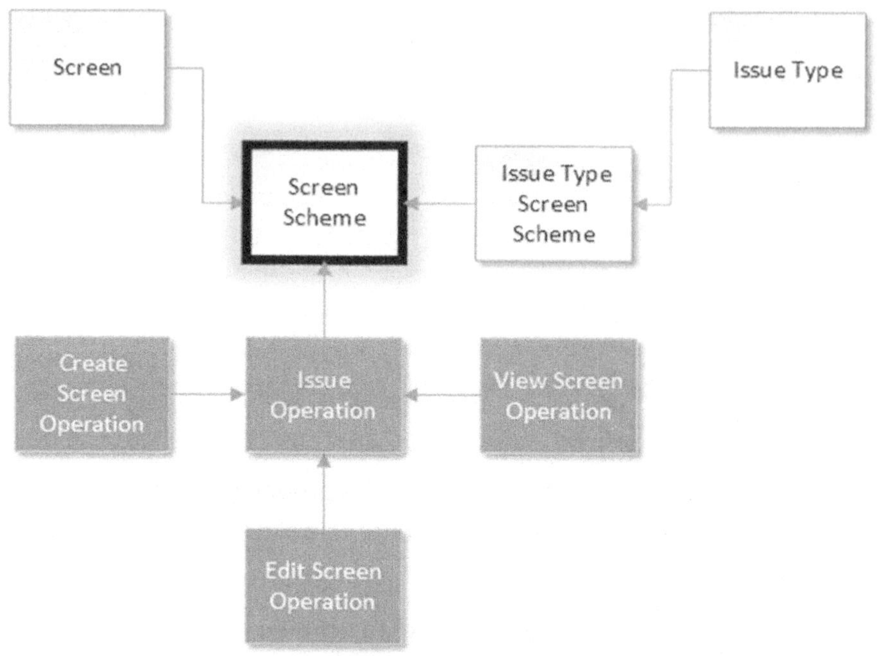

A Screen Scheme does two things. First, it ties a Screen to an Issue Operation. Second, it enables the creation of an Issue Type Screen Scheme. Issue Type Screen Schemes will be discussed soon in this chapter. But for now, let's look at Issue Operation in more details.

Issue Operations

Screen Schemes dictate what a User can do with a Screen during an **Issue Operation**.

There are three Issue Operations:

Create Issue = Screen shown when issue is **being created**

Edit Issue = Screen shown when the issue is being **edited**

View Issue = Screen shown when User is interacting with the Issue Details View

Why do we need different Issue Operations?

Almost every beginner, including myself, has no idea what an Issue Operation is; and what Create, Edit, and View an Issue means in this context. But the answer is fairly simple.

Create Issue Operation

As you remember, when you create an Issue, a screen pops up where you enter data and then click Create. This is, unsurprisingly, the **Create Screen** and it is also the **Create an Issue Operation**. A Create Issue Operation occurs only once for each issue you create.

Edit Issue Operation

When you want to Edit the data in an Issue, you click the Edit button in the upper left corner of the Issue Detail View:

At that point the Edit Issue pop-up opens and you can add more data or edit existing data. This is the **Edit Screen**, also known as the **Edit Issue Operation**. Here are a few examples as to why you may use the Edit Operation:

1. **Confirm or Change.** Let's pretend an insurance claim Issue is created. A number of the fields on the Screen are populated with the medical history of the client already on file. The assignee may be asked to confirm the accuracy of the data or to make a change in the appropriate field where the history is no longer correct.
2. **One-time Complete**. Many times an issue will be created and then assigned to a new User for completion. For example, the

assignee may be asked to add information about the conditions of a specific work site. Adding the information is technically an editing operation.

3. **Multi-phase Complete**. In this case, an issue is created that requires multiple departments to complete the screen based on the workflow. For example, when you enter a hospital the admittance nurse creates a new issue and enters in administration data (first of which is probably the payment method) and some basic triage information. The doctor who sees you enters more information into that issue Screen, and maybe the x-ray technician adds additional data, etc. Auto repair is similar. The front desk technician enters your details - about you and your car - and some diagnostic information. The technician who fixes your car adds additional information, as does the auto parts counter person who orders the parts. In these last two examples each department has edit permissions, but is restricted to only 'their' fields.

View Issue Operation

Finally, you can view the Issue's data in the Issue Detail View screen. This is the **Issue Details View Screen** and is also the **View Issue Operation**.

You can also, if you have the permission, edit most of the data fields directly, but only with two conditions: 1) if the field is visible, and 2) if data had been previously entered during the Create or Edit operations (if not, the field will not be visible).

You are probably asking yourself, "What's the big deal? Aren't they basically all the same screen? Why are they overcomplicating things?" Good question. Many times, the three screens will, indeed, be the same. However, and this is a big however, the three screens can be quite different if you wish them to be.

Here is how I often use the three different operations. Let's say I have a complicated process requiring many fields. First, I often give Customers the permission to create Issues. This Create Issue Operation opens the Create Issue screen which has a handful of fields all of which are mandatory. I also make sure the Customer does *not* have permission to Edit the screens.

Next, I create the Edit Operation Screen which contains *all* the necessary fields for the Issue. Employees have the permission to enter data into the fields in this screen. In other words, they are able to Edit.

Finally, since a Customer can Create an Issue they also, by default, have the ability to View the Issue. There are often fields in the Edit screen that I don't want them to see. So, I create an Issue View Operation screen that contains the fields from the original Create Issue Screen, and a limited number of the fields from the Edit Issue Operation screen; see the Diagram below:

Create Screen	Edit Screen	View Screen
• Field 1	• Field 1	• Field 1
• Field 2	• Field 2	• Field 2
	• Field 3	
	• Field 4	
	↓	
	• Field 89	
	• Field 90	• Field 90
	• Field 91	• Field 91

In the example above the Customer Creates an Issue and completes fields 1 and 2. This may be Customer's information such as name and phone number. The Edit screen is used by the Specialists assigned to work with that issue. It contains the original 2 fields filled in by the Customer plus fields 3 to 91 which are necessary by the Specialists to complete their work on the Issue. The View screen, which the Customer can see, contains just 4 fields: the original 2 she first filled when creating the Issue and fields 90 and 91 which may contain information she should see such as Due Date and Cost to Customer. She doesn't need to see all the other fields that the Specialists completed so, they are not included in the View screen.

If this process sounds a little ugly to you, then you are not alone. That's one reason Jira created Service Desk. Jira Service Desk allows you to create "Customer" screens that contain fields necessary for the customer, and then allows the "Specialists" to manage the Jira Issue as normal (i.e. Create, Edit, and View screens are all the same) in Jira Core.

More about Jira Service Desk

If you want to know more about Jira Service Desk please buy my book **Jira Service Desk Basics**. It contains 226 pages where you will learn how Jira Service Desk works, how it interacts with Jira Core, and how to create and configure Jira Service Desk screens. Available at Amazon.

And now back to business, to our Screen Scheme and Issue Operations.

Exercise: Associate Screen Schemes and Issue Operations

The objectives of this exercise are

- Associate a **Screen to a Screen Scheme**
- Associate the **Screen Scheme to an Issue Operation**

1. Navigate to ⚙ > Issues >| **Screen Schemes** (on the sidebar)
2. In the View Screen Schemes page, click on **Add Screen Scheme** button

3. In the Add Screen Scheme pop-up enter *'Shopping List Screen Scheme'* in the **Name** field
4. Enter 'Screen Scheme for the Shopping List Screen' in the **Description** field
5. Select *Shopping List Screen* in the **Default Screen** Field
6. Click **Add**
7. In the Configure Screen Scheme page click on **Associate an Issue Operation with a Screen** button

Configure Screen Scheme — Shopping List Screen Scheme

Associate an issue operation with a screen

Please use the table and the form below to select which screen will be displayed for each issue operation. The *Default* entry is used to indicate which screen should be used for operations that do not have a specific mapping in this scheme.

To activate this screen scheme, map it to one or more issue types using an Issue Type Screen Scheme and then associate the Issue Type Screen Scheme with one or more projects.

Note: a screen scheme can only be deleted if it is not a default scheme and is not associated with any projects.

- **View all screen schemes**

Issue Operation	Screen	Actions
Default Used for all unmapped operations	Shopping List Screen	Edit

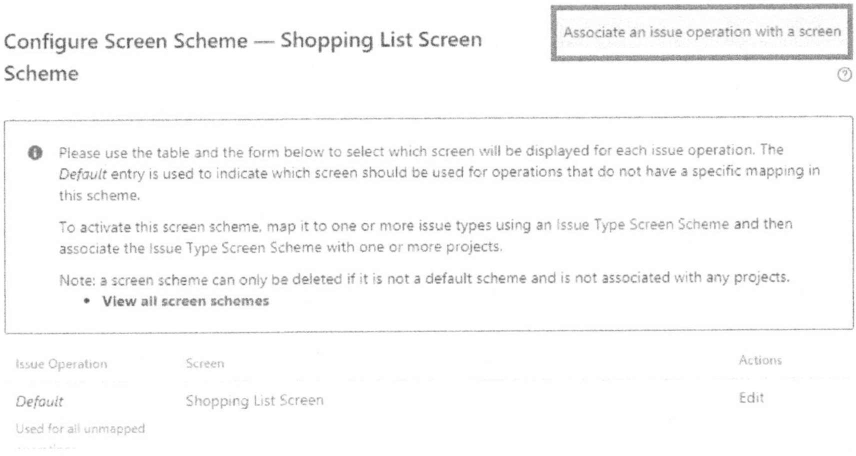

8. In the Associate an Issue Operation with a Screen pop-up, Select Create Issue from the **Issue Operation** list
9. Select *Shopping List Screen* from the **Screen** list
10. Click **Add**

You have now associated a Create Issue Operation with a Screen. When you next create an issue with this project the Shopping List Screen will appear. Unfortunately, your Edit and View screens will show nothing. So, we need to associate this same screen with the Edit and View Operations.

11. In the Configure Screen Scheme page click on **Associate an Issue Operation with a Screen** button
12. In the Associate an Issue Operation with a Screen pop-up, Select **Edit Issue** from the **Issue Operation** list

13. Select *Shopping List Screen* from the **Screen** list
14. Click **ADD**
15. In the Configure Screen Scheme page click on **Associate an Issue Operation with a Screen** button
16. In the Associate an Issue Operation with a Screen pop-up, Select **View Issue** from the **Issue Operation** list
17. Select *Shopping List Screen* from the **Screen** list and click **ADD**

Create Issue	Shopping List Screen	Edit Delete
Edit Issue	Shopping List Screen	Edit Delete
View Issue	Shopping List Screen	Edit Delete

Issue Type Screen Schemes

So, you have built a **screen** and associated the screen with various **Issue Operations** using a **Screen Scheme**. But you still need to associate your screen and screen scheme with an **Issue Type**; otherwise the Issue Type and the Project will never know which screen to use. That is done using an **Issue Type Screen Scheme**.

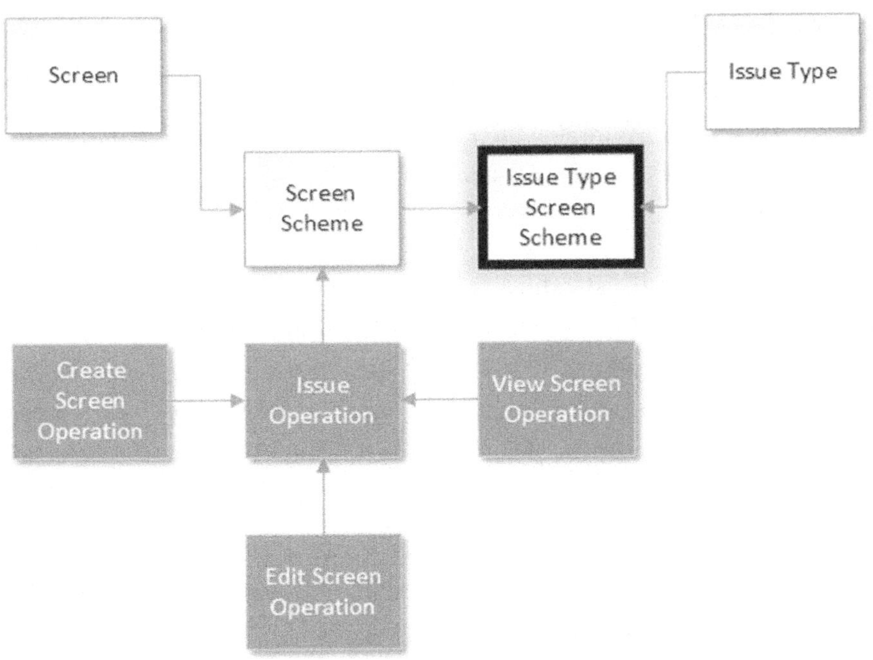

We find the **Issue Type Screen Scheme** link underneath the Screen Schemes link in the Administration > Issues > Sidebar. Clicking that link opens the Issue Type Screen Scheme page. The Issue Type Screen Scheme page has three columns: **Name Projects,** and **Actions.**

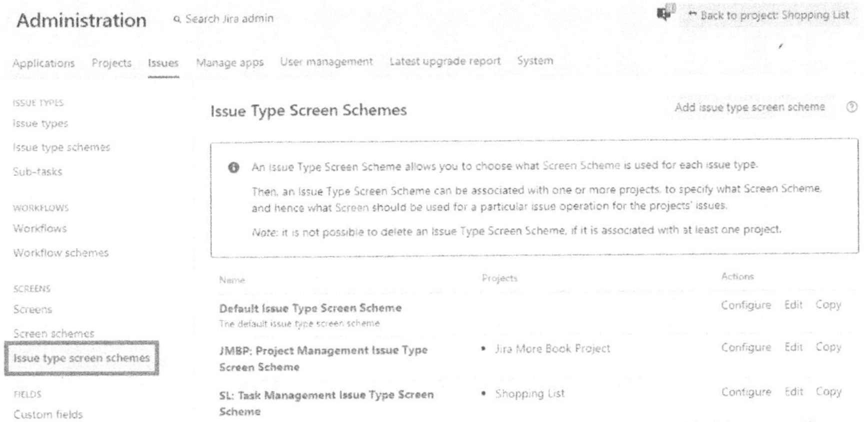

NAME

This column contains the names of the Issue Type Screen Scheme. Issue Type Screen Schemes are listed in alphabetical order.

PROJECTS

This column lists the projects associated with the Issue Type Screen Scheme. You can have only one Issue Type Screen Scheme per project. While multiple projects can be associated with a single Issue Type Screen Scheme, I believe it is easier to create a new Issue Type Screen Scheme for each project. That makes it easier later on to change something in only one project.

CAUTION: You cannot associate an Issue Type Screen Scheme with a project in this page; instead, you need do it through the **Project's Settings** view.

ACTIONS

The Actions column allows you to **Configure, Edit, Copy,** and **Delete** the Issue Type Screen Scheme.

Configure

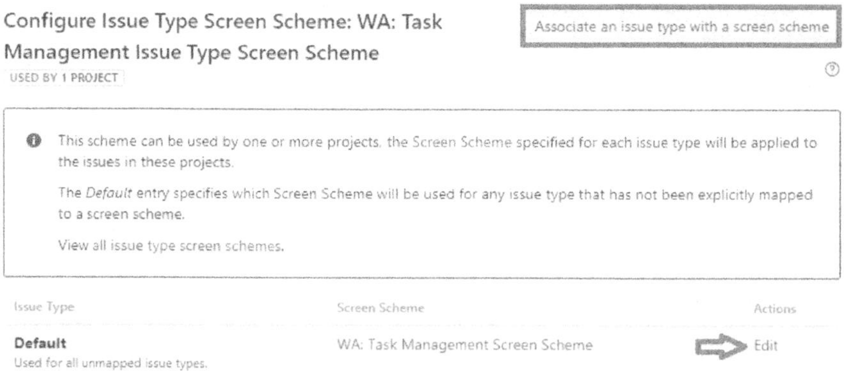

Configure Issue Type Screen Scheme: WA: Task Management Issue Type Screen Scheme

USED BY 1 PROJECT

Associate an issue type with a screen scheme

This scheme can be used by one or more projects, the Screen Scheme specified for each issue type will be applied to the issues in these projects.

The *Default* entry specifies which Screen Scheme will be used for any issue type that has not been explicitly mapped to a screen scheme.

View all issue type screen schemes.

Issue Type	Screen Scheme	Actions
Default Used for all unmapped issue types.	WA: Task Management Screen Scheme	Edit

You can do two things in the **Configure Issue Type Screen Scheme** page. First, you can change the Screen Scheme associated with the Issue Type Screen Scheme by clicking **Edit** link and selecting another Screen Scheme in the pop-up.

Second, on this page you associate another **Issue Type** with a different **Screen Scheme** by clicking **Associate an Issue Type with a Screen Scheme**. You can associate as many different Issue Types with Screen Schemes as you want, as long as they are all unique. Indeed, typically you will have a different Screen Scheme for each Issue Type in your project.

Edit

You can change the name and description of the Issue Type Screen Scheme by selecting the **Edit** link.

Copy

Copy is used to make a duplicate of the Issue Type Screen Scheme. You may want to do this for a number of reasons. You may want to test a new Issue Type Screen Scheme without the risk of damaging your existing Issue Type Screen Scheme. You may want to reuse it in another project and believe, as I do, that it is a good practice to have "a one Issue Type Screen Scheme to one Project" relationship. Or, you may want to use the Issue Type Screen Scheme as a starting point for a slightly different Issue Type Screen Scheme version.

Delete

You can delete your Issue Type Screen Scheme if it is not associated with any project.

Add a New Issue Type Screen Scheme

You can create a new Issue Type Screen Scheme by clicking on the **Add Issue Type Screen Scheme** button located at the upper right corner of the page.

Add Issue Type Screen Scheme

Name*

Description

Screen Scheme: Default Screen Scheme

The screen scheme to use for unmapped issue types

Add Cancel

The pop-up will ask you for the **Name, Description** AND, most importantly, the **Screen Scheme** you want associated with this new Issue Type Screen Scheme.

Exercise: Link Screen to Issue Type and Project

We will now:

- Link a **Screen to an Issue Type** by associating the Screen Scheme to an Issue Type Screen Scheme
- Associate the **Issue Type Screen Scheme to a Project**

1. Navigate to > Issues > **Issue Type Screen Schemes** (on the sidebar)
2. In the opened Issue Type Screen Schemes, click on **Add Issue Type Screen Scheme** button
3. In the **Add Issue Type Screen Scheme** pop-up, type in '*Shopping List Issue Type Screen Scheme*' in the **Name** field
4. Enter 'Issue Type Screen Scheme for Grocery Shopping List Issue Type and Shopping List Screen Scheme' in the **Description** field

5. SELECT *SHOPPING LIST SCREEN SCHEME* FROM THE **SCREEN SCHEME** LIST
6. CLICK **ADD**

You have now linked a **Screen** to an **Issue Type** by associating the **Screen Scheme** to an **Issue Type Screen Scheme.**

Next, you will link the newly created Issue Type Screen Scheme to your project.

7. NAVIGATE TO MAIN MENU BAR >**PROJECTS** > SHOPPING LIST (SL)
8. IN THE SHOPPING LIST PROJECT SIDEBAR CLICK THE **PROJECT SETTINGS**
9. IN THE MAIN AREA OF THE PROJECT SETTINGS, FIND THE **SCREENS** SECTION AND CLICK ON THE SCHEME SHOWN:

Project settings

Summary

Details

Re-index project

Delete project

Issue types

Grocery Shopping List

Workflows

Screens

Fields

Priorities

Versions

Components

Users and roles

Permissions

Issue Security

Notifications

Hipchat integration

Issue collectors

Edit your project's workflows and screens

If your workflows or screens are only used by yo
make sure they suit the way your team works. G
they're currently set up, and to make any chang
documentation for more info, or talk to your Jira

Issue types

These issue types are available in your project.
Each issue type can be configured differently.

Scheme:

GROCERY SHOPPING LIST ISSUE TYPE SCHEME

Grocery Shopping List

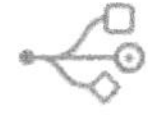

Workflows

A workflow defines which statuses and transitions an issue type can use within a project.

Scheme:

SL: Task Management Workflow Scheme

SL: Task Management Workflow

A screen defines how fields are displayed for an issue. Different screens can be used when an issue is created, viewed, edited, or transitioned through a workflow.

Scheme:

SL: Task Management Issue Type Screen Scheme

10. IN THE OPENED **SCREENS** VIEW CLICK ON **ACTIONS** BUTTON IN THE UPPER RIGHT CORNER
11. SELECT *USE A DIFFERENT SCHEME* FROM THE **ACTIONS** DROP DOWN LIST
12. IN THE **ISSUE TYPE SCREEN SCHEME ASSOCIATION** PAGE SELECT *SHOPPING LIST ISSUE TYPE SCREEN SCHEME* FROM THE **SCHEME** DROP DOWN LIST:

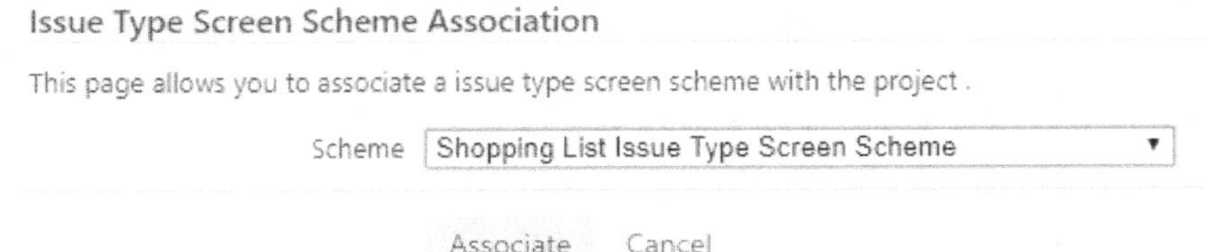

13. CLICK ASSOCIATE

You have completed all of your Screen associations! Congratulations, that was not an easy journey. Test your work by creating a new Shopping List Issue Type.

Chapter 8 – Fields

Chapter Objectives

In the Fields chapter you will gain a deeper understanding of Fields, Field Configurations and Field Configuration Schemes.

You will also be given a brief overview of the remainder of the Issues Screen's Sidebar items: Issue Features, Issue Attributes, and Notifications.

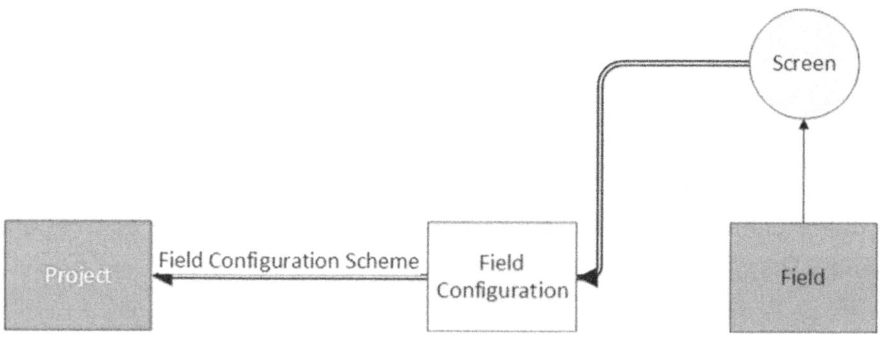

Fields

Fields are the boxes on a screen where you enter, select, edit, or view information. Jira has a number of different types of fields available, such as:

- **Single line or multi line text** boxes where you enter details (your name, for example)
- **Number** fields
- **Calendar** fields where you select a date or a date and time combination
- **Multiple choice, single choice,** and **Cascading** Select lists
- **Radio Button** lists

- **Labels, URL,** and **User Picker**

Jira Core also comes with a great many standard fields (called 'System' fields), which you can use when building screens. Some examples are:

- Summary (text field)
- Type (single select list)
- Due (calendar)
- Labels (labels)
- Description (multi line text field)
- Assignee (User picker)

Custom Fields

Jira Core also allows you to create **Custom Fields**. For example, you may want to create a list of sports activity options for your buddies to choose from. In this case, you could create a custom 'drop down list' field with activities such as: *Golf, Tennis, Hunting, Fishing, Poker, Tiddlywinks, Needlepoint*, etc.

You can reach the Custom Fields view by navigating:

Main Menu Bar ⚙ > Issues > **Custom Fields** in the sidebar:

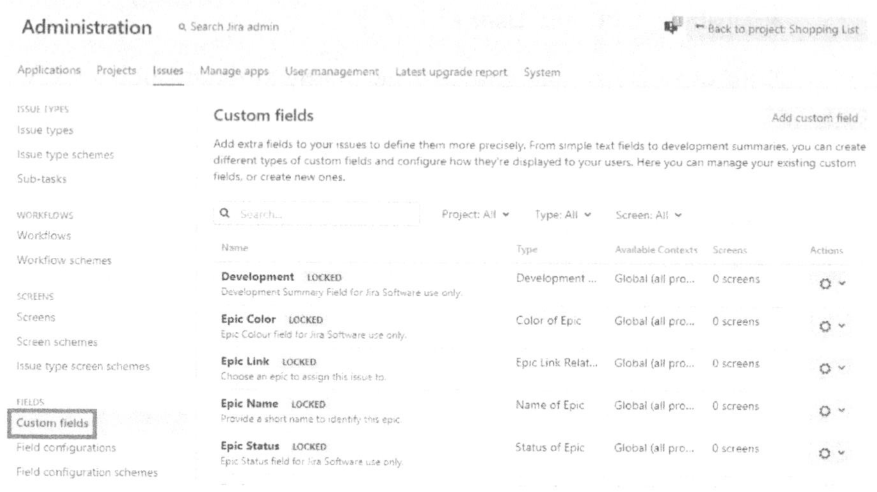

In the opened Custom Fields view you have a Search box and filters such as Project, Type, and Screen. They are here to help you find your field(s). Type the field name, or key words of the field, in the Search box, or click filters' drop-downs and select the options.

Below the Search/Filters row there are five columns: **Name, Type, Available Contexts) Screens,** and **Actions**.

NAME

The **Name** column includes Jira's system fields and those custom fields already built by you or your organization. You may also see a number of 'LOCKED' fields. These are fields available to you if you purchase Jira Service Desk or Jira Software licenses.

This column does NOT include a list of the *types* of custom fields available; those are found in the Add Custom field pop-up when you click the **Add Custom Field** or the **Find More Custom Fields** link.

TYPE

This column indicates the **type** of field used, such as Text, Number, Date, Checkbox, Radio buttons, Select list (single choice), etc.

There are over 20 different types of custom fields available with your purchased version of Jira Core.

You can find more custom field types by clicking on the **Find More Custom Fields** button which will connect you with the **Atlassian Marketplace**.

Available Contexts

Custom Field context is a combination of two things: the **Issue Type** with which the Custom Field is associated and the **Projects** associated with the Custom Field. If a Custom Field is not associated with a specific Issue Type, it is available to all Issue Types (i.e. **Global (all issues)**).

Screens

This column lists the **Screens** associated with the Custom Field.

Actions

In the Actions column (with fields that are not Locked), when you click the **COG** down arrow five options will be listed: **Configure, Edit, Translate, Screens,** and **Delete.**

Configure

The most common Custom Field **Configurations** are: **Add New Context, View Custom Fields, Edit Configuration, Edit Default Value,** and **Edit Options**.

Add New Context

Sometimes you may have a screen with custom fields that you want to reuse in another project but need to change some of the data options in one or more fields. For example, you may have a Jira project that you use in Eastern USA which contains a list of employees who can be assigned to inspect factory equipment. You want to duplicate this project for Western USA but use a different list of employees for that region. That's where a Context comes into play.

Add New Context is fundamentally **a copy function**. It lets you add a new context to the Custom Field by adding a new Configuration Scheme **Label and Description**. You can associate different **Issue Types and Projects** to the new **Context.** In addition, you can change the default value and the options within that field. Just remember that with the Add New Context operation you are keeping the original field too.

You can only have one custom field context per project.

View Custom Fields

This link takes you back to the **Custom Fields** view.

Edit Configuration

This is similar to the Add New Context operation. However, instead of 'copying' your Custom Field configuration scheme, you **modify** the **Label** and **Description** of the existing scheme**.** In addition, you can change the **Issue Type(s)** and **Project**(s) associated with the Custom Field configuration scheme.

Edit Default Value

The Edit Default Value function allows you to set Custom Field Defaults by selecting the value from your existing list of options. Let's say you have a list of three addresses, but your users most often select address number three. Jira allows you to select one value to place first in a Select List (dropdown list). This will become the **first value**, the **Default Value**, the user sees when selecting from the list.

Edit Options

Here you can change the options in your list of items or add new custom field options.

Edit

The Edit link brings you to the Edit Custom Field Details view. Here you can change the name of the **Custom Field** and its **Description**.

Translate

Here you have the option to enter a Custom Field name in a different language, as long as it is one of the twenty in the drop-down list.

Screens

This link takes you to the **Associate field to screens** view. Here you can add the Custom Field to more screens, or change the current Custom Field/Screen association. When you are done, do not forget click on **Update** at the bottom of the view.

Delete

And of course, you can always **Delete** a Custom Field if you no longer need it.

When you click on the Custom **Locked** Field **COG** down arrow, you will see the only two options: View and Screens.

ADD CUSTOM FIELD

To create a custom field, you start by clicking on the **Add custom field** button in the upper right corner of the Custom Fields view. When you do so, the **Select a Field Type** pop-up opens. This is where you start creating a Custom Field:

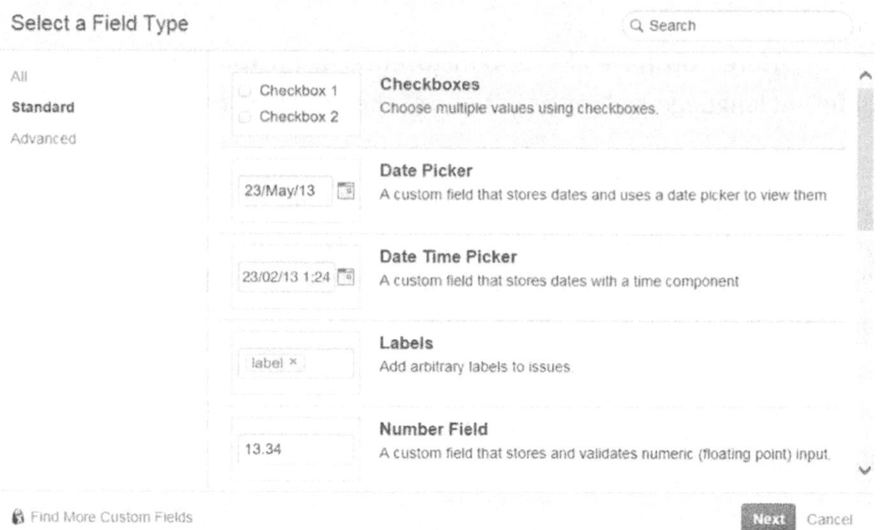

When creating a Custom Field, you go through three steps:

1. Select the type of Custom Field
2. Configure the Custom Field
3. Associate the Custom Field to a Screen

The image above is Step 1 of the Create a Custom Field process. After selecting the Custom Field, you click **Next**, and in the opened **Configure** pop-up add a **Name** and **Description** (Step 2). Clicking on **Create** brings you to the view below, where you associate the newly created Custom Field to your desired Screen(s) (Step 3) by checking the relevant check box in the **Select** column:

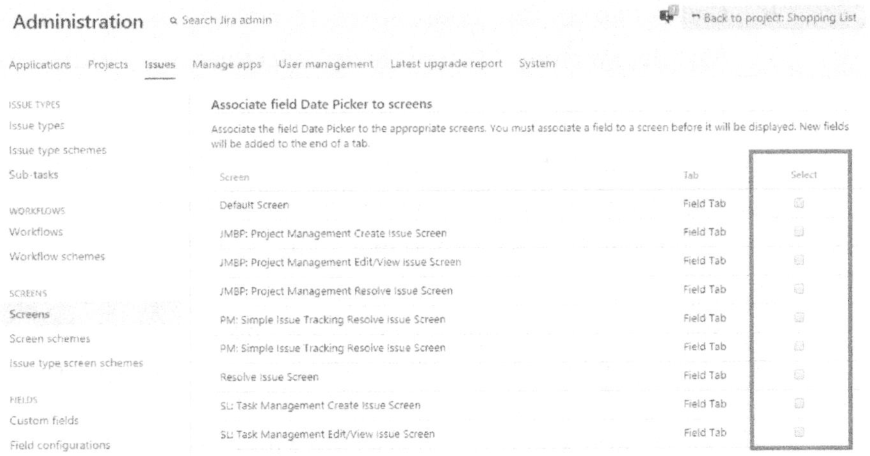

Administration   Search Jira admin   Back to project: Shopping List

Applications   Projects   Issues   Manage apps   User management   Latest upgrade report   System

ISSUE TYPES
Issue types
Issue type schemes
Sub-tasks

WORKFLOWS
Workflows
Workflow schemes

SCREENS
Screens
Screen schemes
Issue type screen schemes

FIELDS
Custom fields
Field configurations

Associate field Date Picker to screens

Associate the field Date Picker to the appropriate screens. You must associate a field to a screen before it will be displayed. New fields will be added to the end of a tab.

Screen	Tab	Select
Default Screen	Field Tab	☐
JMBP: Project Management Create Issue Screen	Field Tab	☐
JMBP: Project Management Edit/View Issue Screen	Field Tab	☐
JMBP: Project Management Resolve Issue Screen	Field Tab	☐
PM: Simple Issue Tracking Resolve Issue Screen	Field Tab	☐
PM: Simple Issue Tracking Resolve Issue Screen	Field Tab	☐
Resolve Issue Screen	Field Tab	☐
SL: Task Management Create Issue Screen	Field Tab	☐
SL: Task Management Edit/View Issue Screen	Field Tab	☐

But what happens if you have **multiple tabs** in your screen and you want the field to appear only in tab three? If your screen *does* have multiple tabs, then the tab column will display a drop-down list for the tabs in that screen. You simply select the relevant tab and check the **Select** checkbox. Once again, do not forget to click on the **Update** button when you finished.

In addition, remember that when you add a custom field to a screen with this method, the field will be added to the bottom of that screen. If you want the field to be somewhere else in the screen you need, first, to open View Screens page (COG Jira Administration > Issues > Screens on the sidebar). Second, find your screen in the Name column and then click on the Configure link in the Actions column.

Find More Custom Fields

If you cannot find the Custom Field you need in the **Add Custom Field** list of Field Types, you can always go to the **Atlassian Marketplace** by clicking on the **Find More Custom Fields** link. Some are free, more are not.

Exercise: Create Custom Fields

In this exercise we will:

- Create two custom Fields
- Associate the new Custom Fields to Screens

We will start by making a check list of commonly purchased grocery items for a fictitious store. Please feel free to alter the list and store name to meet your real-life needs.

1. Navigate Main Menu Bar > ⚙ >**Issues**
2. In the **Administration Issue** view, Select **Custom Fields** from the sidebar
3. In the Custom Field view click on **Add Custom Field**
4. In the **Select A Field Type** pop-up, click on **Checkboxes** and select **Next**
5. In the **Configure 'Checkboxes' Field** pop-up, Enter *Commonly Shopped ACME Store Items* in the **Name** Field
6. Enter the purpose of the list in the **Description** field
7. In the **Options** field, Enter the Following, Click **Add** after each entry:
    - Northern Himalayan Organic Yak Milk
    - Island of Elba Goat Butter
    - 27 Grain Bread
    - Siberian Free Range Quail Eggs
    - Escargot
    - Brussels Sprouts from Brussels
    - Caviar
    - Kobe Beef
    - Champagne
    - Cognac
8. Click **Create**

   NOTE: After you create a custom field, Jira will ask you to **re-index.** Wait until you have completed all the instructions in this exercise. Once you have completed, do re-index.

9. In the **Associate field <Name of your new Field> to Screens** view, find the *Shopping List Screen* in the **Screen** column and check its **Select** box
10. Click **Update** at the bottom of the view

You have just added the new field to your Shopping List Screen. There are two ways to confirm this:

First,

1. Navigate Main Menu Bar > > **Issues**
2. In the **Administration Issue** view, Select **Screens** from the sidebar
3. Locate the *Shopping List Screen*, and click on the **Configure** link in the **Actions** Column

You should see your newly created field in the list of fields for that screen:

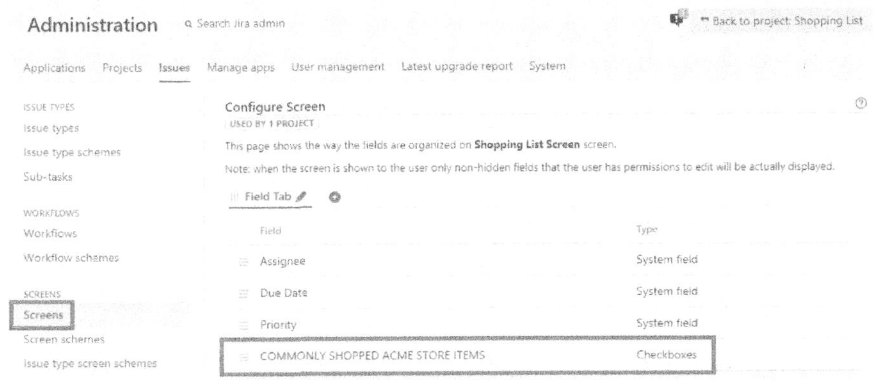

Second,

1. Navigate to Main Menu Bar > **Projects** > *Shopping List*
2. In the *Shopping List* **Project** click **Create** on the Main Menu Bar
3. Make sure *Grocery Shopping List* **Issue Type** is selected in the **Issue Type Field**, and that *Shopping List* is the **project.**

Your specialized list should appear at the bottom of the pop up.

CAUTION: If your field is not there, click on the **Configure Fields button** (in the Create Issue pop up) to make sure your field is available. If the check box next to your custom field is unchecked, then check it and your field will appear on the **Create Issue** pop-up:

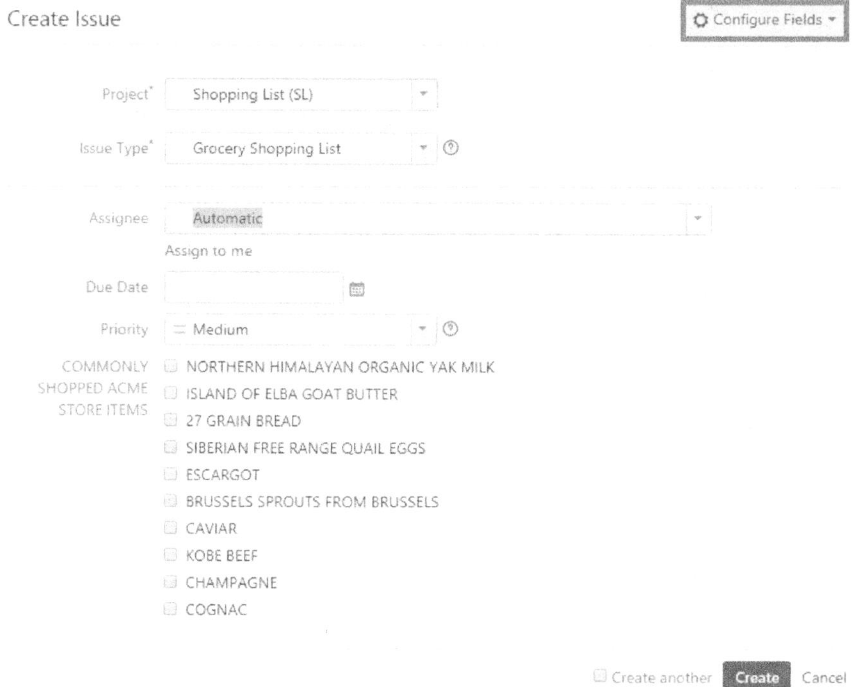

It is convenient to have a list of commonly purchased grocery items; however, you probably purchase other items when you run out of stock. So, now you will create a multi-line text box where you can enter additional items for a specific shopping trip.

EXERCISE: CREATE MULTI-LINE TEXT BOX

1. NAVIGATE MAIN MENU BAR > ⚙ >**ISSUES**

2. In the **Administration issue** view, select **Custom Fields** from the sidebar
3. In the Custom Field view click on **Add Custom Field** button
4. In the **Select A Field Type** pop-up, scroll down to **Text Field (multi-line),** click on it, and select **Next**
5. In the **Configure 'Text Field (multi-line)' Field** pop-up, enter *'Additional Acme Grocery Store items'* in the **Name** field
6. Enter 'additional items to be purchased at the Acme Grocery Store' in the **Description** field
7. Click **Create**
8. In the **Associate field <Name of new field> to Screens** view, locate Shopping List Screen in the **Screen** column and check the **Select** box
9. Click **Update** at the bottom of the Screen

You have now created two new custom fields for your *Shopping List Screen*: a **checkbox field** with commonly shopped grocery items, and a **text box field** where you can enter additional food items for your shopping. Congratulations!

Field Configuration

Field Configuration allows you to modify fields. Here you decide if a field will be visible or hidden, optional or required, and where the field will be positioned on the Screen.

Field Configuration Schemes

Field Configuration Schemes link **Field Configurations** to specific **Issue Types** and from there to specific **Projects**. Field configurations allows you to:

1. Create custom descriptions that will appear below, or next to, a field
2. Show or hide a field
3. Make a field required or optional
4. Determine which renderer to use for text fields

Priorities

Here you can create your own priorities. Just fill in the Add New Priority on the bottom of the View Priorities page and click Add.

> CAUTION: When you add or delete a priority you affect every project in your Jira system. So, **this is an item that should only be managed by the System Administrator** or by the most Senior Jira administrator in your organization.

Priority Schemes

As we have just seen, when you create a new priority, it affects every project in your Jira Core program. You can, however, create a priority scheme that allows you to restrict the priorities a User will see in a particular project. Let's say your priority list includes the five Jira Core default priorities (Highest, High, Medium, Low, Lowest) plus three custom priorities you have created (Level 1, Level 2, and Level 3). You can set up a Priority Scheme for a specific project(s) that will show the User only the Level 1, 2, and 3 priorities.

Having said that, remember that any project NOT using a priority scheme will be able to choose from all eight priorities, which may cause some confusion. I recommend that if you are going to add custom priorities, then you create priority schemes for ALL your projects (e.g. one priority scheme using your new custom priorities, and a second scheme that uses **only** the Jira default priorities).

Setting priorities should be done by your Jira System Admin or most Sr. Jira Administrator.

Issue Features

Time Tracking

Time tracking is an extremely powerful tool in Jira.

If you happen to click on the Time Tracking link in the **COG Administration Issues > Time Tracking** on the sidebar (under Issue Features), you will be taken to the Time Tracking view. The screen will tell you if your Time Tracking is ON or OFF. It will also tell you the default working hours per day, working days per week, and some other key metrics.

You can change these metrics by clicking on the Activate/Deactivate button. In the Time Tracking view you can change:

- Number of working hours per day
- Number of working days per week
- Time format
- Default time unit (e.g. minutes, hours, days, etc.)
- Copying of comments

Once you have made changes, make sure to click the Activate button (if your Time Tracking screen is OFF) or Deactivate (if it is ON). You will also need to do a re-index of the program for changes to take an effect.

We dedicate a chapter to Time tracking later in this book.

Issue Linking

Issue linking allows you to associate one issue to another. It lets you know, for example, if you need to complete Issue X before starting work on Issue Y. The good news is that the program informs you about this in the Issue Detail View. The bad news is that it doesn't take any action. In other words, Issue Linking is simply a notification technique.

Issue Attributes

Statuses

Most workflow design is done in the workflow section, so I am not quite sure why Statuses is included here. I would avoid it altogether in order to keep things simpler. However, if you need to translate a status this is the right location to do so.

Resolutions

In Jira, resolution tells the software – and others - you are finished with the issue, and it can now be closed out. A resolution is NOT a status. Jira has four default resolutions, two of which (Duplicate and Cannot Reproduce) are designed primarily for software purposes. You can add your own Resolutions at the bottom of the View Resolutions page. For example, I have added a resolution in my Jira called "Issue Canceled". This lets me close out an Issue from any status in the workflow.

Issue Security Schemes

Issue Security Schemes are described in more detail in the next chapter.

Notifications and Notification Schemes

One of the great strengths of Jira is its ability to create automated email notifications to specific people based on events that happen during the lifecycle of an issue. For example, you may have an automated email go to the next person in the process once you click an issue's "**Resolved'** status. Or, you can set it up so that an automated email will be sent to the project manager or Issue Owner's boss indicating the issue is late and should be checked into.

There are a number of defaults set up in the program. The most obvious is that you will get an email as soon as you are assigned to a project issue. However, you can also bespoke notifications based on almost any condition or event that might occur in your project.

Notifications need Notification schemes in order to be associated with a project.

Permissions and Schemes

You probably don't want anyone and everyone to see all the details of your project and make any change they want. Imagine if someone from sales started making changes to the manufacturing process, or vice versa. The Permissions (and Security) areas are where you assign people to Groups and Roles, and where you decide the Screens they can see, or not, and the things they can edit, or not.

Why not just assign those things directly to individuals; I hear you ask. That's because individuals often leave the organization or change jobs. You could spend a whole bunch of time giving an individual specific permissions and security clearances, only to see that person win the lottery. You would have to redo all that work for the person who replaces her. Better to create a **Role**, assign all the permissions to the role and simply link the individual to the Role.

Of course, Permissions need Permission schemes to work with a Project.

We look at permissions and schemes in more detail in the next chapter.

Chapter 9- Users, Roles, and Groups

Chapter Objectives

By the end of this Chapter you will have a working understanding of Users, Roles and Groups.

You will be able to:

- **create a User**
- **assign Users to a Role**
- **create a Group and assign a User to the Group**
- **assign a Global Permission to a Group**
- **Create a Project Permission Scheme**
- **Create a Project Admin Role**

Overview

While Jira Core is fantastic at automating a great many tasks and operations, a project still involves people, and there needs to be a way of managing people within Jira and within specific projects.

Jira manages people in two ways: with Permissions and with Groups/Roles. A permission is an authorization, or approval, to do something. In Jira you need permission to do anything. Literally. Want to create an Issue? You need permission. Want to edit an Issue? You need permission. Want to comment, view, see other users? Permission. Permission. Permission. You cannot breathe in Jira without a permission.

There are 39 different permission/security settings available in Jira Core. Jira permits you, or more specifically your username, to be directly assigned to projects or issues or both, meaning every time you are assigned to a new project or issue type, someone needs to go in and go through that 39-permission checklist and determine what you can and cannot do in that project or issue.

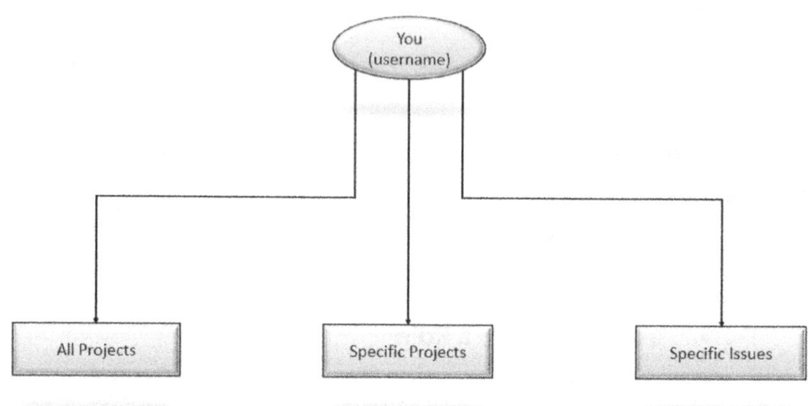

It might be manageable if you have only five or six people in your organization, but you can imagine the headaches if you have 1,000 employees. And what happens when you win the lottery, and the supervisor has to go through that same permission checklist for your replacement. Things get ugly real fast using this method. That's why Jira implemented **Groups and Roles**.

Groups and Roles are ways of easily managing permissions and users. There are four dimensions here to consider:

1. Groups or Roles are created
2. Permissions are associated with the Group or Role
3. Users are then assigned to those Groups or Roles
4. Groups are associated with Jira, and Roles with Projects and Issues.

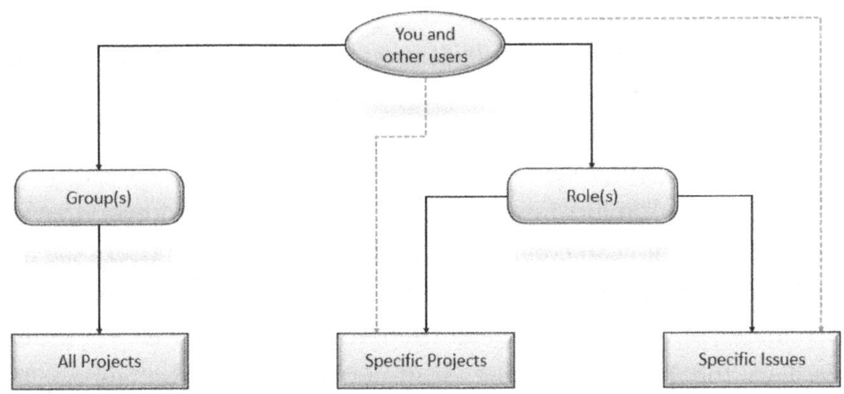

The advantage to this approach is that when people change jobs or leave the organization you simply remove – from the group or role - the username of the person who left and replace it with the new username. You don't need to go through that long permission checklist again.

But what's the **difference between a Group and a Role in Jira**? Great question.

A group is the same as a role with one major difference. Groups have what are called 'global' permissions. This means they can work with all projects, no exceptions. You cannot say, I want this group to work with these 99 projects but not this one project over here. It is all or nothing. In addition, some groups (Jira System Admin and Jira Admin) can work behind the scenes doing the I.T. stuff or designing/ building Projects, Issues, Screens, Fields, etc. Other groups can be limited to simply using the software.

A Role is not global. Roles are meant for specific projects. For example, you might create a Role called 'Denver Sales Representative' and associate it with the Denver project. Or, you may design a Human Resources role that can be used in a number of projects.

Jira Core Default Groups

Jira comes with two default groups: Jira Administrator and Jira-Core-Users.

Jira Administrator

The Jira Administrator has access to anything and everything in Jira. The Jira Admin can create all the front-end stuff that Users see and use: Projects, Issue Types, Screens, Fields, Workflows, etc. In addition, the Jira Admin can also work with all the back-end stuff, what we usually regard as the hardware or I.T. stuff: installing and configuring Jira, connecting Jira to email systems, employee systems, external databases, etc.

Depending on the size of your organization and your needs, you probably want to take the time to seriously consider who should, and who should not, have the Jira Admin permissions. Do you really want to give your idiot nephew Bernard (who spent 3 years in Grade 9 and who truly believes the world is flat) the ability to change anything in the program? I think not.

Luckily, Jira has resolved this problem by creating two other types of Administrators.

Jira System Admin

If you want all of your I.T. (system) access limited to your I.T. department, you can create a new group called Jira System Admin and grant it Jira System Administrator permissions. Of course, after that you will need to remove Jira System Admin permissions from those people you want as Jira Admins.

If you create a Jira System Admin group, make sure to have at least 2 people in that group at all times. What happens if you only have one Jira System Admin, and she wins the lottery and leaves for Bora Bora the next day? There will be no one else who can get into the system.

Jira Project Admin

Prior to Jira Core 7.2 if you wanted to create screens, fields, workflows, etc. you had to be a Jira Admin or Jira System Admin. That created problems because screens, workflows, etc. were often shared across multiple projects. Novice Jira Admins would make a change to a workflow, for example, and wreak havoc among all other projects using that same workflow. Starting with Jira Core 7.2, Atlassian implemented the concept of the Jira Project Admin. Project Admins have the ability to administer a project, but they are restricted to that project.

A Jira Admin will create a project (a Jira Project Admin cannot create projects). The Jira Admin will then assign a person to the project and give that individual Jira Project Admin permissions. The Project Admin then has the ability to edit project role memberships, create screens and workflows, change some project details and versions, etc.

Jira-Core-Users

While the Jira Admin groups tend to focus behind the scenes, the Jira-Core-Users group is limited to the 'front end' of the software. They can work with projects and issues but cannot create anything other than an Issue.

When an individual is invited to be a licensed user, they are added to the Jira-Core-Users group by default. If they are not included in the Jira-Core-Users group, then they will not be given access to Jira Core and will not be able to log in.

By default, any user who is licensed is assigned to the Jira-Core-Users Group AND is given Application Access (a permission). That means they can view and work with any Issue in any project. That's actually not a bad idea if you have a small company and everybody does everything. You don't need to go through all the bother of creating Roles, permission schemes, and then assigning people to those roles and projects. But as you grow, you are likely to find it necessary to restrict what your team members can see and do. Do you really want Sam in Distribution to have access to the Finance project?

Roles vs. Groups

As we saw earlier, a Role is a means of managing permissions and users, but is designed to work only with specific projects.

Personally, I would think of the difference between Roles and Groups this way: Groups are associated with permission and security rules that are applicable regardless of Role. A Role has job specific rules. For example, you may create two Roles, one a Supply Chain Analyst and one a Quality Control Analyst. Just by the titles you can see each will have different requirements and need diverse restrictions. The most obvious Role specific requirements and restrictions may be that the Supply Chain Analyst will have access to Supply Chain projects and no other, while the QC Analyst can work only with QC projects.

Now that we have a good idea of the differentiation between Users, Roles, and Groups lets look at each in more detail.

Users

Exercise: View User Management

1. Navigate to Main Menu Bar > ⚙ > **User management**
2. The **Users** view will open:

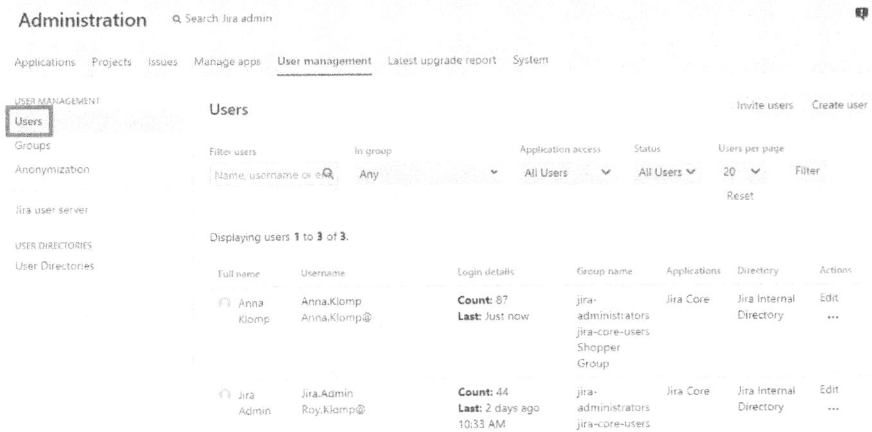

In the Users view you can:

- create and invite new users
- find users
- see details about the Users

Exercise: Create User

1. Click on the **Create User** button in the upper right corner of the view:

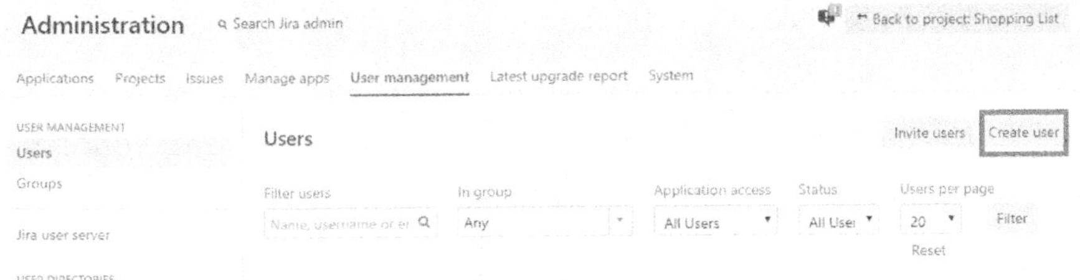

Create new user

Email address* E.g. charlie@atlassian.com

Full name* User's full name

Username* Desired username

Password Password if required

Send notification email

Application access JIRA Core

Create another

Create user Cancel

The fields in the **Create New User** pop-up are obvious, and we won't cover them in detail. Make sure to click the **Send Notification Email**. Doing so allows the User to log on and change their password if they wish.

> CAUTION: The Send Notification Email is only valid for 24 hours. If the user has not responded in that time you will need to resend the notification.

Needless to say (but I'll say it anyway), if you are over your limit of licenses you will not be able to add any new users unless you delete existing users or you purchase more licenses. More importantly, **if you are over your limit of licenses, no one can create an Issue**; you are all locked out until you reduce the number of Users to your license limit.

Invite Users

Another way of adding a User is to invite them, but before you do, you must have set up your **Outgoing Mail Server.** Your Jira System Administrator should do this.

Invite users

You must first configure your Outgoing Mail Server before you can invite users.

Assuming your Outgoing Mail Server has been set up, the following message will pop up when you click the **Invite users** button:

Invite Users

You can invite new users to sign up by entering their email addresses below. An invitation will be sent to each email address. Only the recipient of the invitation will be able to sign up.

Email Addresses*

Enter each email address on a new line or separate addresses using commas.
Note, you cannot invite users by sending an invitation to a mailing list.

Send Cancel

Here you simply include one or more email addresses (use a comma to separate the addresses or enter each address on a separate line) and click Send. An automated email is sent to each invitee, which includes a link to the Jira signup view where they can enter a User name, password, etc.

CAUTION: The invitation is valid for seven days. If the invitee has not responded in that time, you will need to re-invite the individual.

Filter Users

If you have a great many Users, the **Filter users** feature is quite handy. Simply fill in one, some, or all, of the appropriate fields: **Name, user name or email**, or **In group** (simply select the appropriate Group from the "In group" drop down list, or **Application access** (Jira Core is the application in our case), or **Status** (keep here all users or select only active/inactive), or any combination of the four fields. When done, click the **Filter** button.

Filter users | In group | Application access | Status | Users per page
Name, username or em: | Any | All Users | All Users | 20 | Filter | Reset

Clicking the **Reset** link clears all the fields and makes all Users visible again.

The Users Columns

The **Users** view has seven columns: **Full Name, Username, Login Details, Group name, Applications, Directory** and **Actions**.

Full Name

Here you see the complete name of the User or his/her project role (as defined in the User's Profile). Clicking on a full name or a role will take you to the User's detailed information page.

Username

This column contains the **Usernames** of Jira Core licensed users and a hyperlink to their email address.

Login Details

This column indicates how many times the User has logged In, when they last logged in, or never logged in, and any problems that may have occurred when the User tried to log in.

The column is helpful if you have security concerns or are trying to find 'inactive' users.

Group Name

Here are the **Groups' names** to which the User belongs. Clicking on the related Group name will NOT open a list of Users belonging to that Group. Instead, you will be taken to a page showing the various schemes (**Permission, Notification, Issue Security**) associated with the Group.

Applications

That is very obvious: Jira Core. If you have Jira Service Desk or Jira Software licenses they would show up here also.

Directory

By default, Jira adds users to the Jira Internal Directory. However, you may have had your organization's directory also installed. Or you may have had other directories added (e.g. client directory, vendor directory). The Username may appear in any of those associated directories.

Actions

The **Actions** column contains the **Edit link** and a menu button. Clicking on the menu will open the drop-down list allowing you to choose one of three options: **Edit user groups**, **View project roles,** and **Delete user:**

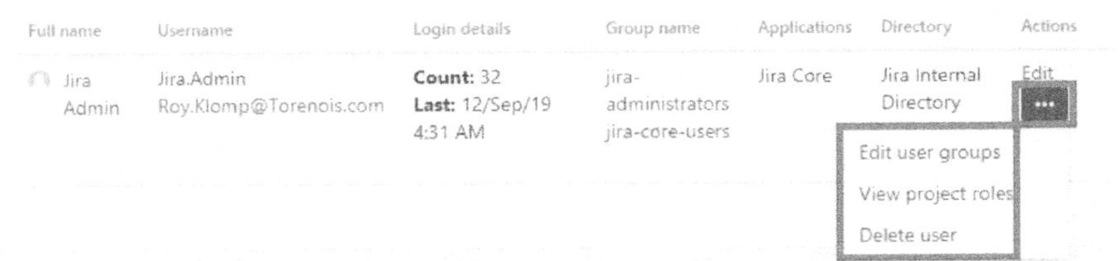

Edit

In the Edit Profile pop-up, which opens when you click **Edit** link, you will be able to change the Username, Full Name, and Email address of the User.

You can also make the User Inactive by removing the check mark in the **Active** Box.

Edit user profile

Username* Jira.Admin

Full name* Jira Admin

Email* Roy.Klomp@

Active

Update Cancel

This is very helpful if you don't want to delete the User, for example a User who has gone on sabbatical or pregnancy leave. An **Inactive** User cannot access Jira and will not receive any further email notifications. Possibly most important, an **Inactive User no longer counts as a Licensed User**, which is quite beneficial if you are near or at your License limit.

Edit user groups

Clicking on **Edit user groups** menu button option will open the **Manage user groups** pop-up:

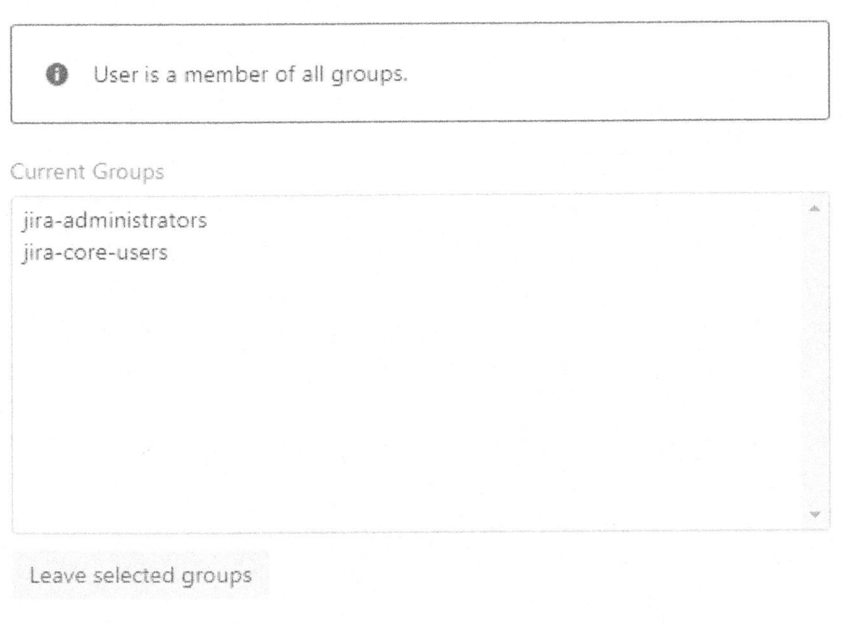

Here you can add the **User** to other groups. Start to type a group name in the “Type to start searching” box to see available groups, then select that group/s from the drop-down list and click on the **Join selected groups** button. You can also remove him or her from the **Current Groups** to which s/he belongs by clicking on the **Leave selected groups** button.

View project roles

Clicking on this link takes you to the **View Project Roles for User** page. Here you see the Projects in which the User is participating and the Roles s/he is assigned to within the Project.

We will discuss **Roles** in more detail in the next section.

Delete user

Finally, you can delete a User by clicking the **Delete user** link. As the warning will tell you, Deleting a User cannot be undone.

Exercise: Create New User

In this exercise you will:

- Create a new User

NOTE: the exercise assumes you have enough licenses to add an additional User *and* you have the Jira permission to add a User.

1. Navigate to Main Menu Bar > ⚙ > **User management**
2. In the opened **Users** view, click on the **Create User** button
3. In the **Create New User** pop-up form, fill in the Fields including the Password field
4. Check the Send Notification Email box
5. Click on the **Create user** button

You have successfully created a **User** and have sent the User a Notification email.

Groups

A **Group** is a collection of individuals in Jira who have the same **Security**, **Notification**, and **Permission** schemes, *regardless* of their **Project Role**. Indeed, the benefits of a Group are many. Groups can be associated with:

- Global permissions
- Project roles
- Workflows
- Permission Schemes
- Email Notification Schemes
- Issue Security Schemes

- Issue Filters
- Dashboards

Group Permissions

There are six global permissions available:

Global Permission	Comments
Jira System Administrator	Can do anything and everything in Jira Core. Typically, is an I.T. group and limits itself to maintaining the software.
Jira Administrator	Can do almost all of the Jira Administration functions. Is restricted from doing the pure I.T. stuff.
Browse Users	A permission to view all Jira user names and group names. Also, to share Issues.
Create Shared Object	A permission to share a filter or dashboard globally or with specific groups. Many organizations have people who specialize in creating all the filters and dashboards for the organization.
Manage Group Filter Subscriptions	A permission to create and delete group filter subscriptions.
Bulk Change	A permission for the bulk operations: -Bulk Edit -Bulk Move -Bulk Workflow Transition

	-Bulk Delete

Often large organizations will create specific groups for: Browse Users, Create Shared Object, Manage Group Filter Subscriptions, and Bulk Change. They then assign specialists to each of these groups. This tends to limit the potential for chaos that may occur if everyone is given the ability to Bulk Change (for example).

GROUP VIEW

EXERCISE: VIEW GROUP

1. NAVIGATE TO MAIN MENU BAR > ⚙ >**USER MANAGEMENT**
2. IN THE ADMINISTRATION USER MANAGEMENT'S SIDEBAR CLICK ON **GROUPS:**

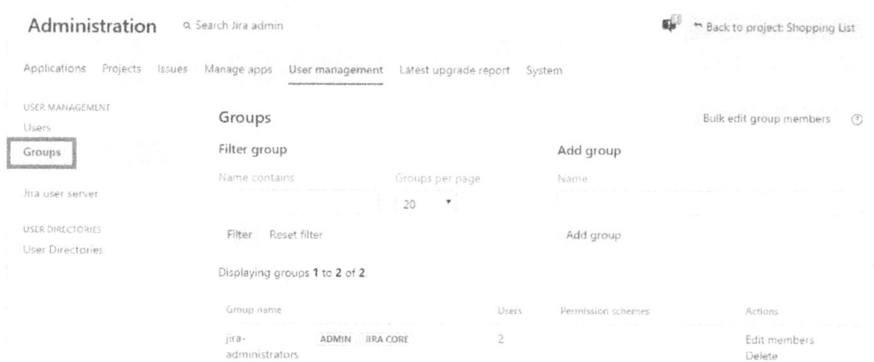

I like this view as it has all the 'Group stuff' in one place. Here you can: Add a group, use a Filter to narrow your group search, Bulk Edit Group Members, Edit or Delete Members, and see a listing of all of your Groups.

Add Group

In the **Add Group** text box simply type in the name of the Group and click the Add Group button. That's it. Your new Group appears instantly in the Group Name list below.

Filter Group

Type in the name, or partial name, of a **Group** in the **Filter Group** text box and click **Filter** button to narrow your range of Group Names.

Click **Reset Filter** link to clear the Filter and have all Group Names reappear.

Bulk Edit Group Members

This is a nice feature if you need to make changes affecting a number of Users at one time.

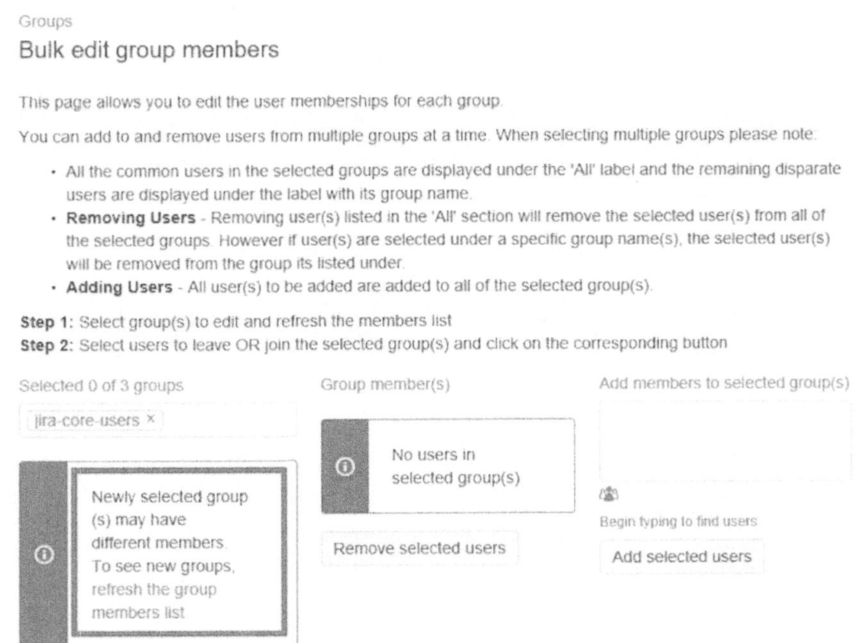

The **Bulk edit group members** page has three texts-boxes: Selected groups, Group member(s), and Add members to selected group(s).

In the first, **Selected groups**, text-box start to type the name of the group and then select that group from the drop-down list.

You should see a note appear below the list. Click on the blue *'refresh the group members list'* link. This will fill the **Group Member(s)** box (the middle box) with a list of the members. From this Group Member(s) box you can delete one, some, or all member(s) from the group. Hold down the **control (Ctrl)** key to select multiple members. Click the **Remove Selected Users** button to, well, remove the selected users.

In the right text box, you can type in the name of a User or Multiple Users (separated by commas), and click the **Add selected users** button to add them to the Group. Before you click the button, make sure the group to which you want to add them is actually selected in the **Group name** text box.

> TIP: If the autotype function is not working (as it is sometimes inclined to do) click on the little icon below the text box. That will open up a list of all available users where you can select the name(s).

The Groups Columns

The **Groups** view contains four columns: **Group Name, Users, Permission Schemes,** and **Actions.**

Group Name

This listing contains the names of your **Groups**. You cannot have duplicate names.

Users

The number of **Users** in the Group is displayed here.

PERMISSION SCHEMES

This column contains the names of any permission schemes associated with the group. If none are listed, and the space is blank, then the default applies.

ACTIONS

The Actions column has links to **Delete** and **Edit Members**.

Delete

Clicking this link will take you to the **Delete Group** page. Be aware that **deleting a Group will not delete Users**.

Edit Members

If you click on the **Edit Members** link you will be taken to the same **Bulk Edit Group Members** page we just discussed.

In the exercises below you will:

- Create a Group
- Add a User to a Group
- Give the Group a Global Permission

EXERCISE: CREATE GROUP

1. NAVIGATE TO MAIN MENU BAR > ⚙ >**USER MANAGEMENT**
2. IN THE ADMINISTRATION USER MANAGEMENT'S SIDEBAR CLICK ON **GROUPS**
3. IN THE GROUPS VIEW, ENTER *SHOPPER GROUP* IN THE **ADD GROUP** TEXT BOX
4. CLICK THE **ADD GROUP** BUTTON

You have created the Group.
Next, you will add a User to the Group.

EXERCISE: ADD USER TO GROUP

1. STAYING IN THE **GROUPS** VIEW, FIND THE *SHOPPER GROUP* AND CLICK ON **EDIT MEMBERS** LINK IN THE **ACTIONS** COLUMN

2. IN THE BULK EDIT GROUP MEMBERS PAGE, ENTER YOUR NAME IN THE ADD MEMBERS TO SELECTED GROUP(S) TEXT BOX

TIP: if the autotype function is not working, click on the little icon below the text box. That will open up a list of all available users and then simply select your name from the list.

3. CLICK THE ADD SELECTED USERS BUTTON

You have just added your name to the newly created Shopper Group.

Next, we will give the Group a Global Permission:

EXERCISE: GRANT GROUP GLOBAL PERMISSION

1. NAVIGATE TO MAIN MENU BAR > ⚙ > **SYSTEM**
2. IN THE ADMINISTRATION SYSTEM'S SIDEBAR CLICK ON **GLOBAL PERMISSIONS** IN THE SECURITY SECTION
3. GO TO THE BOTTOM OF THE **GLOBAL PERMISSIONS** VIEW TO THE **ADD PERMISSION** AREA
4. SELECT *JIRA ADMINISTRATORS* IN THE **PERMISSION** DROP DOWN LIST

IMPORTANT: do not select Jira SYSTEM Administrators

5. SELECT *SHOPPER GROUP* IN THE **GROUP** DROP DOWN LIST
6. CLICK THE **ADD** BUTTON

You have associated your newly created group to a Global Permission.

At the beginning of the Group section of this chapter you saw a list of all the things in Jira Core you could associate with a Group. The good news is that you can indeed associate them. The bad news is that it is not easy to do as it sounds. Needless to say, if you want help associating them, please don't hesitate to contact us where we will be pleased to discuss how Toreno Information Solutions can help you.

ROLES

Users are typically connected to specific Projects through **Roles**.

EXERCISE: VIEW USER'S PROJECT ROLES

1. NAVIGATE TO MAIN MENU BAR > > **USER MANAGEMENT**

IN THE OPENED **USERS** VIEW FIND YOUR **USERNAME**

2. CLICK ON THE MENU BUTTON IN THE **ACTIONS** COLUMN AND SELECT **VIEW PROJECT ROLES**

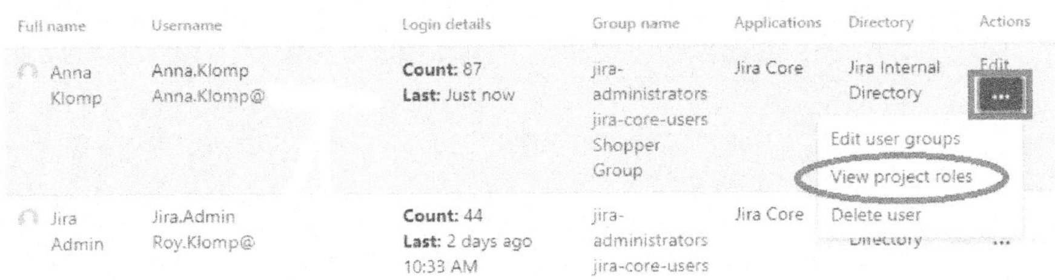

In the opened **View Project Roles for User** page you see the projects to which you belong. Your project Role is indicated by a green checkmark in one or more of the Roles' columns.

You can have more than one Role in a Project.

3. *CLICK* THE **EDIT PROJECT ROLES** BUTTON LOCATED AT THE UPPER RIGHT CORNER OF THE PAGE:

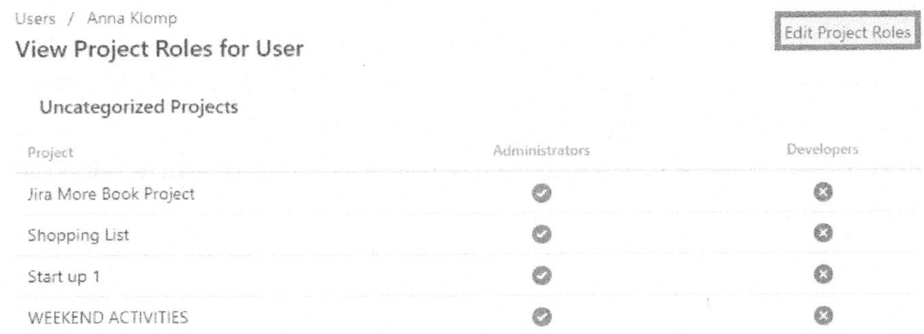

If you are a Jira Admin and you select your own name, you are going to see a list of all projects, because – as a Jira Admin – you are automatically given access to all projects. So, try and find someone who is restricted to a few projects. Once the **Edit Project Roles for User** view opens the user should see a list of the projects s/he is assigned to. In addition, s/he should see an information box above the list. Click on **Display Project** link to see all projects' names:

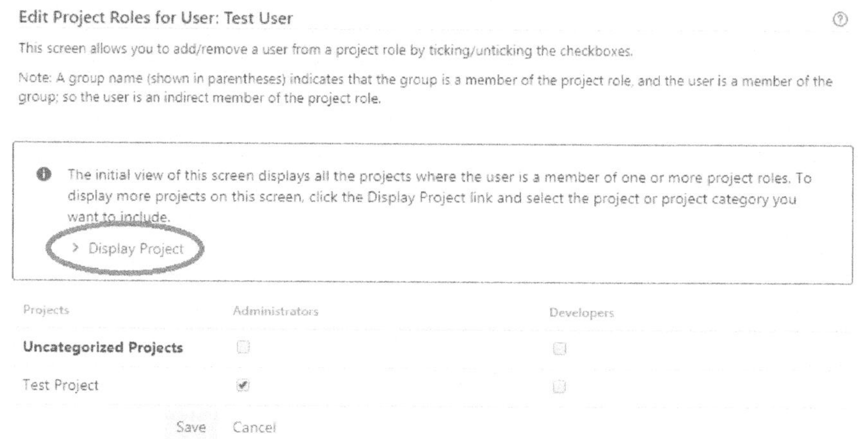

A list of available projects opens. Click one and it will be added to the list in the Edit Project Roles for User view. You can now assign the User to a Role in that newly added project.

Creating and Editing Project Roles

You would think the place to create, edit, and delete project **Roles** would be in the User Management area, but it is actually located in the **System** area. The reason for creating roles in the System area is that at this point we are starting to deal with security issues, which fall under the System authority.

Exercise: View Add Project Roles

1. Navigate to Main Menu Bar > ⚙ >**System**

2. IN THE **ADMINISTRATION SYSTEM'S** SIDEBAR CLICK ON **PROJECT ROLES** IN THE SECURITY SECTION

The **Project Role Browser** view is now open. You can do a lot of stuff here; so, let's spend some time on this view.

The most obvious function is that you can create a new **Project Role** by filling the **Add Project Role** fields at the bottom of the view:

Project Role Browser

You can use project roles to associate users and/or groups with specific projects. The table below shows all the project roles that are available in Jira. Use this screen to add, edit and delete project roles. You can also click 'View Usage' to see which projects, permission schemes and notification schemes are using project roles.

Project Role Name	Description	Actions
Administrators	A project role that represents administrators in a project	View Usage Manage Default Members Edit Delete
Developers		View Usage Manage Default Members Edit Delete

Add Project Role

Name

Description

Add Project Role

PROJECT ROLE BROWSER

The view has three columns: **Project Role Name, Description,** and **Actions**.

PROJECT ROLE NAME

Here, unsurprisingly, are the names of your Project Roles. I advise you consider applying a standard format for Project Role Names, so you can easily identify them later.

I recommend, whenever possible, creating Project Role names by duplicating existing Job Titles within your organization. For example, in your organization you may have a Marketing Analyst job title with five employees as well as a Marketing Analyst Manager with one employee. Each job title, if done correctly in your organization, should have a very clear job description associated with it. I suggest you follow the same practice. After all, the work of defining a Role and determining what the User does within the Role has already been done for you by the organization. Additionally, why would you create Roles that are different from existing job titles? Doing so will: a) just confuse people, and b) make employees very suspicious if they see themselves attached to a different job title (Role). *'Does this mean my job is changing?' 'Will I have to learn new tasks?' 'Will I have new responsibilities?'* Why would you want to risk trouble by making up new Role names?

Of course, speaking out of the other side of my mouth, part of the reason for implementing Jira Core may be because you want to change work processes **and** Roles, or create new ones. In this case, I recommend you create a dramatically different Project Role names. Do you want to send a clear message that this is a different job? Just don't forget to implement your **Change Management** strategy before you do.

The second thing to consider when creating Project Role names is the name of your Project. If the role is meant for only one project, then you should include the role name *and* abbreviation of the **project name**, as the first part of the Project Role name; for example, ACME Project Supply Chain Analyst.

Description

The **Description** of a Project Role should include both an expanded explanation of the Project Role Name and more details around the role itself. If the Project Role is going to be integrated into a workflow, it is recommended you add a warning line informing that, for example, deleting the role or editing its name will cause the workflow to fail.

Actions

The Actions column has four links: **View Usage, Manage Default Members, Edit,** and **Delete**.

View Usage

View Usage for Project Role: Administrators

This page shows which notification schemes, permission schemes, issue security schemes and workflows are currently using the **Administrators** project role. This page also shows which projects are using each scheme.

- **Return to Project Role Browser**

Project role **Administrators** is used by **1 permission** schemes:

Permission Scheme	Associated Projects	Project Role Members Per Project
Default Permission Scheme	Jira More Book Project	1 (View)
	Shopping List	1 (View)
	Start up 1	1 (View)
	Test Project	2 (View)
	WEEKEND ACTIVITIES	1 (View)

This page shows the various schemes, workflows, Projects, and Project Role Members and their relationship to one another.

Manage Default Members

In many organizations there is typically a single person or team of people assigned to a particular role. The **Manage Default Members** link allows you to assign a User, or number of Users, as the default individual(s) for the Project Role. In this approach you don't need to search through your entire database of Users to assign someone to the project role every time you create a new project.

Edit Default Members for Project Role: Administrators

The table below shows the default members (i.e. users, groups) for a project role

NOTE: When a new project is created, it will be assigned these 'default members' for the 'Administrators' project role. Note that 'default members' apply only when a project is created. Changing the 'default members' for a project role will not affect role membership for existing projects.

- Return to Project Role Browser

Default Users	Default Groups
None selected. Edit	jira-administrators Edit

As you can see, assigning a **Default User** to a Project Role is straight forward. You can also change the **Default Group** associated with a Project Role.

A good thing to keep in mind is that any changes you make to the Default User will not affect existing projects.

Edit

The Edit link brings you to a page that allows you to change the **Name** and **Description** of the **Project Role**.

CAUTION: Be very careful when making a Name change, especially if the existing Name is deeply integrated with **workflows and permission schemes.**

Delete

You can **Delete** a project role.

CAUTION: Remember that when you delete a project role you are not just deleting it from the current project, you will also delete it from **all projects** and **all schemes** with which the project role is associated.

In these exercises you will:

- Create a Project Role
- Assign a User to a specific Project

Exercise: Create Project Role

1. Navigate to Main Menu Bar > >**System**
2. In the **Administration System's** sidebar click on **Project Roles** in the Security section
3. in the **Project Role Browser** view, go to the bottom to the **Add Project Role**
4. Enter *Shopper*, in the **Name** Field
5. Enter Shopper Role for the Shopping List Project in the **Description** Field
6. Click the **Add Project Role** button

You have just created your first Project Role.
Next, you will assign yourself to that Role.

Exercise: Assign User to Project Role

1. Navigate to Main Menu Bar > ⚙ >**User management**
2. In the **Administration Users** view find your Username and click on **menu button** in the Actions column
3. Select View project roles
4. In the **View Project Roles for User** page, click on the **Edit Project Roles** button in the upper right corner
5. In the **Edit Project Roles for User** page, find the *Shopping List* Project and click the **checkbox** in the Shopper Column
6. Click the **Save** button

Congratulations you have assigned yourself to the role of Shopper in the Shopping List Project.

Permissions

Earlier in this chapter we explained how to create users, assign them to Roles and then assign them to Projects. Well, that's fine, but is a complete waste of time unless we also address project permissions. Here is a scenario of what happens quite frequently with new Jira Admins working with roles. First, you create a new 'Top-Secret' project. Then you create a 'Top-Secret Scientist' Role. Then you assign George to the Role. You finish by associating the Role with the Project. All is good, now only George can work on the Top-Secret project. But a little while later you find, by accident, that everyone can see and work with the Top-Secret project and its Issues. What's going on?

The problem is with the original sign up process. Remember, when a User is created s/he is associated with the Jira-Core-Users Group and is given 'Application Access'. This is typically where the difficulty lies. Let's take a look.

Exercise: View Default Permission Scheme

1. Navigate Main Menu Bar > ⚙ > **Issues**
2. In the Issues Sidebar, Click on **Permission Schemes** (should be the last option in the Sidebar)
3. In the Permission Schemes view, locate the **Default Permission Scheme**, and click on **Permissions** link in the Actions column
4. In the Default Permission Scheme view, Scroll down a little bit to the **Issue Permissions** area

You will notice that most of the Permissions are granted to "Any logged in user". That means that anyone who is a licensed Jira user can see and work on any Jira Project and Issue.

In order to ensure that only George can work on your Top-Secret Project you need to create a project specific permission scheme. A Project Permission Scheme does a couple of things:

- It ensures only George, and only those roles or other individuals associated with that permission scheme, has visibility and access to the Project and its Issues
- It blocks Jira's Default Permission Scheme from the project. A Default Scheme only works with projects that do not have a Project Permission Scheme.

Why don't we create a Project Permission Scheme and see how it works.

Exercise: Create a Project Permission Scheme

1. Navigate Main Menu Bar > > **Issues**
2. In the Issues Sidebar, click on **Permission Schemes** (should be the last option in the Sidebar)
3. In the **Permission Schemes** view, click on **Add Permission Scheme** button (in the upper right corner)
4. In the Add permission scheme page, enter *Weekend Activity Permission Scheme* in the **Name** field
5. Click **Add**
6. Back in the **Permission Schemes** view, find our newly created *Weekend Activity Permission Scheme* and click on **Permissions** link in the **Actions** column
7. In the opened Weekend Activity Permission Scheme page, Click **edit** link in the **Administer Projects** row
8. In the **Grant Permission** pop up, click **Show more** link
9. In the extended "Granted To" list, click on **Single User**, then enter your name in the field that appears below
10. Click **Grant**
11. Back in the Weekend Activity Permission Scheme page note that you now have the permission to Administer the Project.

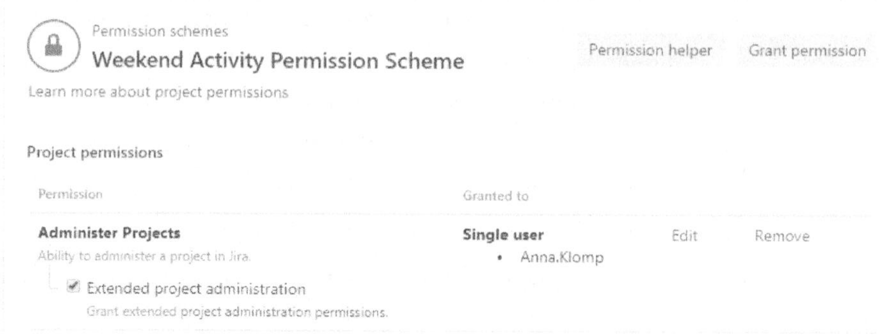

Permission schemes
Weekend Activity Permission Scheme
Learn more about project permissions

Permission helper Grant permission

Project permissions

Permission	Granted to		
Administer Projects Ability to administer a project in Jira. Extended project administration Grant extended project administration permissions.	**Single user** • Anna.Klomp	Edit	Remove

You have just created your first Project Permission Scheme, and, by the way, we have also made you a project administrator for this project. But a couple of things to be aware. First, this is actually a duplicate permission, because – as a Jira Admin – you still have access to the project. Second, any other Jira Admin also has access to the project. Remember, **Jira Admins have global permissions that are not affected by project permission schemes.**

The second thing to keep in mind, is that you can add other users, roles, groups, etc. to your permission scheme. Just don't forget that the permission scheme is where you give permissions. I have to admit that when first starting Jira I would get so frustrated with permissions. First, I would go to the username and try to find where to add permissions. When it didn't work, I would go to the Roles area to try and add those permissions. I kept forgetting that I needed to go to the Permission schemes in the Administration Issues view.

Next, we need to associate the new permission scheme to your Weekend Activity scheme.

Exercise: Associate the Permission Scheme with the Project

1. Open your *Weekend Activities* Project
2. Open the **Project Settings** found in the Project Sidebar
3. In the **Project Settings** page, scroll down to the **Permissions** area, and click on the **Default Permission Scheme** link

4. IN THE **PROJECT PERMISSIONS** VIEW, CLICK ON **ACTIONS** BUTTON (IN THE UPPER RIGHT CORNER)
5. SELECT 'USE A DIFFERENT SCHEME'
6. IN THE **ASSOCIATE PERMISSION SCHEME TO PROJECT** PAGE, SELECT *WEEKEND ACTIVITY PERMISSION SCHEME* IN THE **SCHEME** DROP-DOWN LIST
7. CLICK ASSOCIATE

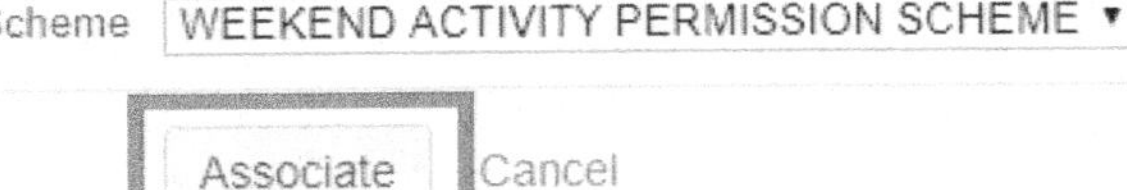

And that's all. You have now created your first Permission scheme and associated it with your project.

PROJECT PERMISSIONS

Let's finish this segment by looking at all the Project Permissions.

There are 33 Jira Core Project Permissions divided into six areas.

PROJECT PERMISSIONS

Administer Projects

Granted to a licensed user in order to manage a project in Jira Core. The individual (typically called a Project Administrator) can edit the project role membership, components, versions, and some of the high-level project details such as Project Name, Project Lead, Project Description, URL.

Users with this permission cannot create projects. A Jira Admin or Jira System Admin must create the project and then assign a Project Admin by giving him or her the Administer Projects permission.

This permission is great if you have 'traditional' Project Managers or Department Managers and you want them to be able *to manage* the project, but don't want them have the ability *to create* projects, fields, schemes, screens, workflows, etc.

Extended Project Administration

The Extended Project Administration permission is a sub-set of the Administer Projects permission. You must have the Administer Projects permission before you can get the Extended permission. This permission gives the Project Administrator the ability to edit the Project's workflows and screens, as long as those workflows and screens are not shared with any other projects. There are some other minor restrictions, but the share restriction is the big one.

Browse Projects

This permission is more important than it sounds. Yes, it gives you the permission to view all projects and issues (unless there is an Issue Security block). It also allows you access to the Issue Navigator.

In addition, other types of permissions (Work on Issues, for example) only work if you have this permission.

If you don't give the 'Browse Issue' permission, then the user will be restricted to viewing only the issues with which they are actively involved.

Manage Sprints

This is only available to Jira Software users (i.e. not Jira Core users).

View Development Tools

This is only available to Jira Software users (i.e. not Jira Core users).

View Read-Only Workflow

This limits the User to seeing the 'view-only' workflow of an issue. What this really means is that the user cannot edit the workflow.

Issue Permissions

Issue permissions give the user the ability to edit (and view) issues for his or her projects. If a user has global permissions, then the Issue permissions are global. If the user is assigned to specific projects, rather than *all* projects, then the permissions apply only to those projects to which the user is assigned.

Assignable User

This means the User is available to be assigned to Issues. It does not give the User the ability to Assign Users. You might toggle this permission in circumstances where workers are unavailable for long periods because they are working on other projects, for example. Once finished that other Issue, they can be brought back into the work que by making them Assignable.

Assign Issues

This allows the User to assign Issues to other Users, which is helpful if you have a manager, or work coordinator, whose role is to assign work - but not much more - on the project.

Close Issues

You may want to restrict the ability to close Issues to specific Roles. For example, you may want only Supervisors, or Quality Control, to have the ability to close an Issue.

Create Issues

This permission limits who can create an Issue. This is helpful if you have a functional workflow such as Customer Request, where you want the ability to create an Issue restricted to a specific Role.

A Create Issue permission also gives the user permission to create sub-tasks, if they are enabled.

Delete Issues

This is a risky permission. Make sure that you don't hand out this permission like candy at Halloween. It seems reasonable to give people the ability to delete issues and therefore keep projects 'clean'. Unfortunately, what happens too often is that user delete issues by accident; or even worse they try to hide their mistakes by deleting the offending Issue.

Edit Issues

Generally speaking, if you have the ability to Create an Issue you probably have the permission to Edit the issue. This is logical. But there may be instances where you want to give an individual the right to Create but not Edit an Issue. Imagine if you have a project where a customer can create an Issue for product defects, but then keeps changing the cause of the problem. So, don't just automatically give your users the permission to Edit, think about the possible consequences.

Edit Issues does not give the User the permission to edit the **Due Date** field.

This permission also gives the user the ability to convert sub-tasks to tasks, and tasks to sub-tasks, if sub-tasks are enabled (Navigate **Main Menu Bar >** ⚙ **> Issues > Issue Types** area (on the sidebar) **> Sub-tasks**).

You cannot delete Issues with this permission.

If you are concerned about an 'audit trail', remember that any time an Issue is edited, a notation of that edit is recorded in the History tab in the Activity area of the Issue Details View.

Link Issues

Just as it sounds. Of course, you need to have Issue Linking enabled (Navigate **Main Menu Bar >** ⚙ **> Issues > Issue Features** area (on the sidebar) **> Issue Linking**).

Modify Reporter

This permission allows user A to create issues on behalf of user B. Jira Core recommends that this permission be granted only to administrators. While I understand their caution, I don't quite agree with it. For example, most Administrative Assistants/Secretaries have delegated authority over their boss's email, calendar, and schedule and are trusted with those sensitive areas. It is probably safe to assume that they can also be trusted with the Modify Reporter permission. Just use common sense when delegating.

Move Issues

If a user has the Create Issue permission, then they can also have the Move Issues permission. This allows the user to move an Issue from either project to project, or from workflow to workflow within the same project.

Resolve Issues

With this permission, the user can resolve *and* can reopen Issues.

Schedule Issues

This permission lets user edit the Due Date of an Issue. I have never liked giving this permission to the Current Assignee for the obvious reasons. I always recommend that this ability be limited to supervisors.

Set Issue Security

The Set Issue Security permission allows the user to set the security level on an Issue. Recommended for Administrators or someone in a supervisory position.

Transition Issues

This allows the user to change the status of a workflow. Depending on the type of work you may want to give this permission to a team member or restrict it to a supervisory role.

Voters & Watchers Permissions

Manage Watchers

When a user is on a Watch List they will receive updates whenever something changes with the issue they are watching.

With the Manage Watcher List the user can see who is watching an issue; and, can add users to, or remove from, the watcher list of an issue.

View Voters and Watchers

This allows the user to see who is on the Voter List and Watcher List of an Issue. This doesn't give them permission to edit either list.

Comments Permissions

Add Comments

This gives the user the ability to add comments but does not give him or her the permission to edit or delete comments.

Delete All Comments

This gives permission to delete all comments in an issue, regardless of who wrote the comment. Be careful with this one. Are you going to want an audit trail? Ask yourself why you need to give someone the ability to delete all comments? What is the business reason?

Delete Own Comments

This permission restricts the ability to delete comments to the user's own comments. Again, do you want an audit trail? What is the business reason for allowing a user to delete his or her own comments? Because a person regrets creating a 'flame mail' type of comment, doesn't necessarily mean the individual should have the ability to delete any of their own comments.

Edit All Comments

Another permission to approach with caution. Do you really want to give a user the ability to edit any comment in an Issue, regardless of who made the comment?

When a comment is edited, a notation will appear in the comment field that the comment was indeed edited, but it will not show *what* was edited.

Edit Own Comments

This allows the user to Edit his or her own comments. Again, is this something you want?

When a comment is edited, a notation will appear in the comment field that the comment was indeed edited, but it will not show *what* was edited.

Attachments Permissions

Create Attachments

With this permission, the user has the ability to attach files to an issue. Of course, you will need to have attachments enabled (Navigate **Main Menu Bar >** ⚙ **> System > Advanced** area (on the sidebar) **> Attachments**).

Delete All Attachments

This gives the user the ability to delete any and all Attachments.

Delete Own Attachments

This limits the user to being able to delete only the attachments s/he attached.

Time Tracking Permissions

NOTE: **all Time Tracking Permissions will only work if Time Tracking is enabled.**

Delete All Worklogs

This gives the user the ability to delete any and all worklogs by any user working on the Issue. I don't need to remind you to be cautious with who gets this permission, especially if you use worklogs for audit, budget, or billing purposes.

Delete Own Worklogs

Again, do you want to give a user the ability to delete his or her own worklogs?

Edit All Worklogs

You can also give a user the ability to Edit all worklogs, regardless of who created them. Needless to say, be careful with this permission.

Edit Own Worklogs

If need be, you can give a user the permission to edit his or her own worklogs. To be annoyingly repetitive, is this something you really want to allow?

Work on Issues

While a bit of a confusing Permission name, this really means that the user can log work (track time) on an issue. It does not give the user the ability to work on an Issue, that permission is covered in the Issue Permissions section in the next chapter.

Issue Security Level

Sometimes, you have Issues and Issue Types that are quite sensitive, and you want to restrict who can see those Issues within the project. That's where Issue Security Levels come into play.

Issue Security Levels are fairly complex to set up and manage. And, if done incorrectly, they can cause havoc in your project. I strongly recommend that if you really need to set up a security level, you do so in the company of an experienced Jira Admin or Jira System Admin.

Chapter 10: Managing Time

"Oh! Do not attack me with your watch. A watch is always too fast or too slow. I cannot be dictated to by a watch."
Jane Austen (1775 – 1817)

Chapter Objectives

In this chapter you will develop expertise with:

- **Activating Jira's Time Tracking**
- **Setting Jira Core work hours**
- **Setting Time Tracking Permissions**
- **Logging Work**
- **Tracking time**
- **Tracking time with Issues and Sub-tasks**
- **Generating a project time tracking report**

Many companies require employees to track how much time they work on tasks in one of two ways.

First, in many instances the User is simply required to track how much time it takes to complete a task. This is often the case, where customers are billed by the hour.

Second, the User may be required to provide an estimate of how long the task will take. That estimate must then be approved, either by management or by the customer. After that, the User must track time against the estimate.

Jira is very good at managing both types of time tracking.

ACTIVATING TIME TRACKING

Before we can get started with Time Tracking, Logging work, and all the stuff, we need to make sure that Time Tracking is activated in Jira Core. By default, it is, but let's make sure.

EXERCISE: CONFIRM TIME TRACKING IS 'CURRENTLY ON'

1. NAVIGATE MAIN MENU BAR > ⚙ >**ISSUES**
2. IN THE ADMINISTRATION ISSUES VIEW, SELECT **TIME TRACKING** IN THE SIDEBAR IN THE ISSUE FEATURES SECTION

   - IF THE TOP OF THE PAGE READS, "*TIME TRACKING IS CURRENTLY ON.*", ALL IS GOOD.
   - IF THE TOP OF THE PAGE READS, "*TIME TRACKING IS CURRENTLY OFF.*", THEN CLICK ON THE **ACTIVATE** BUTTON AT THE BOTTOM OF THE PAGE.

CHANGING DEFAULT TIME TRACKING SETTINGS

While we are in the Time Tracking page, notice that we can also change the default Time Tracking settings. Be aware that you need **to deactivate Time Tracking before** you can make any changes. The good news is that you will not lose any existing time tracking data if you deactivate Time Tracking in order to make settings changes.

NOTE: If you change the current Time Tracking settings, you will affect every Jira Core project. So, if there are multiple Jira Admins in your organization, make sure you have consensus before making any changes.

EXERCISE: CHANGE TIME TRACKING SETTINGS

1. NAVIGATE MAIN MENU BAR > ⚙ > **ISSUES**
2. IN THE ISSUE FEATURES AREA OF THE ADMINISTRATION ISSUES VIEW SIDEBAR, SELECT **TIME TRACKING**
3. CLICK THE **DEACTIVATE** BUTTON

4. In the Time Tracking is Currently OFF page you can:
    i. Change Hours per day
    ii. Change Days per week
    iii. Choose the Time format
    iv. Change the default unit
    v. Select legacy mode (ignore this)
    vi. Copy Comment to Work Description
5. Click the **Activate** button when done
6. **Re-index** the program

Jira Core does not have the ability to set up a calendar, nor does it have the ability to define non-work statutory holidays.

Time Tracking Permissions

In addition to ensuring Time Tracking is ON, you (as the Jira Admin) will need to make sure the proper permissions are set for Time Tracking. There are five Time Tracking Permissions:

- Work on Issues: This allows the user to log work
- Edit own worklogs: Allows the user to edit own worklog
- Delete own worklogs: Allows the user to delete own worklogs
- Edit all worklogs: Allows the user to edit ALL worklogs; it doesn't matter who logged the work
- Delete all worklogs: Allows the user to delete ALL worklogs; it doesn't matter who logged the work

In each of these cases, the user must have permission to work on Issues **AND** Time Tracking is ON.

How to Log Work

Some Jira Core projects or Issue Types simply require the user to record the amount of time worked on an Issue. There are no special fields or screens to set up, this time tracking ability is built right into the program and available in the **More** drop-down list in an Issue Details View. In other words, you don't have to do anything to configure Log Work (other than making sure the Time Tracking function is ON).

Before we go much farther, let's create a new project for our Time exercises.

In the exercises in this chapter we will:

1. Create a Time Project
2. Create a standard Task Issue
3. Demonstrate Time tracking
4. Create a Time Estimate Issue Type
5. Create a Time Estimate Screen
6. Create a Time Estimate Screen Scheme
7. Create a Time Estimate Issue Type Screen Scheme
8. Demonstrate Time Estimating

Exercise: Create Project and Issue

1. Navigate Main menu Bar > Projects > **Create Project**
2. In the Create Project Pop-Up, select **Project Management**
3. In the Project Management Pop-Up, click **Select**
4. In the Project Management Data Entry Pop-Up, enter *ACME Machine Company* in the **Name** field, and click **Submit**
5. With the *ACME Machine Company* project open, click the Blue **Create** Button on the Main Menu Bar
6. Ensure *ACME Machine Company* is selected in the **Project** Field
7. Ensure **Task** is selected in the **Issue Type** field

8. ENTER *LOG TIME DEMO* IN THE **SUMMARY** FIELD
9. ENSURE YOU ARE THE **REPORTER**
10. ENSURE YOU ARE THE **ASSIGNEE**

NOTE: If the Reporter and Assignee fields are not displayed on the Create Issue pop-up, click on the Configure Fields and select them.

11. CLICK **CREATE**

Now that the Project and related Issue have been created, we want to start logging time.

EXERCISE: LOG TIME

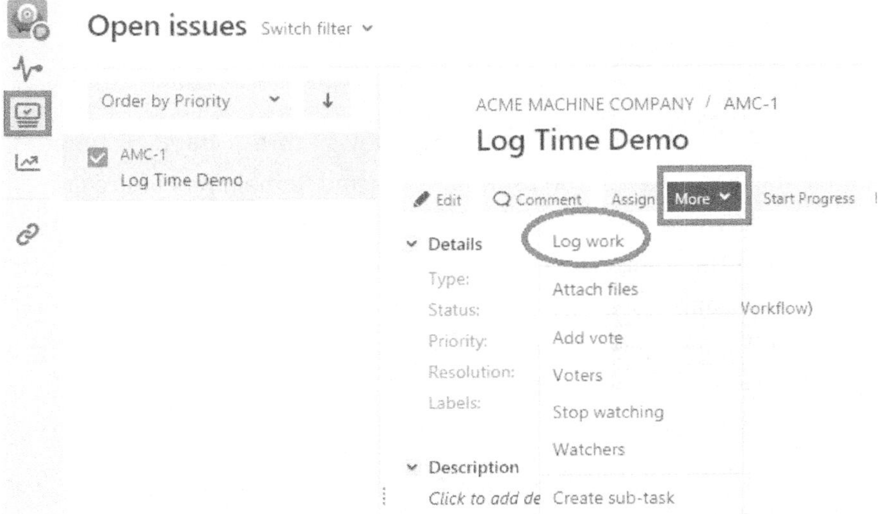

1. OPEN THE NEWLY CREATED *LOG TIME DEMO* ISSUE
2. IN THE *LOG TIME DEMO* **ISSUE DETAILS VIEW**, CLICK THE **MORE** DROP-DOWN LIST AND SELECT **LOG WORK**
3. IN THE **TIME SPENT** FIELD, ENTER 3.5D
4. IN THE **WORK DESCRIPTION** FIELD, ENTER *DID STUFF*
5. CLICK THE **LOG** BUTTON

Back in the *Log Time Demo* Issue Details View notice that a Time Tracking section has been added on the right side of the view, below the People and Dates sections:

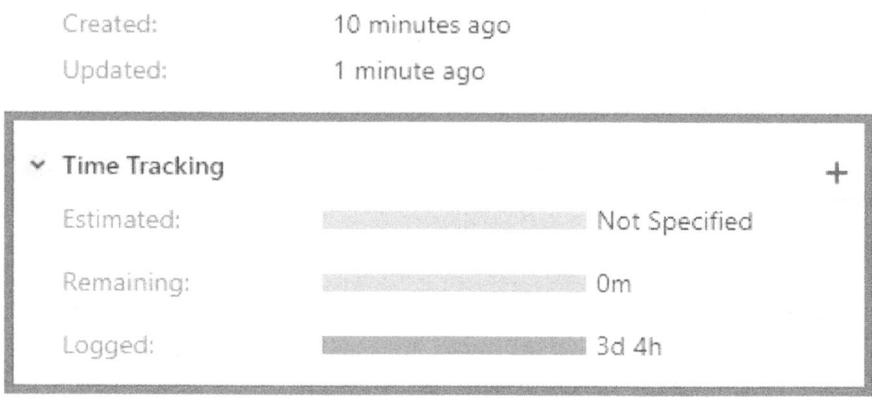

The Time Tracking section shows three bars: Estimated, Remaining, and Logged. The Estimated bar and Remaining bar are grayed out because we did not put in an estimate as to how long it should take to complete the Issue. The Logged bar should be green, and should also show the amount of time you logged (translated into days and hours). This logged time figure will increase every time the user Logs Work. The logged time area will show time in weeks / days / hours / and minutes (e.g 2w 3d 4h 17m).

But where is the Work Description you entered when you Logged work? This is found in the **Work Log tab** of the **Activity** area. If you click on this tab you will find all the work log details recorded:

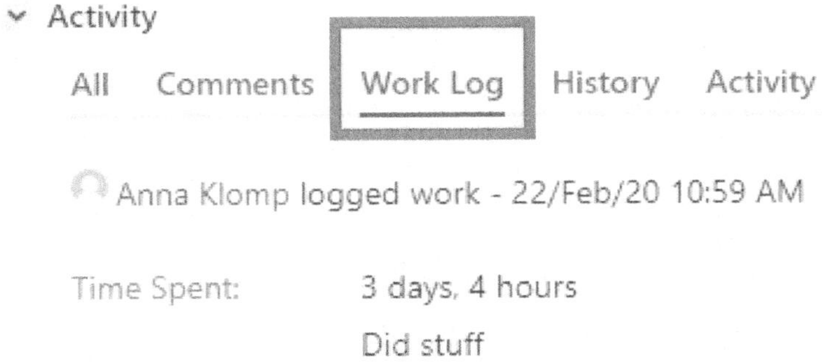

Any time a user logs additional work, it will be recorded here. Let's see what happens when we do.

EXERCISE: LOG ADDITIONAL WORK

1. IN THE *LOG TIME DEMO* **ISSUE DETAILS VIEW**, CLICK ON THE **MORE** MENU AND SELECT **LOG WORK**
2. IN THE **LOG WORK** POP UP, ENTER *12M* IN THE **TIME SPENT** FIELD
3. IN THE **WORK DESCRIPTION** FIELD, ENTER *DID MORE STUFF*
4. CLICK THE **LOG** BUTTON

In the Time Tracking area you will notice that the time logged has now changed to read 3d 4h 12m, which reflects the additional 12 minutes you just logged. **Jira Core will always assume you mean minute in the Time Spent field unless you specify** w (Weeks), d (Days), or h (Hours) after the time entered (e.g. 12h).

In the Work Log Tab of the Activity area, you will see that you logged 12 minutes of work and the log includes a date and time stamp.

Jira Core will time stamp your log **with the date and time when the Log button is clicked**.

Only those users who have the Work On Issues permission for a particular project are able to log work on the issue. However, those who have Browse Project permissions are able to see how much time has been logged. If you don't want everyone to have the ability to log work or edit the log, you will need to set that up with the appropriate Permission Scheme.

At its very basic, this is all the user needs to do to log work.

Logging and Estimating

Of course, you can do much more than just logging work. In many instances it is mandatory to submit an estimate of the time required to complete work (tasks) before the work is approved to begin. When building a project plan, for example, we need to provide an estimate of how much time it will take to complete a specific task or set of tasks. This is done to set a budget for the project. Many businesses will also set estimates for certain types of tasks. Dentists have industry standards for the estimate times of common procedures. Similarly, many auto repair shops will charge a flat rate of 2.5 hours for a brake job (for example) based on an industry standard estimate for the make and model of car. If the actual time to complete the job comes in more than the estimate, the shop loses money. On the other hand, if it took less time to complete (than the estimate) the shop makes additional profit. In cases like this it is essential to record the estimate first and then to track time against that estimate.

Logging Work using the Remaining Field

There are a couple of ways of setting estimates, so let's take them one at a time. The most common method is to insert a Time Tracking field into the Jira Core operations' (Create or Edit) screens. The second method is to use the Log Work pop up (from the MORE menu) to somewhat, kind of, almost, set an estimate. Since we are already working on the Log Work pop up, why don't we look at that method first.

Exercise: Set Work Effort Estimate in Log Work Pop Up

1. Open the ACME Machine Company project

2. **CREATE** A NEW ISSUE AND ENTER *LOG TIME DEMO2* IN THE **SUMMARY** FIELD
3. IN THE NEWLY CREATED *LOG TIME DEMO2*, CLICK ON THE **MORE** BUTTON AND SELECT **LOG WORK**
4. IN THE LOG WORK POP UP, ENTER *1D* IN THE **TIME SPENT** FIELD
5. IN THE **REMAINING ESTIMATE** AREA, CLICK ON THE **SET TO** BUTTON AND ENTER *3W* IN THE **SET TO** FIELD
6. CLICK THE **LOG** BUTTON

Back in the Log Time Demo2 Issue Details View take a look at the Time Tracking area:

We have 1d logged in the Logged area, and we show 3w remaining in the Remaining area. The Estimated is grayed out and "Not Specified" because we didn't actually estimate how long the entire task would take to complete when we created the Issue. This is important to understand.

Let's see what happens when we log more time against this issue.

7. GO TO THE **MORE** MENU, AND SELECT **LOG WORK**
8. ENTER *1W* IN THE **TIME SPENT** FIELD AND CLICK **LOG**

Back in the Issue Details View, notice that the remaining field has decreased to 2w, while the Logged field now reflects 1w1d as the total amount of time logged:

The Log Work pop up may look like we can set an estimate, but in reality we cannot. The total time worked on our Issue will, in this example, be 3 weeks and 1 day. It will be a sum of the work *logged* and work *remaining* fields.

You can only enter data in the Remaining Estimate field after you have logged some work in the Time Spent field. Try it. You cannot enter data in the Set To field and simply Log that as an estimate, the system will not allow it. You must also enter an amount in the Time Spent field, as it is a required field.

But what if you try to cheat the system (as I did) and enter 0 (zero) in the **Time Spent** field and then some data in the **Set To** field? Won't that work for making a work-around estimate? Unfortunately, not. **The validation rules for the Time Spent field do not allow the entry of a zero or negative number.** You could, of course, go in and change the validation rules, but that isn't easy and will probably raise more issues than it solves. Do you really want users to have the ability to go in and start reducing the amount of work hours already recorded on an issue?

Time Estimating

In the previous exercise we noted that using the Log Work pop up to create estimates is an ugly process. The Log Work pop-up does not have an Estimated field. But how do we activate that Estimated field in Time Tracking section? The answer is by using the **Time Tracking function**.

In order to create an Estimate, the Time Tracking field must be added to the Create or Edit views.

Adding the Time Tracking field does four things: first, it adds the Original Estimate field to the Create or Edit view, second, it adds a Remaining Estimate field to that same view; third, it activates the Estimated field in the Time Tracking section of the Issue's Details View; and fourth, it activates a new field in the Log Work pop up.

Let's see how it works and what we need to do:

1. Create a Time Estimate Issue Type
2. Create a Time Estimate Screen
3. Add the Time Tracking field
4. Create a Time Estimate Screen Scheme
5. Create a Time Estimate Issue Type Screen Scheme

First, we will create the Time Estimate Issue Type and Associate it with an Issue Type Scheme.

Exercise 1: Create a Time Estimate Issue Type

1. Navigate Main Menu Bar > > **Issues**
2. In the opened **Issue Types** view, click on **Add Issue Type** button (located in the upper right corner)
3. In the Add Issue Type pop-up, enter *Task w Time Tracking* in the **Name** field
4. Click **Add**
5. In the Administration - Issues sidebar, select **Issue type schemes**
6. In the **Issue type schemes** view, locate *ACME Machine Company* in the **Projects** column and click on **Edit** link in the related **Actions** column
7. In the **Modify Issue Type scheme** page, locate *Task w Time Tracking* in the **Available Issue Types** list and then drag & Drop it over to the **Issue Types for Current Scheme**
8. Click **Save**

Next, we will Create a Time Estimate Screen.

Exercise 2: Create Time Estimate Screen

1. In the Administration - Issues sidebar, select **Screens**
2. In the View Screens page, click **Add screen** button (in the upper right corner)
3. In the Add screen pop-up, enter "*Task w Time Estimate*" in the **Name** Field
4. Click **Add**
5. In the **Configure Screen** page, Add the following fields in the **Field Name** area:
    i. Summary
    ii. Reporter
    iii. Assignee
    iv. Due Date
    v. Time Tracking
6. In the Sidebar click on **Screens**

You may be asking, what about the Estimate field? Don't I need to add that? When you added the Time Tracking field, you actually triggered a sub-program in Jira Core that a) adds two fields to your screen: Original Estimate and Remaining Estimate. At the same time, it also initiates all of the Time Tracking functions.

Next up we need to create our Screen Scheme in order to manage the screen operations.

Exercise 3: Create Screen Schemes for Time Estimate Screen

1. In the sidebar of the Administration - Issues view, select **Screen Schemes**
2. In the View Screen Schemes, click on **Add Screen Scheme** button (in the upper right corner)
3. In the Add Screen Scheme pop-up enter *Task w Time Tracking SS* in the **Name** Field
4. Select *Task w Time Estimate* as the **Default Screen**
5. Click **Add**

6. In the Configure Screen Scheme – Task w Time Tracking SS page, click on **Associate an Issue Operation with a screen** button (located in upper right corner)
7. In the Associate an Issue operation with a screen pop-up, select *Create Issue* as the **Issue Operation**, and *Task w Time Estimate* as the **Screen**
8. Click **Add**
9. In the Configure Screen Scheme – Task w Time Tracking SS page, click on **Associate an Issue Operation with a screen** button (located in upper right corner)
10. In the Associate an Issue operation with a screen pop-up, select *Edit Issue* as the **Issue Operation**, and *Task w Time Estimate* as the **Screen**
11. Click **Add**
12. In the Configure Screen Scheme – Task w Time Tracking SS page, click on **Associate an Issue Operation with a screen** button (located in upper right corner)
13. In the Associate an Issue operation with a screen pop-up, select *View Issue* as the **Issue Operation**, and *Task w Time Estimate* as the **Screen**
14. Click **Add**

Issue Operation	Screen	Actions
Default Used for all unmapped operations.	Task w Time Estimate	Edit
Create Issue	Task w Time Estimate	Edit Delete
Edit Issue	Task w Time Estimate	Edit Delete
View Issue	Task w Time Estimate	Edit Delete

So, we have our screen and Screen Scheme built, now we need to associate them both with our Task w Time Tracking Issue Type and with our ACME project.

Exercise 4: Associate Screen and Screen Scheme with Issue Type and Project

1. In the Administration - Issues sidebar, select **Issue Type Screen Schemes**
2. In the opened Issue Type Screen Schemes, locate *ACME Machine Company* in the **Projects** column, and click on **Configure** link in the related **Actions** column
3. In the Configure Issue Type Screen Scheme page, click on **Associate an issue type with a screen scheme** button (in the upper right corner)
4. In the Associate an Issue Type with a Screen Scheme pop-up, select *Task w Time Tracking* as the **Issue Type**
5. Select *Task w Time Tracking SS* as the **Screen Scheme**
6. Click **Add**

Let's see if we did everything correctly:

Exercise 5: Test Time Tracking function

1. Open the ACME Machine Company **project**
2. Create an **Issue**
3. In the **Create Issue** pop-up, ensure that *ACME Machine Company* is selected as the **Project**
4. Select *Task w Time Tracking* as the **Issue Type**

If everything is done correctly, you should see the two estimate fields at the bottom of the page. Congratulations!

NOTE: If you do not see those fields, click the **Configure Fields** button in the right up corner and select Time Tracking.

Create Issue

Configure Fields

Project* ACME MACHINE COMPANY ...

Issue Type* TASK W TIME TRACKING

Summary*

Reporter* Anna Klomp

Start typing to get a list of possible matches.

Assignee Automatic

Assign to me

Due Date

Original Estimate (eg. 3w 4d 12h)

The original estimate of how much work is involved in resolving this issue.

Remaining Estimate (eg. 3w 4d 12h)

An estimate of how much work remains until this issue will be resolved.

Create another Create Cancel

OK, we're all set, so let's look at how the whole thing works.

Exercise: Create Time Tracking Estimate and Track the Time

1. Open the ACME Machine Company **project**
2. Create an **Issue**
3. In the **Create Issue** pop-up, ensure that *ACME Machine Company* is selected as the **Project**
4. Select *Task w Time Tracking* as the **Issue Type**
5. Enter *Time Tracking Estimate* in the Name **Summary** Field
6. Make sure you are the **Reporter** and **Assignee**
7. Set the **due date** for 3 weeks from now
8. Enter *4d* in the **Original Estimate** Field
9. Leave Remaining Estimate empty
10. Click **Create**

Back in the *Time Tracking Estimate* Issue Details View, you will see that the Estimated bar has been activated and shows a value of 4d. In addition, the Remaining bar also shows a value of 4d. The Logged bar has no value (it says Not Specified) because we haven't logged any work against the task.

Time Tracking

Estimated: 4d

Remaining: 4d

Logged: Not Specified

We will log the work in a minute, but for now go up to the *Time Tracking Estimate* Issue's menu bar and click the **Edit** button.

In the **Edit Issue** pop up, under the Due Date, you see that the original estimate field has the 4d value, but so does the Remaining Estimate field.

11. In the *Time Tracking Estimate* **Edit Issue** pop up, change the Remaining Estimate value to *7d*
12. Click **Update**

Back in the **Time Tracking** area of the Issue Details View a couple of things have occurred. First, the Estimated field has *not* changed. Remember, the purpose of this field is primarily for budgeting or approval purposes. Changing the original estimate after the budget is set or approval given is a really, really, bad way of doing business.

The Remaining field has changed to reflect the new time estimate. And, as before, the Logged field is still empty because we have not yet logged any work against the Issue.

But speaking of Logging the Work, why don't we take a close look at this and see how Log Work interacts with the Estimated and Remaining fields.

Exercise: Log Work Interaction with the Estimated and Remaining fields

1. In the *Time tracking Estimate* Issue Details View, on the menu bar click on the **More** drop-down and select **Log Work**
2. In the **Time Spent** field, enter *4h*
3. Click the **Log** button

In the *Time Tracking Estimate* Issue Details View the Logged field in the Time Tracking area now shows activity. It has recorded the 4 hours logged, and it has decreased the Remaining amount by the same 4 hours. The Estimated remains unchanged at 4 days.

Time Tracking

Estimated: 4d

Remaining: 1w 1d 4h

Logged: 4h

Both the Logged Work and Remaining fields reflect the amount of work logged by a User as s/he continues to log work on the Issue. The only field that will not change is the Estimated field.

Changing the Original Estimate field value

Is there a way of changing the Original Estimate field once it has been entered? Yes, while it is generally not a good idea, indeed there is.

Exercise: Change Original Estimate

1. In the *Time tracking Estimate* Issue Details View, click the **Edit** button on the Issue Menu Bar
2. In the **Original Estimate** field change the current value of *4d* to *3d*
3. Click **Update**

You will see that the Estimated field in the Time Tracking area now reads 3d instead of the original 4d. The Remaining and Logged fields remain unchanged. And while the Activity and History tabs in the **Activity** section do record the change of the original estimate from 4d to 3d, there is no such record in the Work Log tab.

By the way, if you don't like this idea of having the ability to change the Original Estimate, you can always go to Jira's Administration > Issues > Permission Schemes section and restrict the User's ability to Edit Own Worklogs, Edit All Worklogs, Delete All Worklogs, or Delete Own Worklogs. Permissions are discussed in more detail in the *Users, Roles, and Groups* chapter.

Remaining Estimate

As we saw earlier, one way of changing the Remaining Estimate field is in the Edit Issue pop-up. There are other options for changing the estimate and they can be found in the Log Work pop-up. These alternative methods are: Adjust Automatically, Use Existing Estimate, Set to, and Reduce by.

Adjust Automatically

The **Adjust Automatically** option will do two things. First, it will add time to the **Logged** field (bar) in the **Time Tracking** area of the Issue Details View. Second, it will reduce the same amount in the **Remaining** field (bar).

ACTION: Value entered in the Log Work Time Spent field = **2h**		
Time Tracking Fields	**Original Values**	**New Values**
Logged	1h	3h (1+2)
Remaining	8h	6h (8-2)

Be aware that it will not reduce the **Remaining** field number to below zero. For example, if the Remaining field in the Time Tracking area shows 2 hours and the user enters 3 hours in the Log Work Time Spent field, the Remaining field will show zero; it will not show -1.

Needless to say, in order for the **Adjust Automatically** function to work you must have already entered something in the **Time Spent** field.

Use Existing Estimate

The **Use Existing Estimate** option does two things. First, it adds the time entered in the **Log Work** pop up **Time Spent** field to the **Logged** Time field. Second, it leaves the **Remaining** field as it is. Let's say your Time Tracking Remaining field shows 2d 2h, and the Logged field shows 1d. If you then enter 1h in the Log Work Time Spent field, the Logged field will now show 1d 1h, however, the Remaining field will stay unchanged at 2d 2h.

ACTION: Value entered in the Log Work Time Spent field = **1h**		
Time Tracking Fields	**Original Values**	**New Values**
Logged	1d	1d 1h
Remaining	2d 2h	2d 2h

This option tends to be used when the remaining estimate is down to a few hours and the user realizes they may need an hour or two more than is stated in the remaining estimate. The Logged field will continue to record the actual time worked, while the Remaining field will provide any watchers with a more accurate update of the time still remaining to be worked on the Issue.

Reduce By

Often, a task proceeds faster than expected, or estimated. This is where the Reduce by field comes into play. The user may have entered 16h in the Set to field. But while working on the issue, she realizes that she will only need 10 hours. What she can do, the next time she logs work, is enter 6h in the **Reduce by** field. This will reduce the Remaining field result to 10h.

But here is the big caution. When a User enters an amount in the Time Spent field and clicks the Adjust Automatically button, the Time Tracking Remaining field is reduced by that Time Spent value. That does not happen when using the Reduce by field. In other words, when you use the Reduce by field, the Remaining field *will not* recognize what you entered in the Time Spent field.

Let's look at an example to explain this a little better. Lucrezia Borgia is in the process of killing her latest husband. She is one hour into the task and guesses it will take another 5 hours to complete the Issue (6 hours in total). She enters 1h in the **Log Work Time Spent** field and 5h in the **Set to** field:

ACTION: Value entered in the Log Work Time Spent field = **1h** **ACTION:** Value entered in the Set To field = 5h Total time to kill husband = 6h		
Field	**Hours**	**Hours**
Time Spent (in Log Work)	1h	
Logged Time (bar in Time Tracking)	1h	
Set To (in Log Work)		5h
Remaining Time (bar in Time Tracking)		5h

After a couple of hours, she realizes the poison is working faster than expected and she now thinks it will only take another hour to do the evil deed (four hours in total); so, she enters 2 hours in the **Time Spent** field and must also enter 4h in the **Reduce by** field:

ACTION: Value entered in the Log Work Time Spent field = **2h** **ACTION:** Value entered in the Reduce by field = 4h Revised total time to kill husband = 4h "Set to" time still remains the same = 5h		
Field	**Hours**	**Hours**
Time Spent (in Log Work)	1h	
Time Spent (in Log Work)	2h	
Logged Time (bar in Time Tracking)	3h	
Set To (was entered in Log Work)		5h
Reduce by (in Log Work)		4h
Remaining Time (bar in Time Tracking)		1h

It is important to remember that while the Logged time field will continue to add entries from the Time Spent field (from Log Work), the Remaining time field will *not* recognize anything entered in Time Spent.

Once you enter something into Set to, it will (from that point forward) only work with the "Set to" and "Reduce by" fields and will have to be manually adjusted.

I find most users tend to use the Reduce by field when they are down to the last few hours of an issue and want to make minor, fine-tuning, changes to the remaining estimate.

Set To

As you can imagine the Reduce By option is quite challenging and tends to result in a great many errors by Users. Better is to use the Set to option. If you need to make adjustments to the Remaining simply enter that number AFTER you have entered Time Spent.

Time Estimating Odds and Ends

Closing an Issue

You can also log work when you are closing or resolving an issue. Yet, you should be aware that there is no special recording of the status of an issue when you log work. Consequently, if it is important for you to track the time related to closing or resolving an Issue separately, you should either create a separate sub-task, or include a note in the Log Work description field that you are closing the task.

Restricting who can see the Log

Under the Description field in the Log Work pop up there is a little padlock image:

When you click on this icon, a drop-down list appears containing project roles or groups. Clicking on one of these options restricts the view of the log to that role or group. Leaving the lock icon unlocked allows all users, who have permission, to see it.

BEST PRACTICES FOR THE ESTIMATE FIELD

One of the major issues with the Original Estimate field is the ability to change it if it is added to the Edit screen. As stated earlier, the Original Estimate is often used for Budget and Approval purposes. Having the ability to change the field after the fact makes it tempting to 'low ball' the original estimate and raise it after the budget has been approved or approval given.

I find that many managers and users tend to have numerous and creative reasons for needing the ability to edit the Original Estimate field. I also find that senior executives are almost universally adamant that the Original Estimate field must *not* be editable. Guess who wins? Unless there is a compelling reason, and approval by senior management, I would not include the Time Tracking field in the Edit screen. Since the Time Tracking fields cannot be changed in the Issue Details View, that nicely solves the problem.

But what if you do need to change the estimate? After all, a change to the estimate is not uncommon. I recommend you use the **Set**

to field in the Log Work pop up. That way you end up with three more accurate measures. First, you keep, and display, the original estimate. Second, the Remaining field contains the most up to date, or revised, amount of the estimate. And third, the Logged field contains actual work performed. These three measures provide better context to the 'story' of the Issue's work effort.

Typically, when the original estimate is changed (increased), the change needs to be approved by someone authorized to do so. In this case, I would still recommend using the Set to field, but also include a note in the Log Work Description field indicating the reason for the increase, who approved it, and when. A copy of the approval email pasted into the Description field is even better. Of course, you could also use the Comments field to serve the same purpose, but I prefer to keep all related records and comments in the same spot.

So, how should Time Tracking and Log Work be used? My personal preference (and it is just a preference, based on experience) is to keep things as simple as possible.

Don't need an Estimate?

If you don't need an estimate for a job, then simply log work with the Time Spent field. Don't bother with the Remaining Estimate area if it serves no essential business need, if it isn't important to the customer (and that's the ultimate measure), and if it isn't used for budget or approval purposes. So, what would be the point of using it if it does not meet those criteria? The only thing I tend to hear is that managers want it to benchmark their employees. Well, that can be done with the reporting tool. Additionally, I find many users don't understand how to use those Remaining Estimate fields, which results in either mistaken estimates or numerous phone calls to the 'help desk' asking for assistance with the fields.

Need an Estimate?

If you do need an Original Estimate, I recommend two basic steps. First, the Original Estimate field should be completed by the individual who knows the subject matter best. Second, the User, who is doing the work, fills in the Time Spent field (s/he may be the Subject Matter Expert as well as another individual). If the Original Estimate turns out to be inaccurate and must be revised, then I recommend the project manager or administrator adjusts the *Set to* field after receiving approval.

Bottom line, again, keep things as simple as possible.

Time Tracking with Issues and Sub-tasks

I often get calls from Users who complain that the Time Tracking fields seem to show inflated numbers. The first thing I do is check that they are not 'double counting', as this is the most common reason for the problem. Let's say you think it will take five hours for a machine repair: one hour for the estimate, three hours for the repair, and one hour for billing. So, when you create the issue you enter five hours in the Original Estimate field. In the Issue Details View you see that the Time Tracking Estimated field does indeed show 5h. You assign the Estimate to Charles. Charles creates an estimate sub-task (in that repair Issue) and figures it will take him one hour to complete the estimate. He enters 1h in his Estimate sub-task Original Estimate field and clicks Create. Unfortunately, when you check the Parent Issue's Details View, you see that the Time Tracking Estimate field now records 6 hours to complete the Issue. That's because the software has added the Sub-task's original estimate amount to the Parent Issue's Original Estimate. This is a remarkably common problem. I recommend that if you are going to have Sub-tasks, then either use Original Estimate in the parent Issue Create screen, or in the Sub-tasks' Create screen(s), but not both.

Reporting

Time Tracking isn't of much use without the ability to report it. Jira Core has a number of reporting methods, including exporting to a spreadsheet, that you will find quite useful.

The most obvious reporting tools for Time Tracking are those embedded in the Issue Details View: Time Tracking area and the Work Log tab in the Activity section.

Exercise: Create an Issue Time Tracking report

If you need a simple Time Tracking report for a specific Issue:

1. Open the **Issue**, and click the **Export Button** in the Issue Details View (in the right up corner)
2. Select the report format you want: XML, Word (a Word document), or a Printable (Printed copy)

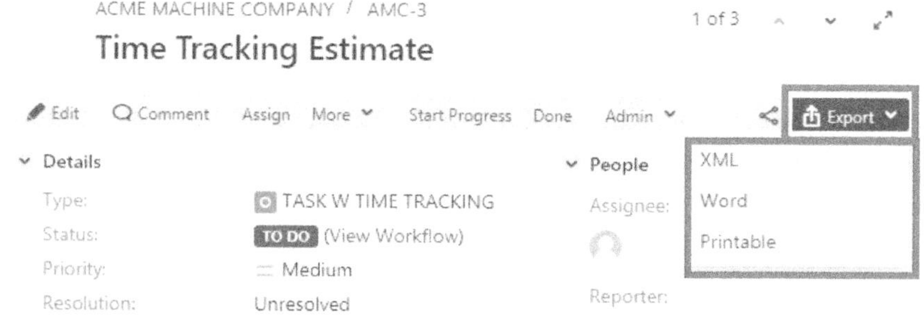

Go ahead and click on any, or all, option(s) to see what the formats look like. In all cases you will see the Original Estimate, Remaining Estimate, and Time Spent results. You will not see a detailed breakdown of the Work Log.

Work Log Report

I must admit that Jira Core's reporting functions for the Work Log are quite weak. A number of companies have built reporting add-ons which include Work Log reporting capability; so, you might want to check them out.

Create a Work Log Report

If you do want a very basic means of creating a Work Log report for a specific issue:

Exercise: Workarounds for Work Log Report

1. Open the **Issue**, and click on the **Work Log tab** in the **Activity** area of the Issue's Details view
2. With the **Work Log tab** open, and work log details showing, use your web Browser's Print method to print the page (or use a snipping tool to cut and save an image)

You can print the details of the Issue Details View as well as the Work Log details. It's not a perfect solution, but it does give you the work log details that you can keep as a record.

Project Time Tracking Report

The final report we want to look at in this chapter is the Jira Core Time Tracking Report for a Project, which is located in the Project report area.

Exercise: Create a Project Time Tracking Report

1. Open the Project for which you want a report
2. In the Project's sidebar, select **Reports**
3. In the All Reports view, scroll down and click on Time Tracking Report link in the Forecast and Management area
4. In the Configure – Time Tracking Report view select the following options:
5. No Fix Version in the **Fix Version** Drop-down

This typically refers to software versions, so you can probably ignore this field and select No Fix version (if not selected)

ii. *Least completed issue* first, in the **Sorting** Drop-down

This sorts your uncompleted tasks from top to bottom based on the amount of Estimated Time Remaining. When selecting Least

Completed, Issues with the greatest amount of Estimated Time Remaining will be shown first. If you select Most Completed, Issues with the least amount of Estimated Time Remaining will be shown first.

iii. *ALL* IN THE **ISSUE** DROP-DOWN

When you select All, you will see all incomplete and completed Issues and Sub-tasks (assuming you selected No Fix Version and are including all Sub-tasks).

If you choose Incomplete Issues only, then Issues where the Estimate Time Remaining field is zero, or Issues that do not have an Original Estimate will be excluded. In this report, "Incomplete" has nothing to do with the Status of the Issue.

iv. *INCLUDING ALL SUB-TASKS* IN THE **SUB-TASK INCLUSION** DROP-DOWN

Two out of the three options are related to Version control; so, you are probably safe simply selecting Include all Sub-tasks.

6. CLICK **NEXT**

The Time Tracking Report for a particular project starts off with Description of the report. More importantly, it contains a link allowing you to create an Excel version of the report (more about that later).

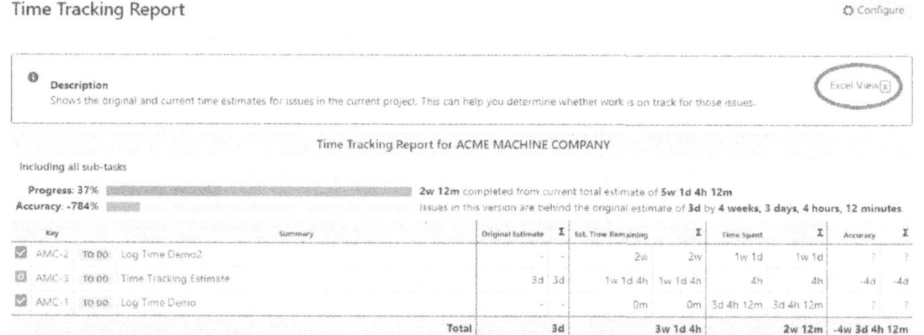

Next are two bars. The top bar shows your project's progress by comparing the percentage of completed issues against incomplete issues.

It does not take into account *what portion* of an incomplete issue is actually completed; if the whole issue is incomplete it gets zero percent.

The second bar measures the overall accuracy of all of the original estimates versus all of the current estimates. The current estimate amount is calculated by adding the Time Spent and Estimated Time Remaining fields.

This two-bars area will also show you if you are on schedule or not, based on estimates:

- If the two bars are of equal length, then you are on schedule.
- If the bottom bar is shorter than the top bar, then you are behind schedule.
- If the top bar is shorter than the bottom bar, then you are ahead of schedule.
- The text area to the right of the bars provides you how much (in weeks, days, and hours) you are ahead or behind schedule.

Now we are moving to the details area, which includes a number of columns. Let's look at them from left to right:

- An Issue type icon indicating whether the row relates to an Issue or Sub-task and type of Issue or Sub-task.
- The Key for the Issue of Sub-task. Clicking on the key will open that Issue or Sub-task Details View. If an Issue has a Sub-task, the Issue will be shown first and its Sub-tasks will be shown directly below it.
- The Status of the Issue or Sub-task.
- The Summary of the Issue or Sub-task. Clicking on the summary will bring you to the same Issue or Sub-task Details View as clicking on its key.
- Original Estimate. The left column will show the Original Estimates for any Issues and Sub-tasks. The right column in the Parent Issue line will show the sum of the Sub-tasks' Original Estimates for that Issue.

- Estimated Time Remaining. The left column will show the Estimated Time Remaining for any Issues and Sub-tasks. The right column in the Parent Issue line will show the sum of the Sub-tasks' Estimated Time Remaining for that Issue.
- Time Spent. The left column will show the Time Spent for any Issues and Sub-tasks. The right column in the Parent Issue Line will show the sum of the Sub-tasks' Time Spent for that Issue.
- Accuracy. The Accuracy column compares the Original estimate against the sum of the Time Spent and Remaining Estimate amounts. It then indicates whether the Sub-task or Issue is On-track or not. The left column will show the Accuracy for any Issues and Sub-tasks. The right column in the Parent Issue line will show the sum of the Sub-tasks' Accuracy for that Issue.

NOTE: when we configured this report, we chose to include Sub-tasks in the report. If you choose to ignore Sub-tasks, then you will only see one column in Original Estimate, Estimated Time Remaining, Time Spent, and Accuracy. You will not see a Sum column (because there are no sub-tasks to sum, of course).

Exporting the Time Tracking Report

At the top of the report we saw that the user has the ability to export the report to an Excel spreadsheet (I find it also works fine with the LibreOffice spreadsheets). Simply click on the link and (assuming you have Excel) a spreadsheet will be created for you. Be aware that depending on your version of Excel you may get a caution pop up. If that occurs, click yes (Legal Warning: I accept no responsibility for any adverse effect).

Timesheet Reporting

You may want to generate a report on the workload of an individual. Currently, Jira Core does not have an effective report for this.

However, there are a number of very good Timesheet or Time Tracking plug-ins that will do a great job for you.

Chapter 11 – Dashboards

Chapter Objectives

In this chapter you will:

- **Explore the Jira Core Dashboards and common Gadgets**
- **Create a custom dashboard**
- **Customize dashboard gadgets**
- **Learn how to share a dashboard**

What is a Jira Core Dashboard?

A Jira dashboard is the User's 'central control' view providing a high-level outlook of his or her Jira Core settings, individual project activities, or issues. It often contains quick links to more commonly used Jira elements. I like Matillion Business Intelligence's definition of a dashboard as "a tool that provides a simplified overview of the key performance indicators" (in their article "How to Create Compelling Business Dashboards").

Types of Jira Core Dashboards

There are two types of Jira Core dashboards: System and Bespoke. Whereas a system dashboard tends to be used as the global default dashboard for the organization or project team, a 'bespoke' dashboard is meant to be customized for individuals, specific projects, or roles.

When you log on to Jira Core, you usually open to a default System Dashboard:

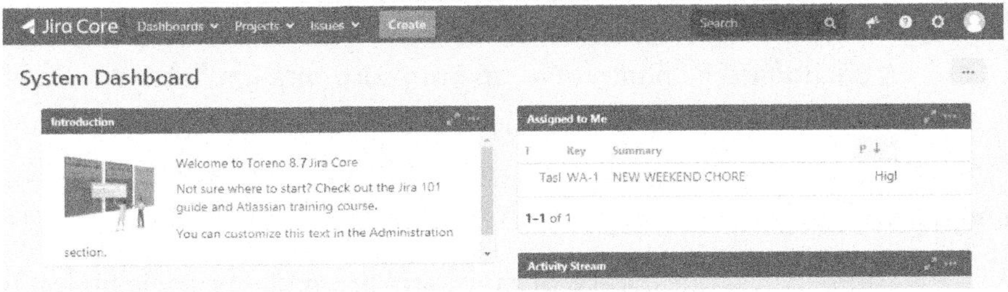

A **System** dashboard is typically used:

- As the default dashboard all members of an organization will see when they first log in, and for those who have not added any customized dashboards
- To provide instruction or training material for the User
- To display Issues assigned to the User
- To display company activity
- To display quick links to other areas of Jira
- To limit views of gadgets based on permission schemes. For example, non-administrators will not see any administration gadgets

A **Bespoke** dashboard can:

- Be customizable to individual Users, projects, roles or groups
- Be created and managed by Users
- Display project status details
- Display a list of Issues
- Provide quick links to other areas within the project

While there is only one system dashboard, any number of Bespoke Dashboards can be created for either an individual User or sets of Users (usually for individuals performing a similar job or task, or working on the same project).

Gadgets

A dashboard is made up of one or more 'Jira gadgets'. A gadget is a small application focused on a specific topic. For example, the default System Dashboard shows three gadgets: Introduction, Assigned to Me, and Activity Stream.

There is a large library of standard Jira gadgets available, and even more can be found in the Atlassian Marketplace.

A Tour of the System Dashboard

Let's take a tour of the default System Dashboard, though I must admit this is going to be a rather short tour as there really isn't that much to show. I should also caution, that your organization may have changed the system dashboard a little, or a lot, depending on requirements.

Main Menu Bar

The Jira Core Main Menu Bar includes Dashboards as one of the menu headings. Opening this Dashboard's menu will show a list of your existing Dashboards and will also contain the link to managing your Dashboards.

CLICK ON **SYSTEM DASHBOARD** IN THE DASHBOARD MENU ITEM (FOR SOME OF YOU IT MAY SAY **'VIEW SYSTEM DASHBOARD'**)

Left Column

In the main System Dashboard view the sidebar on the left contains a list of links to your Dashboards. This column will not appear if you only have the System dashboard.

System Dashboard

The main part of the System Dashboard view includes three elements: the title "System Dashboard", the gadgets, and the Tools menu buttons (see the image at the beginning of the chapter). The view title needs no further explanation, but let's look at the other two areas in more detail.

The Gadgets area

When a User opens the default System Dashboard s/he will see at least three Gadgets: **Introduction, Assigned to Me,** and **Activity Stream.** The **Introduction** gadget can include any message you might want to place there. If you are a Jira Administrator, you will also be shown the **Administrator Guide** gadget, which includes documentation to help you manage or customize Jira, and the **Atlassian Training Course** link.

The gadgets area typically contains operational applications, mostly reports related to your Organization or Users projects.

There are more than 50 standard 'gadgets' available for you to mix and match in order to create your own dashboard. Categories of gadgets include Charts, Jira, and Wallboard gadgets though, truth to tell, many of them are quite similar in function.

Tools

In the upper right corner of the System Dashboard view, you will see the Tools menu (the button with three dots). This list of options (discussed in more detail later) allows you to:

- Copy Dashboard
- Edit Dashboards
- Share Dashboard
- Find Dashboard
- Create Dashboard
- View as Wallboard
- Set Up Wallboard Slideshow

Additionally, after you set up a Wallboard Slideshow you will have another menu option entitled, obviously enough, "View Wallboard Slideshow".

Customizing the System Dashboard

You can customize the System Dashboard as little or as much as you desire. However, as it is a System Dashboard, you will need Jira

Administrator rights to modify it (in other words, a Project Admin does not have permission to change the System Dashboard).

> NOTE: If there is more than one Jira Administrator in your organization, make sure to talk with them before changing the System Dashboard. There should be agreement amongst all Jira Administrators as to any changes. Better yet, there should also be only one System Dashboard "Owner".

How to Modify the System Dashboard

Exercise: View Configure System Dashboard

1. Navigate main menu bar > > **System**
2. In the Administration System sidebar, find the User Interface section and click on System Dashboard

The opened **Configure System Dashboard** displays a copy of the layout of your current System Dashboard:

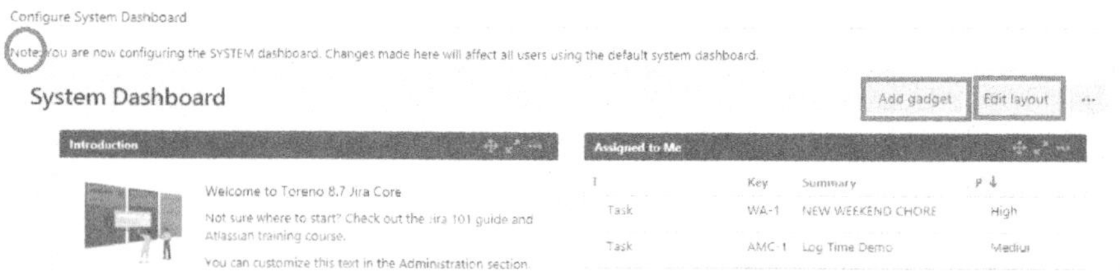

> CAUTION: Notice the warning below the view header, **"You are now configuring the SYSTEM dashboard. Changes made here will affect all users using the default system dashboard."** If you want to make a change affecting all users, then continue. However, if you want to make a change affecting only yourself or a specific group of users, then exit this view as soon as possible and make a local dashboard described in the Local Dashboard section of this chapter.

In the Configure System Dashboard view you will see your current gadgets. Each gadget's title bar has three icons: a four-direction arrow, maximize arrows, and tool icon (three dots):

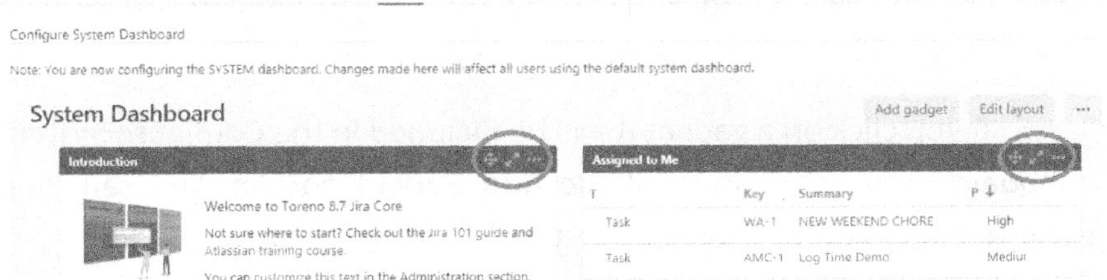

If you hover your mouse over the gadget title bar, you will notice the appearance of a four-direction arrow. The four-direction arrow is used to change the location of your gadget. When you click and hold the four-direction arrow you can drag-and-drop the gadget around the page. As you do so, you will notice a large gray box appear that says, "Drag your gadget here." Depending on the view size you are using, this can sometimes be a challenging exercise; so, I recommend you do this on the largest view available to you.

The next icon is a maximize icon that allows you to maximize the gadget by hiding all other gadgets.

The last icon Tool icon allows you to minimize the gadget, to choose the color of the gadget's title bar, and to delete or edit the gadget.

Near the top of the Configure System Dashboard view, there are three buttons where you can make changes to the system dashboard: **Add Gadget**, **Edit Layout**, and **Tools**:

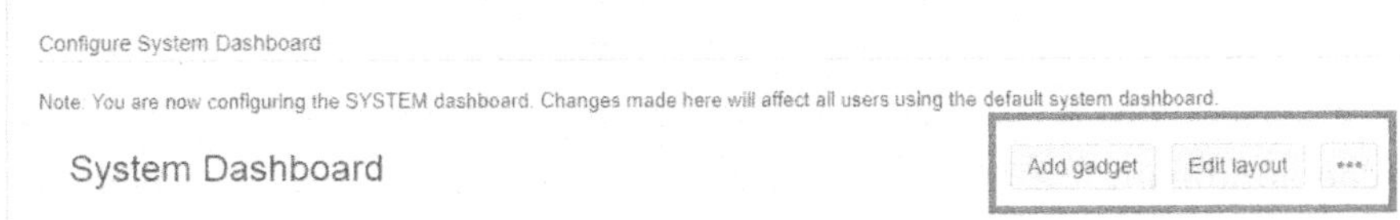

Add Gadget

The **Add Gadget** button brings you to the **Add a gadget** view. At the time of writing there are more 23 gadgets listed in categories such as: Charts, Jira, and Wallboard. You will find most of the gadgets are focused on reporting about specific projects or User activity.

If you click on a gadget it will be included in the Configure System Dashboard view when you exit the **Add Gadget** pop-up. You can then drag it to a location you think best suited to your needs.

One thing to note is that in the default settings you are limited to 20 gadgets per dashboard page.

Edit Layout

The Edit Layout button is a 'one trick pony'. Here you select the number of columns you want for your System Dashboard; and in some cases, the width of some of the columns.

Tools

The final button in the **System Dashboard** provides you with two options: View as Wallboard, or Set Up Wallboard Slideshow.

A wallboard is just as it sounds. A large board hung on a wall. Typically, it is used to show the status of individual tasks in a project. In the ancient days of ten years ago, a classic wallboard using Agile Project Management methodology would have the physical board sorted into four columns: Not Yet Started, In Progress, In Testing, and Complete. In each of these columns would be a number of Post-It notes, with each note representing a task. As the task progressed, the Post-It note would be moved from column to column until it was complete. You can replicate that model with a Jira digital wallboard display if you purchased the Jira Agile bundle (in Jira 7 it is now a standalone software program called Jira Software). Or you can use it to show status reports that are better suited to a larger view environment. It's very flexible.

A Wallboard Slideshow is simply a number of status or report views that display as a slideshow. You can customize the slideshow to display the wallboards in random order, and to have any one of 10 transition effects. You can also set the cycle period (how long each wallboard will be shown before it transitions to the next).

Bespoke Dashboard

In addition to the system dashboard many users want to see a dashboard customized for their own use, a specific project, or for a group of users.

Let's create one now.

Exercise: Create New Dashboard

1. Navigate main menu bar > Dashboards > **Manage Dashboards**

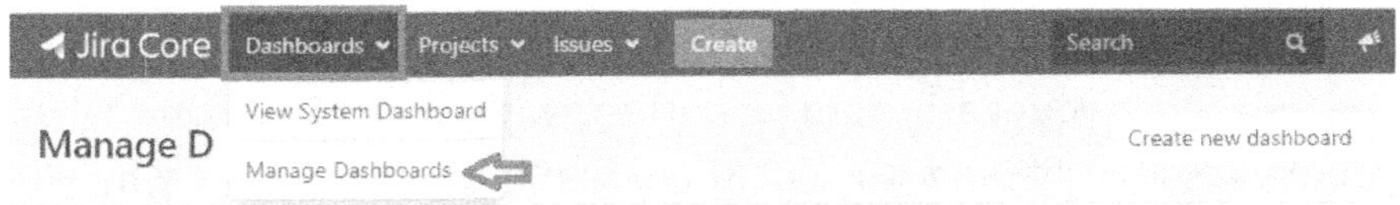

2. In the **Manage Dashboards** view, click on **Create new dashboard** button located in the top right of the view:

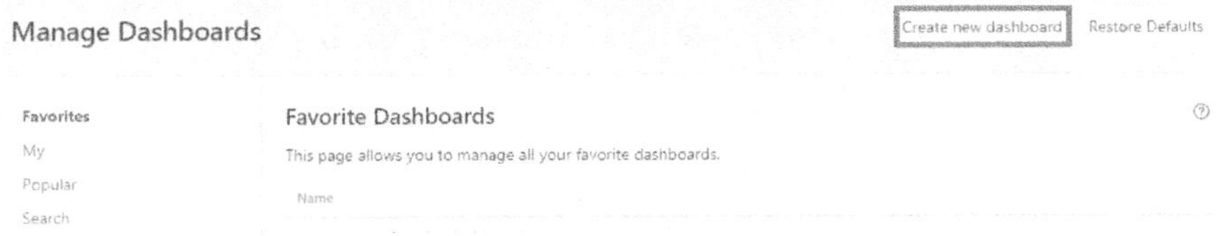

3. In the **Create New Dashboard** view, type the name of the new Dashboard such as "Test Dashboard" in the name field
4. Write a brief description of the Dashboard, if you wish
5. In the **Start From** field, ensure *Blank Dashboard* is selected.

The **Start From** field allows you to start with a Blank Dashboard you can customize. Alternatively, you can start with an existing dashboard, if one of them is similar to what you want to build. If you do start from an existing dashboard, it will make a copy of that dashboard. In other words, it will not overwrite or change the original.

6. LEAVE THE **FAVORITE STAR** AS IS

By default, any new dashboard will become a favorite. This means that it will show up in the Dashboard Menu on the Main Menu Bar. Clicking on the star changes the filled-in star icon to an outline of a star. This indicates the Dashboard is not a favorite. You will still see the Dashboard listed in the Manage Dashboards view, however it will not be shown in the Dashboard Menu.

7. LEAVE THE **VIEWERS (SHARES) ICON** AS IS FOR NOW

Viewers are those who can only view the dashboard, but they are not allowed to make any changes there. The **Viewers** field informs you if you are sharing your dashboard (or not) and with whom. By default, when you create a dashboard it is not shared with anyone. This is why you should see a figure icon with the words "Not shared" next to it. When you do share a dashboard, the details will show up here.

Notice that when you do share, a little **garbage can** icon will appear next to the viewers details. Needless to say, clicking on this garbage can icon will delete the share.

8. IN THE **ADD VIEWERS** DROP-DOWN LIST, SELECT *ANY LOGGED-IN USERS*
9. CLICK THE **+ADD** BUTTON NEXT TO THE **ADD VIEWERS** FIELDS

CAUTION: If you do not click the **+ Add** button your **Add Viewers** selections will not take effect.

Notice that the **Viewers** field has changed from *Not Shared* to *Shared with logged-in users (VIEW)*.

10. Again, click on the down arrow inside the **Add Viewers** drop-down list
11. Select **Group**

When you do so, a new box with a drop-down list of groups' names appear immediately to the right.

12. Click the down arrow in the new drop-down list of **groups' names** and select *jira-administrators*
13. Click the **+Add** button next to the Add Viewers fields

The Jira will ask you to confirm that your chosen share will replace sharing with the logged-in users. Click OK. The Viewers field should have changed from *Shared with logged-in users to Group: Jira-administrators*.

14. Next, select **Project** in the Left Add Viewers drop-down list

This time you should see two additional drop-down lists appear. The second (middle) drop-down list contains a list of Projects from which you can select. The third list will show the roles associated with the project selected in the middle drop-down list.

15. Select a **project** from the middle drop-down list
16. Select a **project Role** in the third list and click the **+ Add** button

The Viewers field should now show a Project name and Role.

17. Add **Editors** in the same way as you did with Viewers. The Editors are those who can make changes to the Dashboard
18. Ensure you are not sharing your experimental dashboard at this time by Clicking all **Garbage Can** icons next to the **Viewers** and **Editors** fields until the Not Shared messages appear
19. Click on the **ADD** button at the bottom of the page

This will bring you back to the Favorite Dashboards view. Let's now customize your new dashboard by adding gadgets.

EXERCISE: BESPOKE THE DASHBOARD

1. CLICK ON THE NEWLY CREATED DASHBOARD

Your new dashboard will appear with a couple of grey boxes each saying: ***Drag your gadgets here or add a new gadget.***

If, when creating a new dashboard, you had selected an existing project in the **Start From** field, then instead of the two grey boxes you would see the gadgets from the original dashboard.

Let's first simplify the view by Editing the Layout.

2. CLICK **EDIT LAYOUT** BUTTON IN THE UPPER RIGHT OF THE VIEW
3. SELECT THE SINGLE COLUMN LAYOUT:

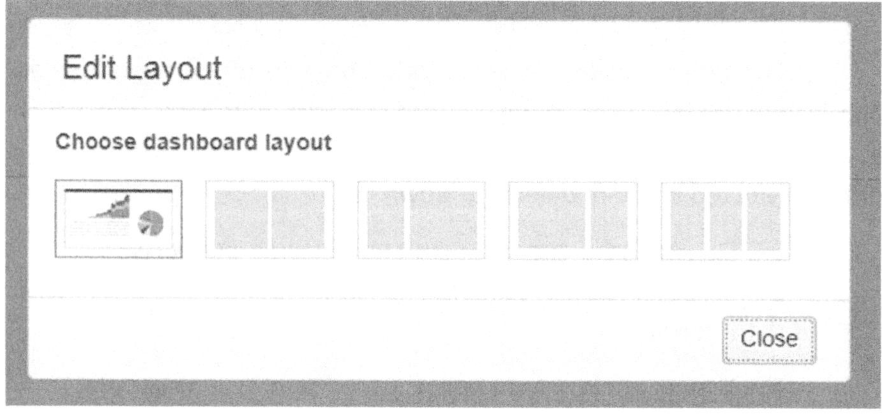

Next, let's add some Gadgets to our Dashboard.

4. CLICK **ADD GADGET** BUTTON IN THE UPPER RIGHT OF THE VIEW:

The left column of the **Add a Gadget** view categorizes the various gadgets. When you open the Add a gadget view by default you will see all of the gadgets available in alphabetical order). Let's add three to our dashboard.

5. FIND **STATISTICS** AND CLICK ON ITS **ADD GADGET** BUTTON
6. CLICK THE **X (CLOSE)** ON THE TOP RIGHT OF THE ADD A GADGET POP-UP
7. DO THE SAME FOR ASSIGNED TO ME AND **CREATED VS. RESOLVED**
8. CLICK THE **X (CLOSE)** ON THE TOP RIGHT OF THE ADD A GADGET POP-UP

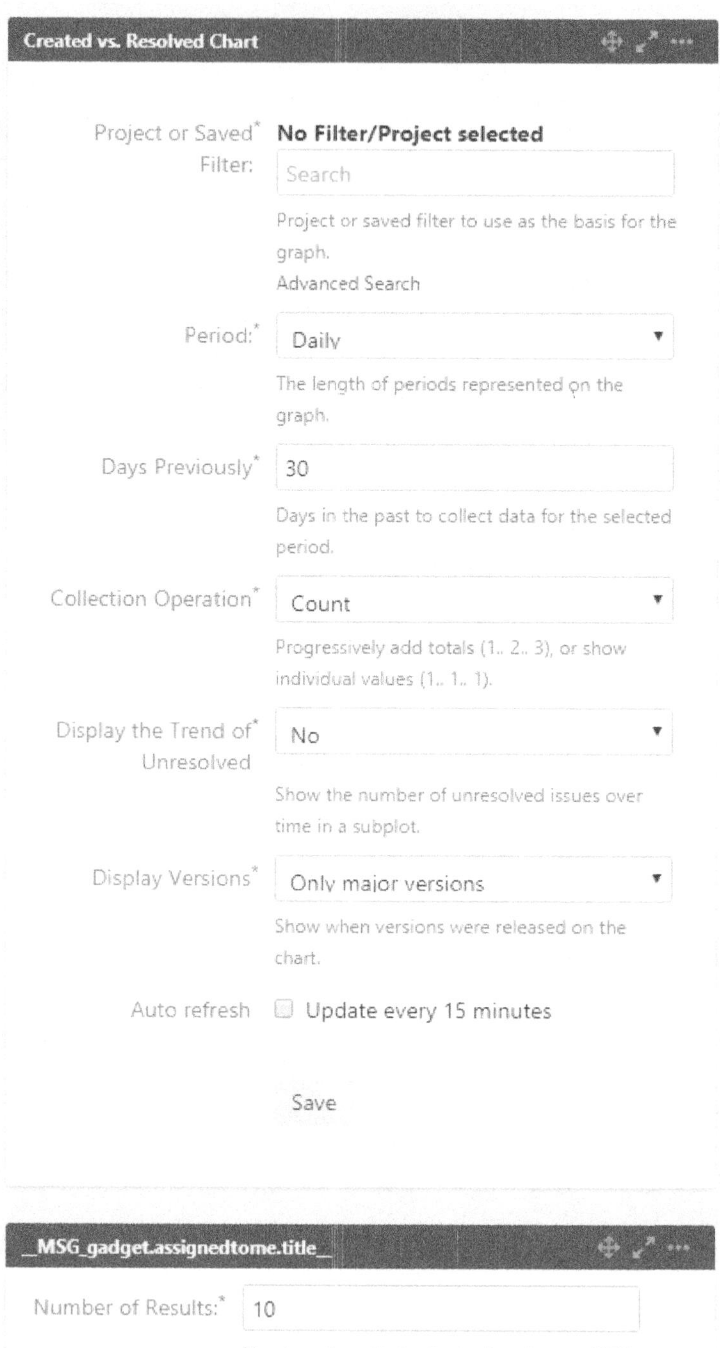
Created vs. Resolved Chart
Project or Saved Filter:
No Filter/Project selected
Search
Project or saved filter to use as the basis for the graph.
Advanced Search
Period:
Daily
The length of periods represented on the graph.
Days Previously
30
Days in the past to collect data for the selected period.
Collection Operation
Count
Progressively add totals (1.. 2.. 3), or show individual values (1.. 1.. 1).
Display the Trend of Unresolved
No
Show the number of unresolved issues over time in a subplot.
Display Versions
Only major versions
Show when versions were released on the chart.
Auto refresh
Update every 15 minutes
Save
_MSG_gadget.assignedtome.title_
Number of Results:
10
Number of results to display (maximum of 50).

As you can see, there is still some work required to set up the gadgets for this particular dashboard. Let's start with the Statistics (Issue Statistic).

EXERCISE: EDIT ISSUE STATISTICS GADGET

1. IN THE **PROJECT OR SAVED FILTER** SEARCH BOX TYPE IN THE NAME OF AN EXISTING PROJECT (OR SAVED FILTER). CLICK **ENTER** WHEN DONE

NOTE: Suggestions will be provided in the Search box as you type:

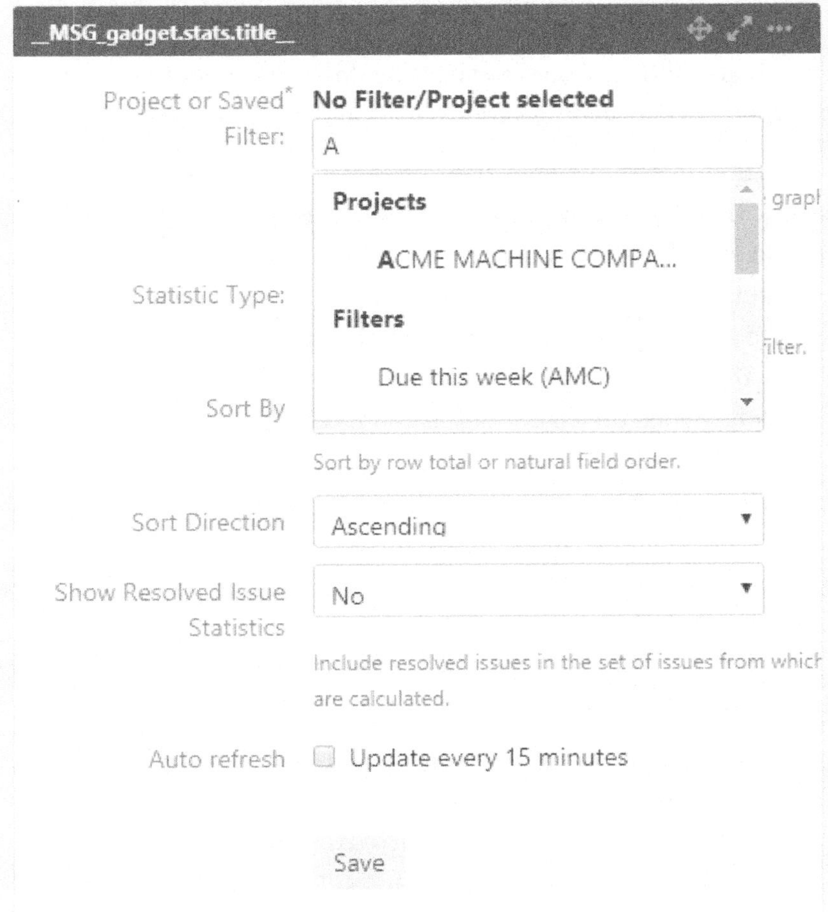

2. IN THE **STATISTIC TYPE** DROP-DOWN LIST SELECT *STATUS*

NOTE: You can select from almost every custom and standard field available to you. Just remember the fields available to you are also based on your Jira Core permissions.

3. IN THE **SORT BY** DROP-DOWN LIST SELECT *NATURAL*
4. IN THE **SORT DIRECTION** DROP DOWN LIST SELECT *ASCENDING*
5. IN THE SHOW RESOLVED ISSUE STATISTICS SELECT *YES*
6. CHECK THE **AUTO REFRESH** BOX SO THAT THE GADGET UPDATES *EVERY 15 MINUTES*
7. CLICK **SAVE**

Take a look at your results. Why don't you get a better sense of this gadget by changing the various fields and observing the outcome.

You can edit the gadget by hovering your mouse over the Issue Statistics Title Band. When you do so three icons will appear near the right-side end of the band. One is a four-sided arrow allowing you to drag the gadget to another location on the view. The second is a view icon which allows you to maximize the gadget by hiding all other gadgets. The third is a three dots menu button. Click on it, this allows you to minimize the gadget, change the colour of the band, edit the gadget, or delete the gadget.

8. CLICK THE **EDIT** OPTION AND SPEND SOME TIME CHANGING THE FIELDS AND OBSERVING THE RESULTS.

EXERCISE: EDIT ASSIGNED TO ME GADGET

This gadget, like the Issue Statistics gadget, needs to be configured before it shows anything. Let's do it now.

1. CLICK ON THE **EDIT** OPTION IN THE ASSIGNED TO ME GADGET'S HEADER BAR
2. LEAVE NUMBER OF RESULTS AT 10
3. DELETE *KEY* FROM THE **COLUMNS TO DISPLAY** LIST (BY CLICKING ON THE TRASH CAN ICON)

4. Select and click on *Created* in the **Add fields** drop-down list
5. Select and click on *Due Date* in the **Add fields** drop-down list
6. Check the **Auto Refresh** check box
7. Click **Save**

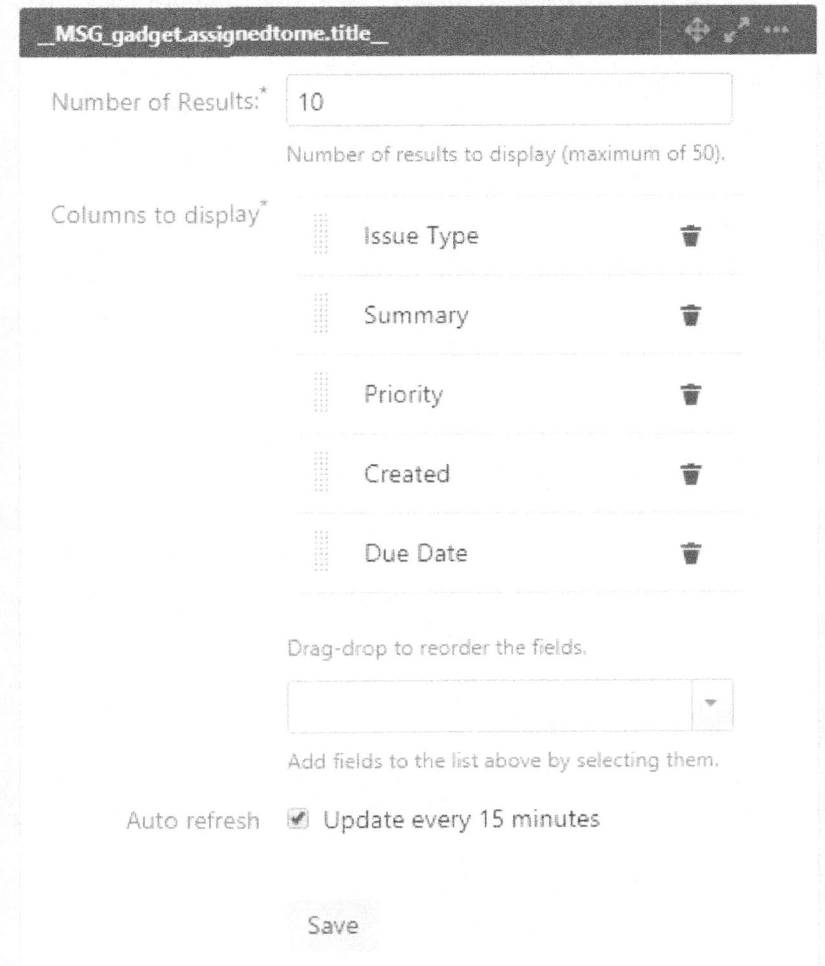

Great! This shows all of my issues along with the summary and priority, when they were created (i.e. how old they are), and when they are due. But, I just realized that I have one field missing. Let's go back and edit the gadget once again.

8. CLICK ON THE **EDIT** OPTION IN THE ASSIGNED TO ME GADGET'S HEADER BAR
9. SELECT AND CLICK ON *PROJECT* IN THE **ADD FIELDS** DROP-DOWN LIST
10. IN THE **COLUMNS TO DISPLAY** LIST, DRAG PROJECT UP SO THAT IT IS BETWEEN SUMMARY AND PRIORITY
11. CLICK **SAVE**

OK, that's better. Since I am working on multiple projects, having this additional column, showing the project associated with the Issue, helps me keep track of things a little easier.

By now you should be comfortable with adding and configuring gadgets; so, go ahead and experiment on your custom, not the system, dashboard.

AGILE GADGETS

You may notice a good many Agile gadgets available and most of them look interesting. The reason I did not include them in the example has to do with the fact that they tend to require a 'sprint' due date. A sprint is a designated period within an Agile project. In a sprint there are a number of tasks to be accomplished. So, when using an Agile gadget, you typically need to a) create an Agile project, b) create a sprint, and c) create a finish date for the sprint.

Having said that, if you have purchased the Jira Software package and have set up a sprint, please feel free to experiment with the Agile gadgets.

SHARING DASHBOARDS

In the previous section we showed how to share a bespoke dashboard when we are in the process of building one. But how do we make share changes *after* we have created a dashboard?

Exercise: Share a Dashboard

1. Navigate Main Menu Bar > Dashboards > **Manage Dashboards**
2. On the **Manage Dashboards** view find the dashboard you created in the previous section (Test Dashboard)
3. Click on the **COG wheel** down arrow in the Selected dashboard's (far right) column and select **Edit**.

NOTE: This will bring you to the **Edit and Share Dashboard** view where you can add additional shares to viewers or editors or modify and delete existing shares. Follow the same instructions you used when you Created the New Dashboard.

4. Click the **Update** button when done.

Project Summary: Activity view vs Dashboard view

As you know each project has its own Summary Activity overview (found if you click on the Summary link of the opened Project's sidebar):

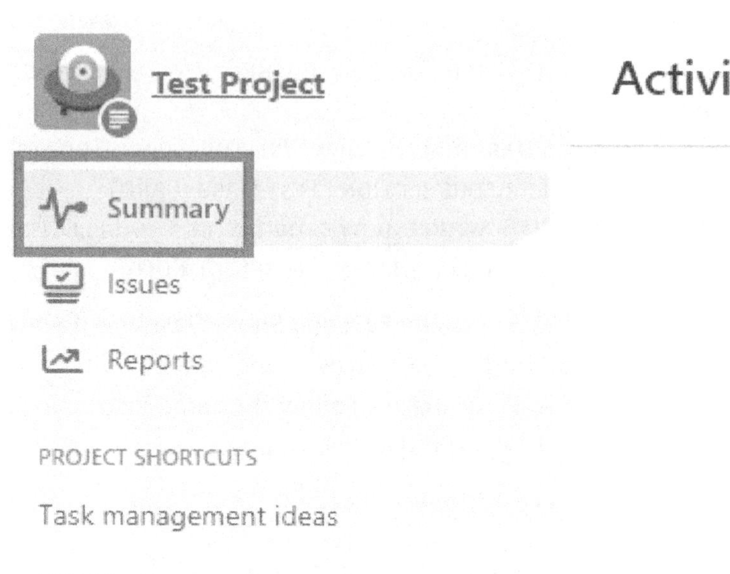

Many users confuse this view with a Dashboard view and spend a good deal of time and frustration trying to add gadgets and configure it. Unfortunately, a project Summary view cannot be changed, at least not at this time.

But let's continue with our custom dashboard.

Tools

In the upper right corner of your custom dashboard you will find the tools menu (the button with three dots). Let's spend some time to cover them.

Copy Dashboard

This is pretty easy. It is the same as the Create Dashboard function we used earlier when we created our custom dashboard. The only difference is that it copies the current dashboard (in the Start From field) instead of starting with a blank dashboard.

Edit Dashboard

This option allows you to edit your dashboard, changing the name, descriptions and shares.

Share Dashboard

You can use this function to change the shares. In reality, this option is the same as the Edit Dashboard option.

Delete Dashboard

Use this to delete your dashboard. You can also delete Dashboards in the **Manage Dashboards** view, as well as Copy and Edit. In other words, clicking on the Copy, Edit and Delete options on the Tools menu button will bring you to the same views as you would click on Copy, Edit and Delete in the COG drop-down list in the last column of the Manage Dashboards view:

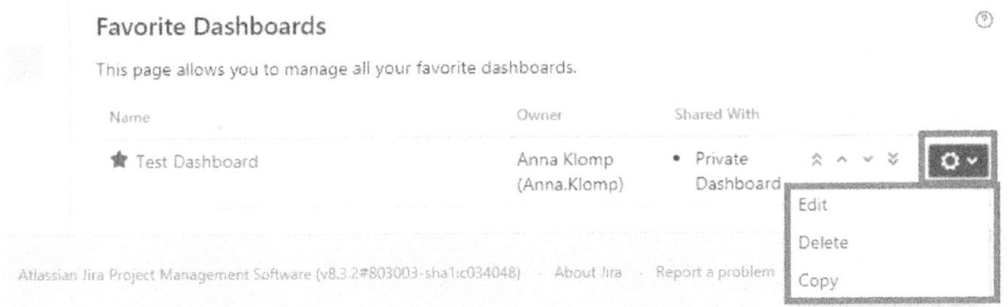

Find Dashboard

Some organizations have so many dashboards they need a Search Dashboards function.

Create Dashboard

Use this option when you want to start with a blank dashboard.

VIEW AS WALLBOARD

This sets up the current dashboard as a wallboard, meaning the gadgets will be displayed as a series of slides.

SET UP WALLBOARD SLIDESHOW

This option allows you to set up a slide show of your dashboards and gadgets. You can select one, some, or all of your dashboards and you have a number of display options to choose from. My recommendation is to avoid the transition effects. Keep it simple and easy to follow.

VIEW WALLBOARD SLIDESHOW

After you create a wallboard slideshow, a new option appears in the tools menu that allows you to view that wallboard slideshow.

MANAGE DASHBOARDS

The last item on the Dashboard menu is Manage Dashboards.

In the Manage Dashboards view, you can create a new dashboard or Restore Defaults (both buttons are found in the upper right corner).

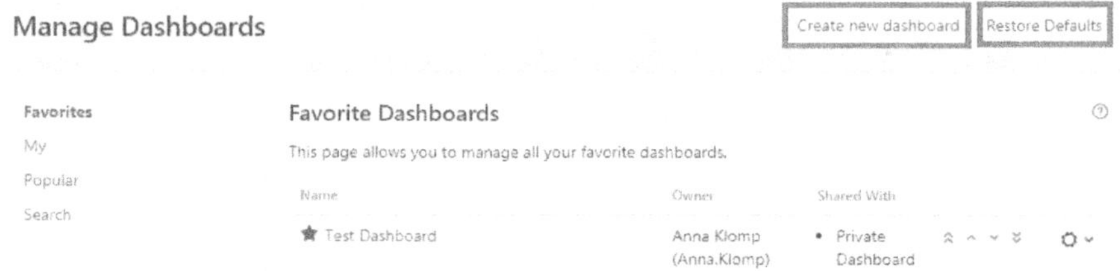

The Manage Dashboards view is divided into a sidebar and main view.

The sidebar contains the links to four pages in the Manage Dashboards area: Favorites, My, Popular, and Search.

Favorites

The Favorites view has a list of your favorite Dashboards. A favorite is designated by a solid star, while a simple star outline indicates that the dashboard is NOT a favorite.

This view contains five columns.

First, we have the name of the Dashboard. That's followed by a column indicating the owner of the Dashboard. The third column lists who the dashboard is shared with.

The fourth column is used to move dashboards up or down in the list. Any changes made here will also be reflected in the Main Menu Bar Dashboard's menu.

The final column allows you to Edit, Delete, or Copy the Dashboard. The exception is the System Dashboard, which you can only copy.

My

The My Dashboards view lists all of your personal dashboards. It is the same as the Favorites dashboard view, except there is no Owner column; because you are the owner.

Popular

The Popular Dashboards view shows all Dashboards. It is similar to the Favorites and My pages, except each Dashboard has a Popularity ranking (meaning how many people have it as a favorite). This is handy when trying to determine if there are dashboards you should consider deleting, or if you don't have it as one of your favorites.

Search

We mentioned this view earlier when we looked at the Tools menu (Find Dashboard option).

Chapter 12 – Filters and Reports

Chapter Objectives

In this chapter you will:

- **Understand Filters in greater detail**
- **Build and save a custom filter**
- **Subscribe to a filter**
- **Build a Dashboard gadget based on a Filter**
- **Build a filter report**
- **Export a filter**

I must admit that when first learning Jira, I didn't spend much time focusing on Filters and Reports. I was too busy just trying to figure out how the program worked. Only later, as I gained experience with Jira, did I realize its flexibility and power.

Filters and Reports are two sides of one coin. Reports cannot exist without filters. Even the reports, charts, and report gadgets included with Jira Core when you purchase the software, are based on filters.

Filters fundamentally do three things. They let you:

- Search for something in Jira Core
- Customize lists of issues
- Create Jira Core reports

Let's start with searching for something in Jira Core.

Search

When opening Jira Core and looking for an issue, most beginners typically click on **Projects** in the **Main Menu Bar** and then click on the **Issues** in the sidebar:

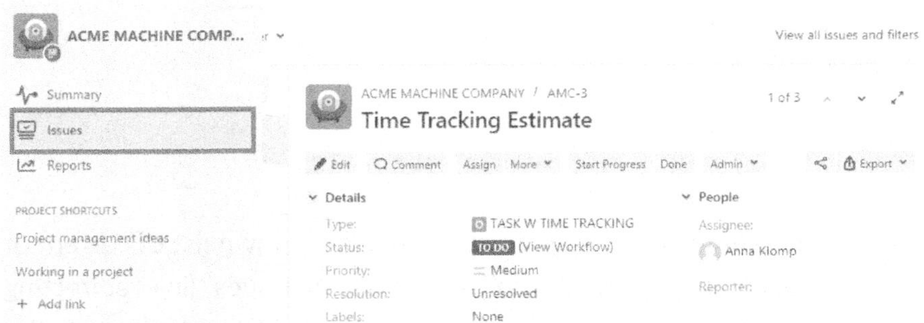

Alternatively, Users might click on **Issues** in the **Main Menu Bar,** and if that issue, hopefully, is listed in the **Recent Issues** section, they would click on it. If not so lucky, they head back to the Projects button described in the previous paragraph and scrounge around until they find the Issue. Bottom line, it usually takes a good number of mouse clicks to get to your specific issue.

So, it is probably a good time to make your life easier by reintroducing the Issue Search functions. As you recall, there are four types of Search functions in Jira Core:

- Quick Search
- Current Search
- Search for Issues (Basic Search)
- Advanced Search

Quick Search

Quick Search is the easiest search method to use when looking for an Issues(s) or a Project(s).

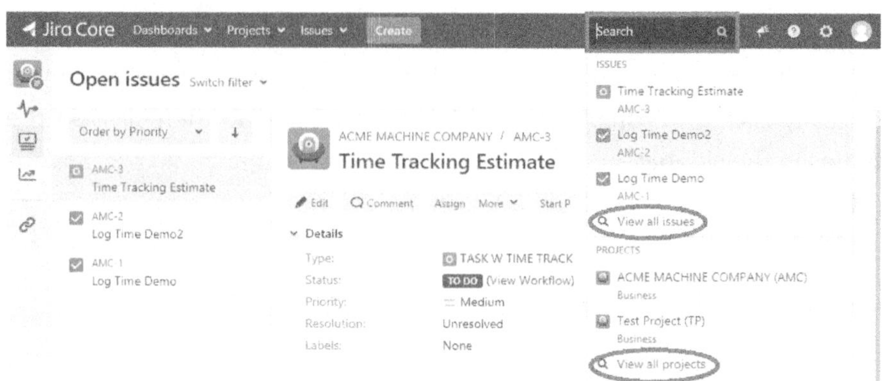

Clicking on Quick Search will open a drop-down list of current or recent issues and projects. It also has a 'View all issues' link redirecting you to the Issue Navigator and 'View all projects' link sending you to the Browse Project view.

Current Search

The Current Search is the first Search option you see when you click on Issue menu item):

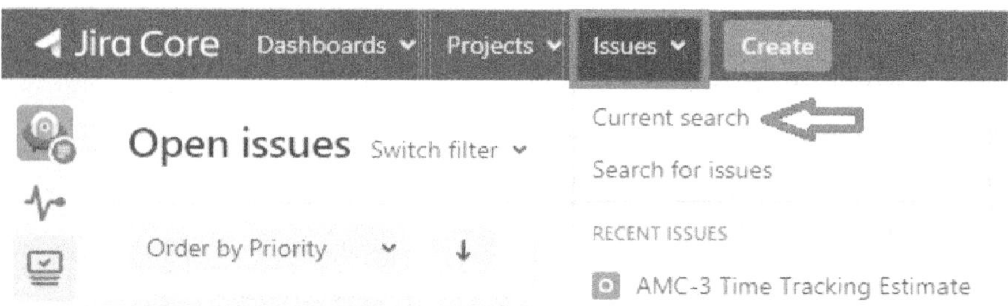

Opening Current search will bring you to the last search you performed. Jira Core simply assumes you will need this search again.

Search for Issues (Basic Search)

If you forgot about the Quick Search box you can always go to **Search for Issues:**

EXERCISE: VIEW 'SEARCH FOR ISSUES'

1. NAVIGATE MAIN MENU BAR >ISSUES > **SEARCH FOR ISSUES**:

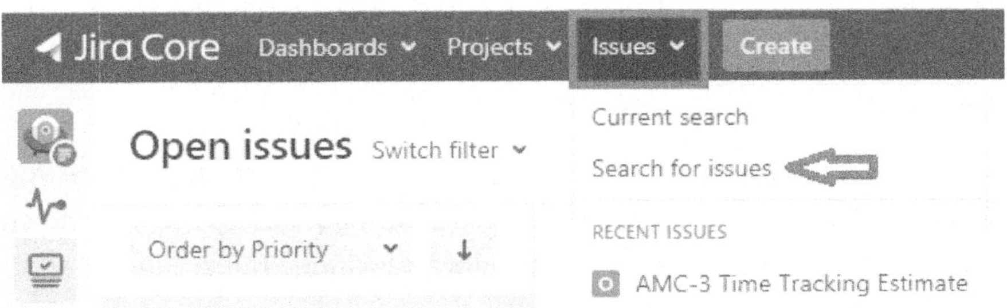

This opens up the **Issue Navigator** (or Search View) listing all of the issues for **all the projects** with which you are associated.

Near the top of the Issue Navigator is a row made up primarily of drop-down lists. Collectively they are called the **Basic Search**.

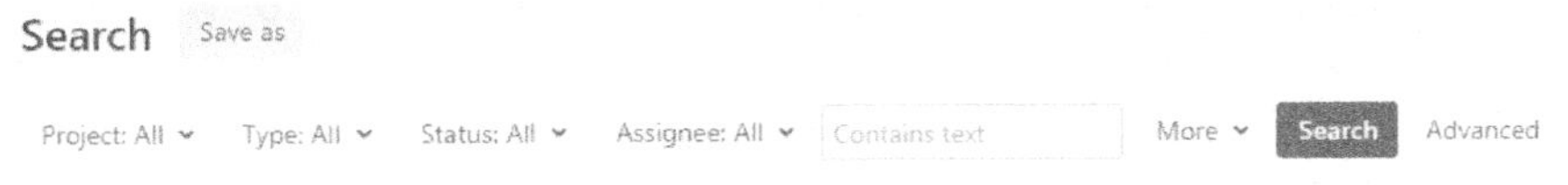

These drop-down lists are nothing more than filters, allowing you to narrow your search as little or as much as you wish.

In the image above, you see that there are five drop-down filters and one text box. It is important to remember that these filters are subsets of other filters. For example, let's say you select "To Do" in the Status filter and then want to select an Assignee in the Assignee filter. Your choices in the Assignee list will be limited to those Issues that have a "To Do" status. **Jira Core builds searches in the order that the filters were selected.** Therefore, when building a multi-filter search, remember to build the search in the proper filter order.

Let's take a closer look at the filters.

Project

This filter will allow you to filter your issues by project. The drop-down list will contain all the projects you have permission to see. The filter is multi-select, which means you can select more than one project if you wish.

If, after you have initially set your project filter, you realize you need to include additional projects, then simply go back to the drop down and select those projects you now want to include. There is no need to clear your filter and start over.

If you are currently viewing issues associated with one project and want to see *all* of your issues across all projects, then uncheck the project. When there are no projects checked, Jira Core will automatically select ALL projects.

You can also filter a project by entering its name or key in the Find Projects search field.

Type

This filter allows you to narrow your search based on Issue Types or Sub-Task Issue Types. Simply check the Issue Type(s) you want to see, or type in the name of the Issue Type in your Find Issue Types search field.

You need to remember that if you have selected a particular project or projects to view, you will only see the Issue Types associated with that project or projects.

If there are no Issue Types selected you will see ALL issues, depending on your Project filter setting.

Status

This filter allows you to narrow your search based on Status type.

Once again, the number of statuses available in this search will be limited if you have already narrowed your search with the Project and Type filters.

If the are no Statuses selected you will see ALL issues depending on your Project and Type filter settings.

Assignee

This filter allows you to narrow your search based on Assignee.

The number of Assignees available in this search will be limited if you have already narrowed your search with other filters.

Contains text (Search Field)

Any criteria (must be text) or key words typed in this search field will be dependent on any previous filters selected.

More

The More filter is quite powerful. It contains all the other standard and custom fields available to you. Well, almost all. It will only show you the fields in your Projects or Issue Types. For example, if you do not have any Epic projects, you won't see any Epic fields.

Since these fields are going to be used in a Filter argument Jira Core calls these fields 'criteria'.

When you select any of these criteria, another pop-up will show up to narrow the search even further. For example, if you select the Due Date field, a pop-up will appear with a number of criteria options you can use to narrow the filter results:

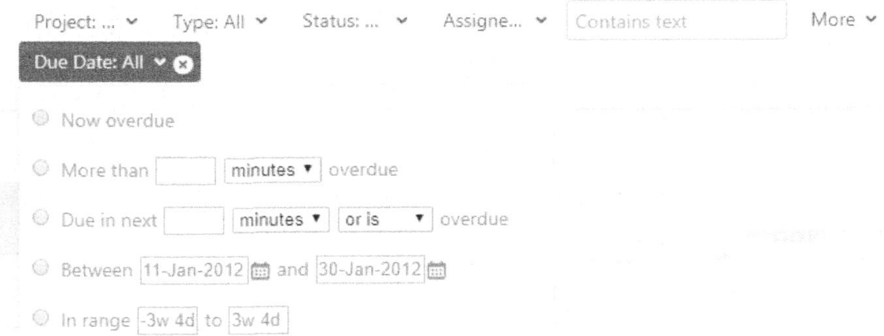

If you have built a Custom Field that contains a list of options, you can also use those options as criteria for your More filter. In the image below, I am using a Custom field called Approved, which has two options. I can select either Yes or No to further narrow my filter:

You can also repeat the More search as many times as you want as long as you remember that each More filter is a subset to previous filters.

If you want to delete a More filter, you will need to unclick the selected field name.

SEARCH BOX

The purpose of the Search box is to execute the search, or refresh the search if you have made a change to any issue.

ADVANCED SEARCH

Clicking on Advance link will replace the basic search filters with the advanced filter field. In this field you would create a search using the Jira Query Language (JQL). If you have experience with Microsoft Excel functions, you will find this quite similar. Using the Advanced function involves creating a JQL command followed by a criterion. Let's try one. But before we do, look at the format below so you don't get confused:

Font	Purpose	Example
Regular	Instruction	Enter
Bold	Specific text to be Entered	**Project**
Regular italic	Something you should enter (such as a project or field name in your Jira program); or should select from the drop-down list	*My first project*
[]	Instruction to enter a space	Project[]=[]*My first project*
= + - > < !	Argument operator	Project =

EXERCISE: VIEW ADVANCED FIELD

1. IN THE ADVANCED FIELD, ENTER (OR SELECT FROM THE DROP-DOWN LIST THAT APPEARS AS YOU START TO TYPE):
2. PROJECT[]=[]SELECT THE NAME OF A PROJECT THAT APPEARS IN THE LIST[]
3. ORDER BY[]ISSUEKEY

After you enter Project and a space, you will see a drop-down list of project names, select one of them. After you enter (or select) Order By, make a space and enter (or select) Issuekey. After you have entered a few of the Issuekey letters a list of words related to Issue will appear. You can select Issuekey from that list or continue to manually enter the word:

Project instructs Jira Core to look for a project name. ORDER BY is a command, and Issuekey is the criteria. In this case, your issues will be sorted by the issue key, with the lowest number Issue key at the top of the list. I like this search as I prefer to see my list of issues **in the order**

they were created, rather than the Jira default that lists issues based on create time (most recent issue listed first).

Notice how, when you are entering the argument, Jira offers options for you to choose from. This makes the building of the argument much easier.

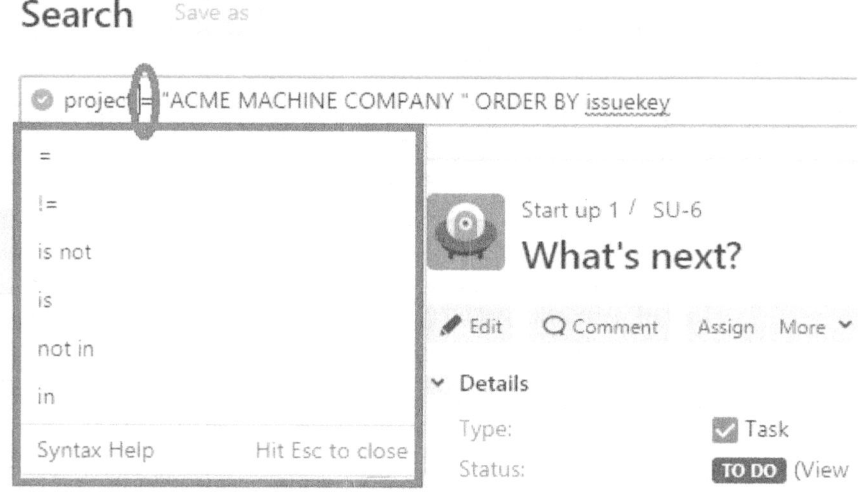

We won't go any further in this book. However, if you are interested in following up, the Jira Core Support Documentation Advanced Searching page contains a great deal of helpful information: https://confluence.atlassian.com/display/Jira/Advanced+Searching

Change View

The last item in the Search row (at the far right) is an icon allowing you to change your issue view:

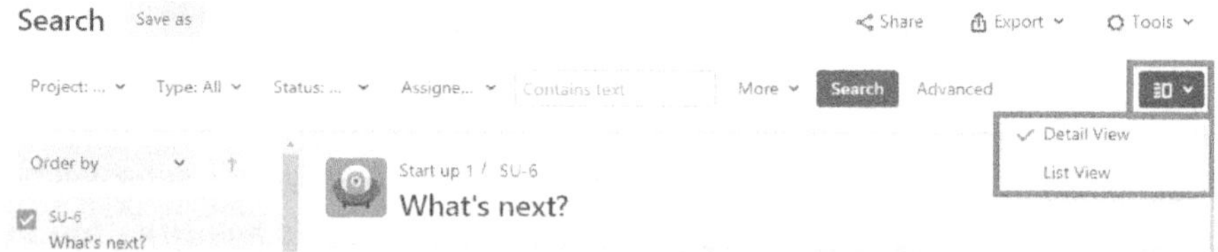

One is a list view of your issues. The other is a combined view with a list of your issues on the left, and a detailed view of the issue selected.

Save Search

Of course, when most people go to the effort of building a search they usually plan on viewing that search a number of times. Saving the search means the user doesn't need to reenter the search criteria every time s/he wants to view it.

Exercise: Save Search As

1. Click on the **Save As** button
2. Type in a Filter Name in the Save Filter Pop Up and click **SAVE**.

Once you click the save button your Search (really a filter) will be saved in the **Favorite Filters** sidebar.

Build a Custom Filter

Technically, any Saved search is defined as a Custom Filter. However, we are going to create one using the More filter.

In this specific filter we want to see those Issues that will be due in two days or less, but not those that are already overdue. Later in this chapter we will create an issue subscription so that you will receive a system generated emails containing all your tasks that are due in two days or less (hopefully you are so organized that the list will be quite small or non-existent).

Exercise: Build a Custom Filter

1. Navigate Main Menu Bar > Issues >**Search for issues**

2. In the Search view, click on the Project drop-down list and make sure no projects are selected. In other words, you want to include **all projects**
3. In the Filter menu bar, click on the **More** drop-down list and select (or start to type in the Search text box) *Due Date*
4. In the Due Date pop up go to the **Due in next** option and click the radio button:

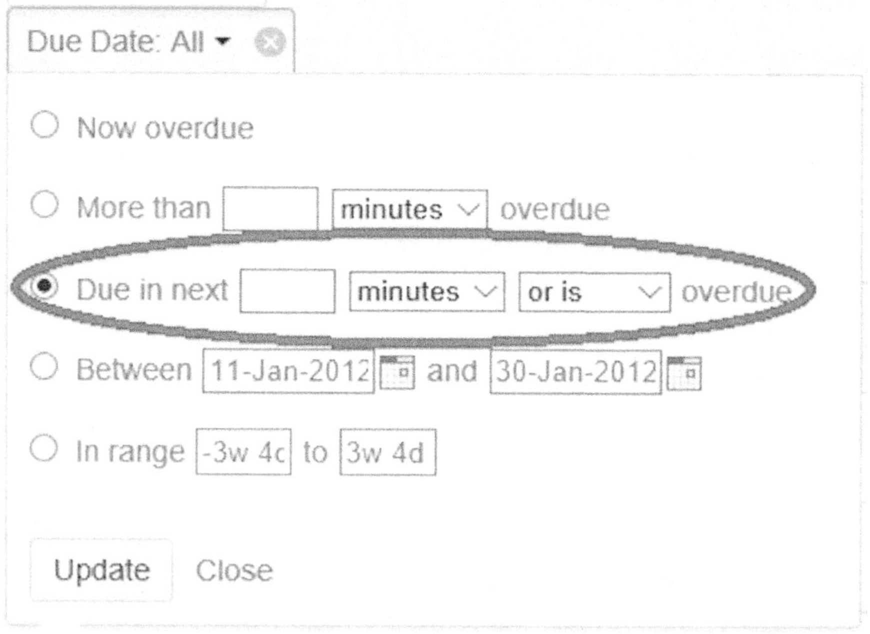

5. In the first entry field in the **Due in next** option, enter the number *2*
6. In the **drop-down** list next to the **Due in next** entry field select *Days*
7. In the **next drop-down list** select *and not* as the option for **Overdue**
8. Click the **Update** Button
9. Click the **Save as** Button

10. In the **Save Filter** pop up **text** field, type *"Issues due in 2 days or less"*
11. Click **Save**

Customizing your Issue List View

One of the really great things you can do in Jira Core is bespoke any of the filters' views by adding or deleting columns in the Issue List view. This allows you to modify your Issue List view so that only the critical fields are shown, and the need to go to each Issue's Detail View is eliminated. For example, I have added my custom 'Follow Up Date' to the Issue List view; so, I can see at a glance those issues that will soon require this action.

You can customize your Issue List view using the **Columns** drop-down. Clicking on Columns will open a drop-down list with three tabs: My Defaults, Filter, and System:

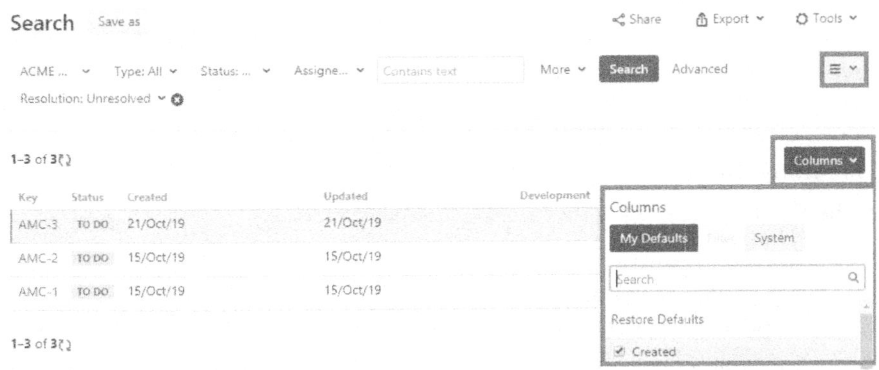

My Defaults allows you to create your own customized list view. It is applicable only to your views.

The **Filter** tab allows you to design Issue List views for specific Saved Filters.

In the **System** tab the Jira Core Administrator can define the columns for *all* users who have not created their own default views.

Having said that, making changes in the System area may over-write the custom views of some users; so, be careful when you use this configuration. To confirm my words, click on the system tab and see the warning note.

Changing the Issue List View

After you click any of the three Column tabs you will see a number of fields accompanied by check marks. Clearing a check box will eliminate that field from the Issue List view.

If you want to add a field to that configuration, simply continue to scroll down to find an option of your interest and select one or more to include them in your view; or, type that option in the Search box right below the My Defaults tab.

Make sure to click **Done** when you are finished.

Just one note of caution. When making your My Defaults configuration, remember you are in the general Search Issues view. Otherwise, you may end up accidentally making a configuration to a Saved Filter.

If you are unhappy for some reasons with your result and want to restore your defaults, click on **Restore Defaults** link under Search box in the Column pop up.

Sorting

You can also reconfigure your list view by clicking on any of the column headings. Doing so will give you an option as to how to sort the column. For example, clicking on the Key column will change the sorting from smallest to largest or largest to smallest Key number.

Re-arranging Columns

You can also move Issue columns (in the List View), by clicking on the column title and then drag-and-drop to the new location.

Subscribe to a Filter

One of the incredible strengths of Jira Core is the ability to be notified, by email, of any issue or issue condition. This is done by subscribing to a filter. Building a custom filter and then subscribing to it is one of the most amazing productivity and risk management tools I have run across. And subscribing is incredibly easy to do.

Exercise: Subscribe to a Filter

1. Navigate Main Menu Bar > Issues >**Manage Filters** (located at the very bottom of the opened Issues Menu)
2. By default, the **Favorite Filters** view will appear
3. In the Favorite Filters, find the **Issues Due in 2 days or less** filter in the **Name** column, then click on the **Subscribe** link in the **Subscriptions** column:

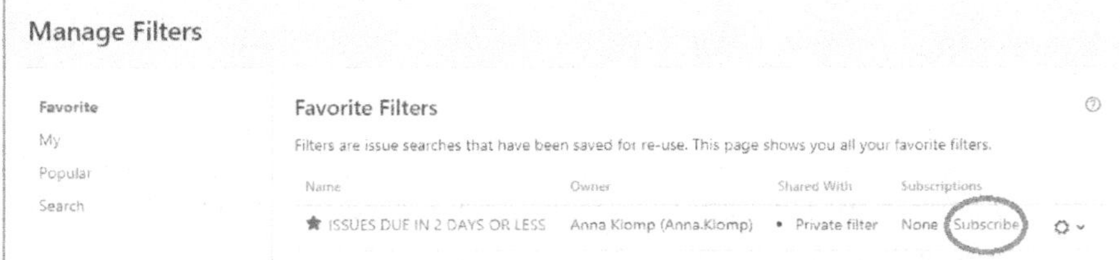

4. In the **Filter Subscription** pop-up, ensure *Personal Subscriptions* is selected in the **Recipients** drop-down list
5. Check *Daily* in the **Schedule** options
6. In the **Interval** area select Once per Day and at 1:00 AM in the following drop-down lists (or select some other time if you wish)
7. Leave the "Email this filter, even if there are no issues found" unchecked
8. Click Subscribe

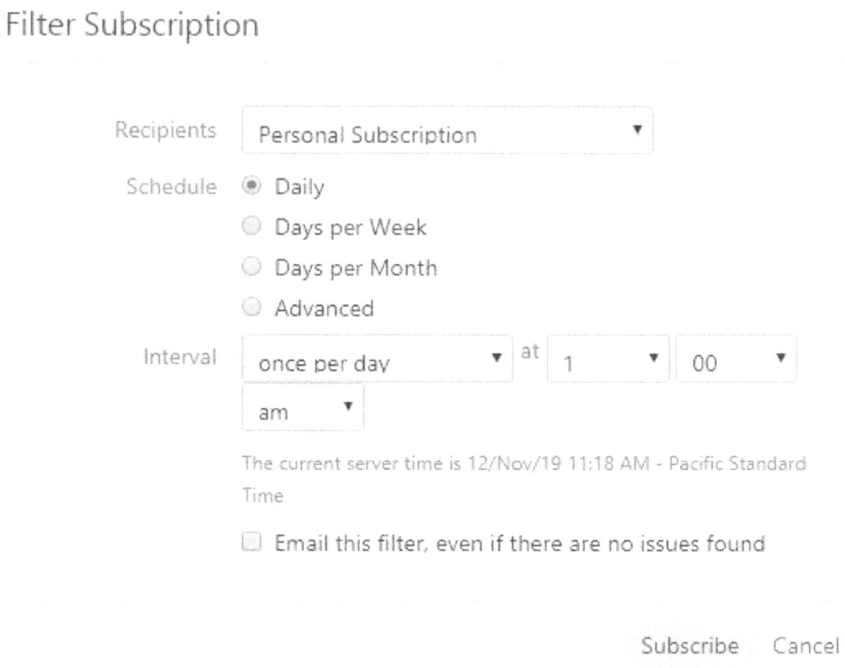

Filter Subscription

Recipients Personal Subscription

Schedule
- Daily
- Days per Week
- Days per Month
- Advanced

Interval once per day at 1 00 am

The current server time is 12/Nov/19 11:18 AM - Pacific Standard Time

Email this filter, even if there are no issues found

Subscribe Cancel

As we went through these various steps rather quickly, let's take a step back and discuss each view in more detail.

MANAGE FILTERS

The Manage Filters view is divided into two sections: the Manage Filters Sidebar and the Main view (Favorite Filters).

MANAGE FILTERS SIDEBAR

The Manage Filters Sidebar has four links: Favorite, My, Popular, and Search.

Manage Filters

Favorite
My
Popular
Search

Favorite Filters

Filters are issue searches that have

Name

Issues due in 2 days or less

Favorite lists all of the Filters you have designated as a Favorite (usually when you first created the Filter). **My** will bring up a view showing all of your Filters (in alphabetical order). **Popular** ranks your Filters by popularity. Truth to tell, the only value I have found with this view is to show my filters I have never, or rarely used. At which point I delete them. The final **Search** option takes you to a view where you search by the filter name or description, the filter owner, or filters that are shared. We will talk more about all of these options a little later.

Manage Filters Main View

Clicking on any option in the Manage Filters sidebar will open the Manage Filters Main view. By default, when you open Manage Filters, the Favorite Filters view will appear:

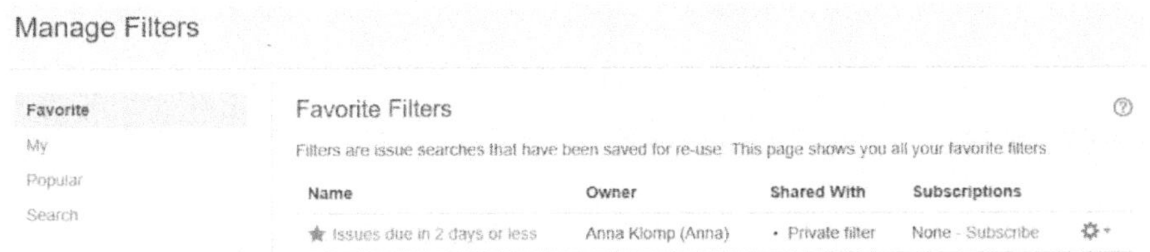

Favorite Filters View

The **Favorite Filters** view has five columns: **Name, Owner, Shared With, Subscriptions**, and the ubiquitous **COG.**

Name

This column lists all of your favorite filters in alphabetical order. If you don't see a filter in this column it is probably not designated as a Favorite. In this case, go to the **Manage Filters Sidebar** and click **My**, which will open a list of all of your Filters. Beside each filter you will see a star. Some stars may be solid, and that indicates they are a favorite. Click any star that is simply a star outline. Once the star is filled in, it becomes a favorite. And of course, the reverse is true.

Owner

This column lists the name of the owner of the filter. Typically, this is the individual who built it. It is handy in the event you want to modify the filter but are not the owner.

Shared With

When the Filter was created, a creator either made it a private filter, or shared it with others. This column simply tells you if it is private or shared; and if shared, then shared with whom.

Subscriptions

The subscriptions column will show one of two things. It will show that no one has subscribed and will include a **Subscribe** link. Alternatively, it will indicate how many subscriptions are associated with that filter, and will include a link that allows you to add more subscribers to that filter or to edit the existing subscription(s).

COG

In the final column you will meet our friend the COG. The COG menu allows you to either Edit the Filter or to Delete it.

My Filters View

The My filters is the essentially the same as the Favorite Filters view except it does not have an Owners column, because, well, You are the owner. The other key difference is that it lists all of your filters, both your favorites and non-favorite filters.

Popular Filters View

The Popular Filters is the same as the Favorite Filters except the COG column is replaced by a Popularity column. This column lists the number of people who have used the filter. This is a helpful feature if you are considering whether or not to delete a filter.

Search Filters View

You can also search for a filter by typing in the name, or part of a name, of the filter; by trying to find the owner; or by determining if a filter is shared with anyone, a group, or a project.

Build a Report

In a previous chapter, we learned how to build Dashboards and add Gadgets to them. Most of the time a Gadget is a type of report, though there are exceptions such as the Administrator User Guide Gadget.

You can also build project specific reports that are located within that project, and that's what we will do now.

Exercise: Build a Project Report

1. Navigate Main Menu Bar> **Projects**
2. Select any project
3. Navigate to the sidebar of the project, click on **Reports** (the Icon with the graph)

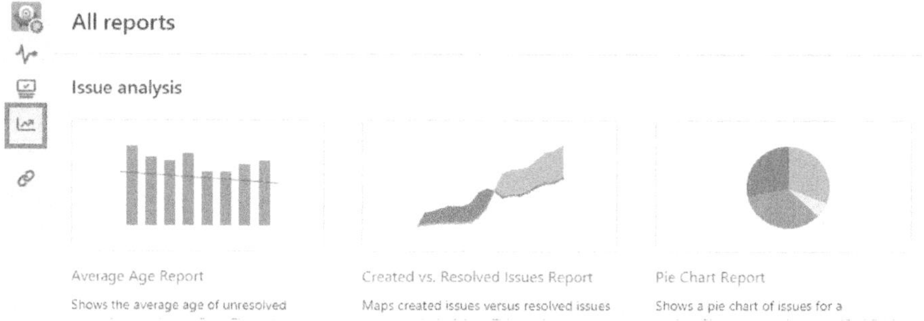

The opened view is full of different report types. However, sometimes there may be only one specific report shown. If that is the case, go to the top of the view and where it says **Reports**, click the down arrow next to it, then click **All Reports** on the menu.

4. Click on any report

Clicking on a report will open its configuration view. Here you will answer a number of questions specific to that report. Since they are all different, we won't try to explain them all here. I recommend you click on a report that seems appropriate for your type of project and then configure it in a number of different ways (e.g. try different reporting periods) to determine what works best for you.

Once you configure a report click the **Next** button to see the results.

After the report is created you can revise the report by clicking on the **Configure** button in the top right of the Report view.

Dashboard Filter Reports

In a previous chapter we created the Test Dashboard using Jira's Core Gadgets. Many of those gadgets are based on Jira Core built-in filters. In this chapter I want to introduce you two Filters gadgets.

Remember that a Project Report will appear only in a Project and will only display information about that project. A Dashboard Filter Report can cover multiple projects and will appear only in a Dashboard.

Exercise: Add a Report Gadget to a Dashboard

1. Navigate Main Menu Bar > **Dashboards**
2. Select any **Dashboard** (except for the System Dashboard)
3. Click on **Add Gadget** button in the upper right corner of the Dashboard
4. Scroll down until you see **Favorite Filters** and **Filter Results**

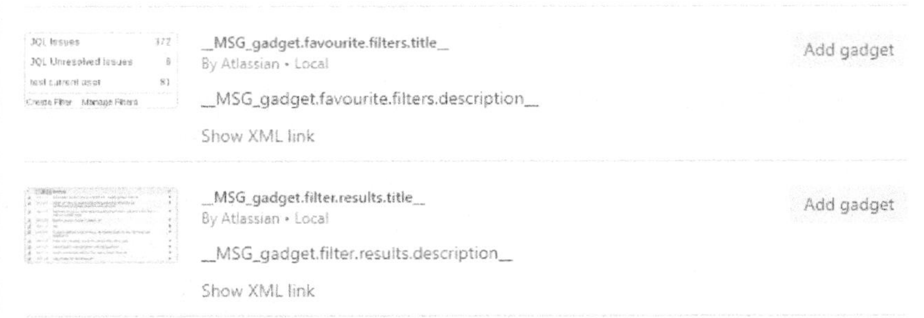

Favorite Filters

Selecting this gadget will place a list of your favorite filters on the dashboard. Clicking any filter will bring up that specific filter report.

Filter Results

This gadget will place a Filter Results configure view on the Dashboard. Select the Saved Filter you want to see, answer the other questions, save the results, and those results will now be shown in the dashboard.

Export a Filter's results

There may be occasions when you need to export the results of a filter. This happens when you need to send the results to someone who isn't licensed for Jira Core. Or you may want to save the Filter results as a snapshot in time, to be reviewed at a later date. One of the many great things about Jira is that you can easily export Filter results in many different ways.

Exercise: Export a report

1. Navigate Main Menu Bar > **Issues**
2. Select **My Open Issues**, or any other **Filter** if you wish
3. click on the **Export** drop-down list in the upper right corner

You will see 11 export options available to you:

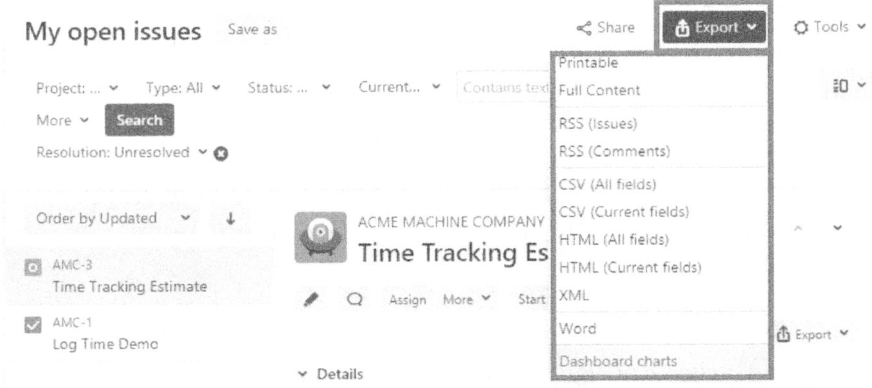

PRINTABLE

Printable option is designed to view your filter's issues in printable format. It has two parts: Header and Body.

Header

The header contains the name of the Organization or Jira Core (i.e. the Title name of your Jira Core program found in the main menu bar), the project or projects (if previously selected), as well as the other filter criteria such as assignee, status, sorted by, etc.

Body

The body of the report contains the filter results. Note that it will only show the columns you have selected to be visible when you configured your column layout in the List View.

Printing

To print the page, use your web-browsers print method (e.g. for Windows 10 click the right mouse button and select Print in the menu that appears).

FULL CONTENT

When you choose **Full Content,** you will be brought to a view that displays, in a table format, all the available fields related to the issues in that saved filter.

Your filter may contain issues that have different fields. This is quite common if your filter includes different projects or issue types. Your report will be divided into sections for each issue and all the fields available for that particular issue will be shown.

If you have created a custom field and there is no data in that field, the report will not show the field.

Printing

To print the page, use your web-browsers print method (e.g. for Windows 10 click the right mouse button and select Print in the menu that appears).

RSS Issues and RSS Comments

RSS means Really Simple Syndication and it can provide constant updates of information (such as Issue Status Updates, etc.). However, you need to set up a place (webpage) to host the RSS feed. And since that is pure I.T. stuff, we will move on to our next Export item.

CSV (All fields)

You can export your Saved Filter report as a CSV (comma separated value) format to a spreadsheet format such as Microsoft Excel. This is great if you want to rearrange or do something with the data. You must have a copy of MS Excel on your computer.

When you select the All fields option, be aware that every field you have permission to see will be exported to the spreadsheet report, even those unrelated to the issues in your saved filter.

Additionally, despite Jira saying it will export All Fields, it does not export the comments related to the issues.

Jira Core limits the number of issues you can export to 1,000.

You may also get a pop-up warning in Excel that the file is corrupted, or something like that. This is because Jira inserts two 'header' rows at the beginning of the spreadsheet, and that tends to confuse Excel. Don't worry about it, import the sheet anyway.

CSV (Current fields)

When selecting the Current Fields option, you will receive an CSV report that only contains the columns you have visible in the Jira Saved Filter.

As with the ALL Fields option, Jira Core limits the number of issues you can export to 1,000.

HTML (All fields)

When selecting this option, a new page will open in your browser (e.g. Google, Firefox, IE Explorer, etc.) and display every *common* Issue field.

What does "common" mean? Well, your HTML page will only display a field if every issue in that filter has that field. For example, let's say your filter contains 10 Issues and 9 of those Issues contains the field Due Date, but the 10th does not. In this case the Due Date field will not appear.

When you select the All fields option, be aware that every field you have permission to see will be exported to the spreadsheet report, even those unrelated to the issues in your saved filter.

Additionally, despite Jira saying it will export All Fields, it does not export the comments related to the issues.

Jira Core limits the number of issues you can export to 1,000.

HTML (Current Fields)

When selecting this option, a new page will open in your browser (e.g. Google, Firefox, IE Explorer, etc.) and display the fields shown in your list view.

Additionally, despite Jira saying it will export All Fields, it does not export the comments related to the issues.

Jira Core limits the number of issues you can export to 1,000.

XML

Selecting XML will open a page containing the HTML code of your Saved Filter. Since this book is written for business users and not I.T. professionals, we will not dive any deeper into this export option.

Word

You can export your Saved Filter report to Microsoft Word. When you do, so the format will look very similar to the Full Content format.

One convenient feature is that Word will insert a page break after each issue. This means each issue will start on a new page. This is quite useful if you want to print out specific issues.

It should go without saying that you must have a copy of MS Word (or program compatible to Word) on your computer for this option to work.

Dashboard Charts

This format allows you to export a Saved Filter as a gadget to any Jira Core Dashboard you have permission to edit.

When you click **Dashboard Charts** you are presented with a number of Gadget options to choose from. Depending on the type of Saved Filter you may not be able to choose all Chart types shown; if that happens, keep experimenting until you find one you like and that works for your Saved Filter.

Once you have selected the Chart you want, click the **Save to Dashboard** button. That will open another view where you will select the Dashboard you want to host your chart. In addition, you can enter the name of the Filter and that title will appear in the header bar of the chart.

After you have selected the Dashboard, click **Save**. The Dashboard you selected will open, and your chart will be inserted as the first (top of page) gadget in the Dashboard. From there you can reposition it if you wish.

Chapter 13 – How To...

Chapter Objective

In this chapter you will find 'scripts' to create or edit the most common Jira Core elements, such as Projects, Issues, Schemes, etc.

NOTE: There are often different ways to accomplish the same thing in Jira Core. To keep it simple, I will present what I believe to be the easiest method for the novice Jira Core Administrator.

NOTE: Many of these scripts require you to log on using your Jira Administrator Access Username and Password.

NOTE: For most elements, Jira Core will not check to see if you have completed everything in order to make your element work. For example, after creating a new Issue Type, there will not be a pop-up message reminding you to associate it with an Issue Type Scheme or a Project. Where relevant, at the end of the script I included a "**What you also need to make it work**" checklist of related items necessary to make sure your element does indeed work.

NOTE: These scripts are based on the assumption that **you have the permission to execute the actions**. For example, when editing an Issue, it assumes you have permission to edit that issue. If you do not, you will not see the Edit link.

Jira Admin vs Jira Project Admin

This book is written for the Jira Admin. The Jira Project Admin may be able to do some of these scripts but only by accessing the administration area via a Project's Project Setting page. For example, a Project Admin can place a custom field on a custom screen, but only if the custom screen and custom field already exist (i.e. made by a Jira Admin).

To make things easier, I will indicate whether a Jira Project Admin can perform the script or not. Of course, even if you can perform the script, you need to ensure you have the permission to do so (as defined by the relevant permission scheme).

Projects

Create a Project

Jira Admin	Yes
Jira Project Admin	No

1. Navigate to Main Menu Bar > **Projects > Create Project**
2. In the Create Project pop-up, Select the Business Project Type you want to use for your project: Project Management, Process Management, or Task Management
3. Click the **Next** button
4. You will be provided with a brief description of the selected business project type and with a preview of the workflow associated with that project type. If satisfied click **Select**. If not satisfied, click **Back** and Repeat step 2 above
5. In the **Project Type Naming** pop-up, enter the **name** of your Project

CAUTION: Project Names must be Unique as must Key names

In the **Project Lead** text box, enter (or select) the name of the project lead

6. Click the **Submit** button

View Project (View Project's Issues)

Jira Admin	Yes
Jira Project Admin	Yes

1. Navigate to Main Menu Bar > **Projects**
2. Choose the name of the Project from the **Current Project** or **Recent Projects** sections and click on it; or click on Business, or View All Projects

Edit Project

Jira Admin	Yes
Jira Project Admin	Yes

1. Navigate to [gear icon] > **Projects**
2. In the Administration Projects view, in the **Projects List** find the Project you want to Edit, click on three dots button in the Action Column, and then click the **Edit** link
3. In the **Details** pop-up you can change:
   i. The Name of the Project
   ii. The Key of the project

CAUTION: Not recommended as it can cause severe database issues if not done correctly

   iii. The URL
   iv. The Project Type
   v. The project category
   vi. The Avatar
   vii. The Description
4. Click the **Save Details** button

Delete Project

Jira Admin	Yes
Jira Project Admin	No

1. Navigate to ⚙ > **Projects**
2. In the Administration Projects view, in the **Projects List** find the Project you want to Delete, click on the three dots button, and then click the **Delete** link
3. You will be taken to the Delete Project page where you will see: WARNING strongly recommending you to save the project data **before you delete** it by creating a back up
4. In the Delete Project page, click the **Delete** button

View Project Settings

Jira Admin	Yes
Jira Project Admin	Yes

1. Navigate to Main Menu Bar > **Projects**
2. Choose the name of the Project from the **Current Project** or **Recent Projects** sections and click on it; or click on Business, or View All Projects
3. Click on the **Project Settings** at the bottom of the Project Sidebar:

⚙ Project settings «

Issue

Create an Issue

Jira Admin	Yes
Jira Project Admin	Yes

1. Navigate to Main Menu Bar
2. Click **Create**
3. In the **Create Issue** pop-up, select the project that will be **associated** with the new Issue from the **Project** drop-down list
4. The default **Issue Type** is **Task** and is already selected. Or, you may select the Issue Type from the Issue Type drop-down list
   i. You must complete those fields having a red asterisk, they are mandatory. Other than that, complete the fields you feel are necessary to your project
   ii. **Note:** Occasionally, Jira Core does not have enough information to display a full Create Issue Screen. In those instances, only two fields might be appear: Project and Issue type. In such a case, select the Project and Issue Type, Click the **Next** button and complete **All Fields**
5. Click the **Create** button

What you also need to make it work

- ✓ Project
- ✓ Issue Type *Note: Jira Core provides Issue Type defaults to select from. If you are not satisfied with them, you can create your own Issue Type*

- ✓ Issue Type Scheme

View Issue Details

Jira Admin	Yes
Jira Project Admin	Yes

1. Navigate Main Menu Bar > **Issues** > **Search for issues**
2. In the **Search** view, locate the **Issue** you wish to View
3. Click on the Issue's link

Edit Issue

Jira Admin	Yes
Jira Project Admin	Yes

1. Navigate Main Menu Bar > **Issues > Search for issues**
2. In the **Search** view, locate the **Issue** you wish to edit
3. click on the selected Issue
4. In the opened **Issue Details** area (on the right) click on the **EDIT** icon on the Issue Details' menu bar
5. In the **Edit Issue** pop-up, change the field information (values) as necessary
6. Click the **Update** button

Delete Issue

Jira Admin	Yes
Jira Project Admin	Yes

1. Navigate Main Menu Bar > **Issues** > **Search for issues**
2. In the **Search** view, locate the **Issue** you wish to Delete
3. click on the selected Issue
4. In the opened **Issue Details** area (on the right) click on the **MORE** button on the Issue Details' menu bar
5. In the More drop-down list click on **Delete**
6. In the **Delete Issue** pop-up, click the **Delete** button

Start up 1 / SU-1

This is your first task

Edit Comment Assign More Start Progress Done Admin

Issue Types

Add Issue Type

Jira Admin	Yes
Jira Project Admin	No

1. Navigate to > **Issues**
2. In the Administration Issues > Issue Types view, click on **Add Issue Type** button located in the upper right corner
3. In the **Add Issue Type** pop-up:
   i. Enter a **Name** for the Issue Type (Required)
   ii. Enter a **Description** for the Issue Type
   iii. Select the **Type** of Issue
      a. Standard Issue Type
      b. Sub-task Issue Type
4. Click **Add**

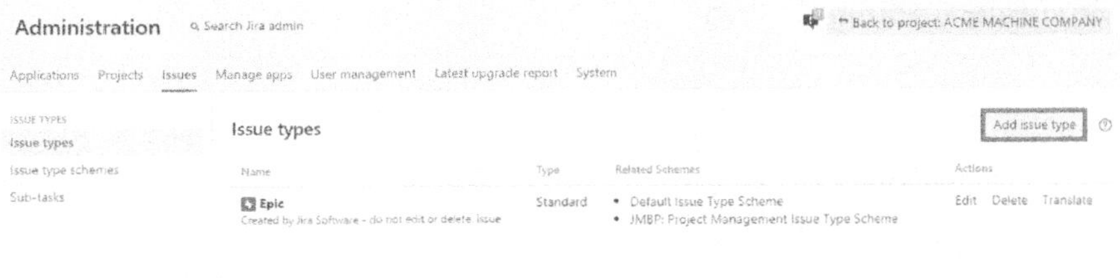

What you also need to make it work

- ✓ Project
- ✓ Issue
- ✓ Issue Type Scheme

Edit Issue Type

Jira Admin	Yes
Jira Project Admin	No

1. Navigate to ⚙ > **Issues**
2. In the Administration Issues > Issue Types view, click **Edit** link in the **Actions** Column for the **Issue Type** you want to edit
3. In the **Edit Issue Type** view you can:
   i. Change the **Name** of the Issue Type
   ii. Change the **Description**
   iii. Change the Issue Type **Avatar**
4. Click the **Update** button

Delete Issue Type

Jira Admin	Yes
Jira Project Admin	No

1. Navigate to ⚙ > **Issues**
2. In the Administration Issues > Issue Types view click **Delete** link in the **Actions** Column for the **Issue Type** you want to delete
3. In the **Delete Issue Type** view Click the **Delete** button

   CAUTION: a) the Issue Type cannot be deleted if there are open issues associated with that Issue Type (Jira Core will provide an error message). b) It is highly recommended you NOT delete an **Issue Type** if it is **associated with Workflow Scheme(s), Field Configuration Scheme(s), or Screen Scheme(s)**, as doing so will really, really, *really* mess up your project(s). If the Issue Type is associated with any of these schemes you will need to migrate them to a new Issue Type.

Issue Type Schemes

Add Issue Type Scheme

Jira Admin	Yes
Jira Project Admin	No

1. Navigate to ⚙ > **Issues**
2. In the Administration Issues view, Select **Issue Type Schemes** from the sidebar
3. In the **Issue Type Schemes** view, click on the **Add Issue Type Scheme** button located in the upper right corner
4. In the Add Issue Type Scheme view:
   i. Enter a Scheme **Name**
   ii. Enter a **Description** of the Scheme
   iii. Drag and drop all **Available Issue Types** you want to **associate with** this **scheme** from the Right Column to the left (**Issue Types for Current Scheme**) column
   iv. Select a **Default Issue Type** from the drop-down list

TIP: If you need a new issue type for this scheme you can create one by clicking on the **+Add Issue Type** button at the top right of the view. If you use this feature, the Issue Type will a) appear in the left column (**Issue Types for Current Scheme**), and b) be added to Jira's Core database.

What you also need to make it work

- ✓ Project
- ✓ Issue Type

Copy Issue Type Scheme

See Add Issue Type Scheme

Jira Admin	Yes
Jira Project Admin	No

Edit Issue Type Scheme

Jira Admin	Yes
Jira Project Admin	No

1. Navigate to [gear icon] > **Issues**
2. In the Administration Issues view, Select **Issue Type Schemes** from the sidebar
3. In the **Issue Type Schemes** view, click the **Edit** link in the **Actions** column for the **Issue Type Scheme** you want to edit
4. In the Modify Issue Type Scheme view you can:
   i. Change the Scheme **Name**
   ii. Change the **Description**
   iii. Change the Default issue Type
   iv. Change the **order** of the **Issue Types for Current Scheme** by dragging and dropping the Issue Types into the order you prefer
   v. Drag and drop issue types from one column to the other to **add** or **remove** an Available Issue Type from the Issue Type Scheme
5. Click the **Save** button

TIP: If you are not happy with any of your changes you can click the **Reset** button and your scheme will revert back to its original form. Reset will only work if you have not already clicked the Save button.

Associate Issue Type Scheme with Project

Jira Admin	Yes
Jira Project Admin	No

1. Navigate Main Menu Bar > ⚙ > **Issues**
2. In the Administration Issues view, Select **Issue Type Schemes** from the sidebar
3. In the **Issue Type Schemes** view, click the **Associate** link in the **Actions** column for the **Issue Type Scheme** you want to associate with a **Project**
4. In the **Associate Issue Type Scheme** view, select the **project**(s) you wish to associate with the scheme from the **Projects list**
5. Click the **Associate** button

Delete Issue Type Scheme

Jira Admin	Yes
Jira Project Admin	No

1. Navigate Main Menu Bar > ⚙ > **Issues**
2. In the Administration Issues view, Select **Issue Type Schemes** from the sidebar
3. In the **Issue Type Schemes** view, click the **Delete** link in the **Actions** column for the **Issue Type Scheme** you want to Delete
4. In the **Delete Issue Type Scheme** view, click the **Delete** button

CAUTION: If you have any **Projects associated with** the **Issue Type Scheme**, once you click **Delete** the projects will use the **Default Global Issue Type Scheme**.

Sub-Task Issue Types

Add Sub-Task Issue Type

Jira Admin	Yes
Jira Project Admin	No

1. Navigate Main Menu Bar > ⚙ > **Issues**
2. In the Administration Issues view, Select **Sub-Tasks** from the sidebar
3. In the Sub-Tasks view, click on **Add Sub-Task Issue Type** button in the upper right corner
4. In the Add Sub-Task Issue Type pop-up:
   i. Enter a **Name** for the Sub-task Issue Type (Required)
   ii. Enter a **Description** for the Sub-Task Issue Type
5. Click the **Add** button

What you also need to make it work

- ✓ Project
- ✓ Issue
- ✓ Issue Type
- ✓ Issue Type Scheme

Edit Sub-Task Issue Type

Jira Admin	Yes
Jira Project Admin	No

1. Navigate Main Menu Bar > ⚙ > **Issues**

2. In the Administration Issues view, Select **Sub-Tasks** from the sidebar
3. In the **Sub-Tasks** view, click the **Edit** link in the **Actions** column for the **Sub-Task** you want to edit
4. In the Edit Sub-Task Issue Type view you can:
   i. Change the **Name** of the Sub-Task
   ii. Change the **Description** of the Sub-Task
   iii. Change the Issue Type **Avatar**
5. Click the **Update** button

Delete Sub-Task Issue Type

Jira Admin	Yes
Jira Project Admin	No

1. Navigate Main Menu Bar > ⚙ > **Issues**
2. In the Administration Issue view, Select **Sub-Tasks** from the sidebar
3. In the **Sub-Tasks** view, click the **Delete** link in the **Actions** column for the **Sub-Task** Issue Type you want to Delete
4. In the Delete Sub-Task Issue Type view, click the **Delete** button

CAUTION: It is highly recommended you NOT delete a **Sub-Task Issue Type** if it is **associated with Workflow Scheme(s), Field Configuration Scheme(s), or Screen Scheme(s)**, as doing so will really, really, *really* mess up your project(s). If the Sub-Task Issue Type is associated with any of these schemes you will need to migrate them to a new Issue Type.

WORKFLOWS

ADD WORKFLOW

Jira Admin	Yes
Jira Project Admin	No

1. NAVIGATE MAIN MENU BAR > ⚙ > **ISSUES**
2. IN THE ADMINISTRATION ISSUES VIEW, SELECT **WORKFLOWS** FROM THE SIDEBAR
3. IN THE **WORKFLOWS** VIEW, CLICK THE **ADD WORKFLOW** BUTTON
4. IN THE **ADD WORKFLOW** POP-UP ENTER:
   i. A **NAME** FOR THE WORKFLOW
   ii. A **DESCRIPTION** FOR THE WORKFLOW
5. CLICK THE **ADD** BUTTON

What you also need to make it work

✓ Project
✓ Workflow Scheme

VIEW WORKFLOW

Jira Admin	Yes
Jira Project Admin	Yes

1. NAVIGATE MAIN MENU BAR > ⚙ > **ISSUES**
2. IN THE ADMINISTRATION ISSUES VIEW, SELECT **WORKFLOWS** FROM THE SIDEBAR

3. IN THE **WORKFLOWS** VIEW, CLICK THE **VIEW** LINK IN THE **ACTIONS** COLUMN FOR THE WORKFLOW YOU WANT TO VIEW

COPY WORKFLOW

Jira Admin	Yes
Jira Project Admin	No

1. NAVIGATE MAIN MENU BAR > ⚙ > **ISSUES**
2. IN THE ADMINISTRATION ISSUES VIEW, SELECT **WORKFLOWS** FROM THE SIDEBAR
3. IN THE **WORKFLOWS** VIEW, CLICK THE **COPY** LINK IN THE **ACTIONS** COLUMN FOR THE WORKFLOW YOU WANT TO COPY
4. IN THE **COPY WORKFLOW** POP-UP ENTER:
   i. A NEW WORKFLOW **NAME**, *OR*, ACCEPT THE DEFAULT NAME WHICH WILL BE, "COPY OF <NAME OF ORIGINAL WORKFLOW>"
   ii. A **DESCRIPTION** OF THE NEW WORKFLOW
5. CLICK THE **COPY** BUTTON

EDIT WORKFLOW

Jira Admin	Yes
Jira Project Admin	Yes, but only if the workflow is restricted to your project (i.e. not shared with any other project)

CAUTION: I strongly suggest you **make a Copy of the original workflow and edit the copy**, rather than edit the working version.

1. NAVIGATE MAIN MENU BAR > ⚙ > **ISSUES**
2. IN THE ADMINISTRATION ISSUES VIEW, SELECT **WORKFLOWS** FROM THE SIDEBAR

3. IN THE **WORKFLOWS** VIEW, CLICK THE **EDIT** LINK IN THE **ACTIONS** COLUMN FOR THE **WORKFLOW** YOU WANT TO EDIT
4. IN THE **WORKFLOWS EDIT** VIEW, EDIT THE WORKFLOW DRAFT
5. WHEN YOU ARE DONE AND WANT TO RE-ACTIVATE THE WORKFLOW, CLICK THE **PUBLISH** BUTTON

DELETE WORKFLOW

Jira Admin	Yes
Jira Project Admin	No

1. NAVIGATE MAIN MENU BAR > ⚙ > **ISSUES**
2. IN THE ADMINISTRATION ISSUES VIEW, SELECT **WORKFLOWS** FROM THE SIDEBAR
3. IN THE **WORKFLOWS** VIEW, CLICK THE **DELETE** LINK IN THE **ACTIONS** COLUMN FOR THE **WORKFLOW** YOU WANT TO DELETE

NOTE: You can only delete **INACTIVE** workflows.

4. IN THE **DELETE WORKFLOW** POP-UP, CLICK THE **DELETE** BUTTON

CAUTION: You cannot delete a **workflow** if it is **associated with** a **Workflow Scheme** or a **Draft Workflow Scheme**. You must first delete the Scheme (see Delete Workflow Scheme)

Workflow Schemes

Add Workflow Scheme

Jira Admin	Yes
Jira Project Admin	No

1. Navigate Main Menu Bar > ⚙ > **Issues**
2. In the Administration Issues view, select **Workflow Schemes** from the sidebar
3. In the Workflow Schemes view, click the **Add Workflow Scheme** button
4. In the **Add Workflow Scheme** pop-up enter:
   i. A **Name** for the Workflow Scheme
   ii. A **Description** for the Workflow Scheme
5. Click the **Add** button

What you also need to make it work

- ✓ Project
- ✓ Issue Type
- ✓ Workflow

Copy Workflow Scheme

Jira Admin	Yes
Jira Project Admin	No

1. Navigate Main Menu Bar > ⚙ > **Issues**

2. IN THE ADMINISTRATION ISSUES VIEW, SELECT **WORKFLOW SCHEMES** FROM THE SIDEBAR
3. IN THE **WORKFLOW SCHEMES** VIEW, CLICK THE **COPY** LINK IN THE **ACTIONS** COLUMN FOR THE **WORKFLOW SCHEME** YOU WANT TO COPY

CAUTION: Click **Copy** only once! As soon as you click 'Copy' a duplicate of the Workflow Scheme will be placed in the Inactive section of the Workflow Schemes view. In other words, a pop-up or new view will NOT appear.

EDIT WORKFLOW SCHEME

Jira Admin	Yes
Jira Project Admin	No

CAUTION: It is highly recommended you **make a Copy of the original workflow scheme and edit the copy**, rather than edit the working version.

1. NAVIGATE MAIN MENU BAR > ⚙ > **ISSUES**
2. IN THE ADMINISTRATION ISSUES VIEW, SELECT **WORKFLOW SCHEMES** FROM THE SIDEBAR
3. IN THE **WORKFLOW SCHEMES** VIEW, CLICK ON THE **EDIT** LINK IN THE **ACTIONS** COLUMN FOR THE **WORKFLOW SCHEME** YOU WANT TO EDIT
4. IN THE SPECIFIC WORKFLOW SCHEME VIEW YOU CAN...

...CHANGE WORKFLOW SCHEME NAME

1. TO CHANGE THE **WORKFLOW SCHEME NAME:** HOVER OVER THE WORKFLOW SCHEME NAME AND CLICK ON IT. IN THE TEXT BOX THAT APPEARS MAKE YOUR CHANGES

...Change Workflow Scheme Description

2. To add or change the **Workflow Scheme description** hover over the *Click to add description* and click on it. In the text box that appears make your changes

...Add another Workflow to the Scheme

3. To **Add** another **Workflow** to the scheme:
    i. Click the **Add Workflow** button
    ii. Select Add Existing
    iii. Follow the steps in the **Add Existing Workflow Wizard** that opens

...Remove a Workflow

4. To Remove a **Workflow** from the **Scheme** click on the **Remove** link in the **Actions** column

CAUTION: If you have only one workflow associated with your workflow scheme, then you must add the replacement workflow before you can delete the current one. In other words, **you must have at least two Workflows associated with the Scheme before you can delete one of them.**

...Add an Issue Type

5. To Add a new Issue Type to the Workflow assigned to the Workflow Scheme:
    i. Click on the **Assign** link in the **Actions** column for the **Workflow** to which you want to add an **Issue Type**
    ii. In the **Issue Type checklist** pop-up, check the **Issue Type(s)** you wish to add to the Workflow
    iii. Click the **Finish** button

...Remove an Issue Type

6. To **Remove** an **Issue Type** from a **Workflow** assigned to the Workflow Scheme click on the '**x**' beside the Issue Type's name

Remove Workflow Scheme from a Project

Jira Admin	Yes
Jira Project Admin	No

1. Navigate Main Menu Bar > ⚙ > **Projects**
2. In the **Administration Projects** view, in the **Project List** click on the **Project** (in the **Project** column) Associated with the Workflow Scheme you want to remove
3. In the Project's **Project Settings Administration** view, select Workflows in the sidebar
4. In the Workflows view, Click on the **Switch Scheme** Button
5. In the **Associate Workflow Scheme to Project**, select *Default* from the Scheme drop-down list
6. Click the **Associate** button
7. Follow the steps in the **Wizard**, which will migrate any **issues associated with** the **old Workflow Scheme** to the Default scheme

Delete Workflow Scheme

Jira Admin	Yes
Jira Project Admin	No

1. Navigate Main Menu Bar > ⚙ > **Issues**
2. In the Administration Issues view, Select **Workflow Schemes** from the sidebar
3. In the **Workflow Scheme** view, click the **Delete** link in the **Actions** column for the **Workflow Scheme** you want to Delete

NOTE: You can only delete INACTIVE workflows.

4. In the **Delete Workflow Scheme** pop-up, click the **Delete** button

CAUTION: You cannot delete a Workflow Scheme if it is associated with a Project. See the note at the end of **Associate Workflow Scheme with a Project** (below) for more details.

Associate Workflow Scheme with a Project

Jira Admin	Yes
Jira Project Admin	No

1. Navigate Main Menu Bar > ⚙ > **Projects**
2. In the **Administration Projects** view, in the **Project List** click on the **project** (in the **Project** column) you want to associate with the workflow scheme
3. In the **Project's Setting Administration** view, select Workflows in the sidebar
4. In the Workflows view, Click the **Switch Scheme** button
5. In the **Associate Workflow Scheme to Project** select **Workflow Scheme** you want to associate with the project from the drop-down list
6. Click the **Associate** button
7. Follow the **next steps** as required (the steps will vary depending on the Issue Types already associated)

TIP: If you want **to delete a Workflow Scheme** but it is associated with a project, then **follow the steps above and switch the Project's workflow scheme to the Jira Core default workflow scheme as described in step 5**.

SCREENS

ADD SCREEN

Jira Admin	Yes
Jira Project Admin	No

1. NAVIGATE MAIN MENU BAR > [gear icon] > **ISSUES**
2. IN THE ADMINISTRATION ISSUES VIEW, SELECT **SCREENS** FROM THE SIDEBAR
3. IN THE **VIEW SCREENS**, CLICK ON THE **ADD SCREEN** BUTTON
4. IN THE **ADD SCREEN** POP-UP ENTER:
   i. THE **NAME** OF THE SCREEN
   ii. THE **DESCRIPTION** OF THE SCREEN
5. CLICK THE **ADD** BUTTON
6. IN THE OPENED **CONFIGURE SCREEN** YOU CAN ADD, REMOVE, MOVE FIELDS, AND CREATE SCREEN TABS. SEE THE CONFIGURE SCREEN FOR DETAILS

NOTES: You cannot use a newly created screen unless:

i. It is **associated with** an **Issue Operation *and* Issue Type** (this is done by creating first a **Screen Scheme**, and then an **Issue Type Screen Scheme**), **or**
ii. It is **associated with** a **Workflow Transition screen (View).**

What you also need to make it work

- ✓ Project
- ✓ Fields
- ✓ For Issue Operation Screens:
  - Screen Scheme

    - Issue Type Screen Scheme
- ✓ For Workflow Transition Screens:
    - Workflow Transition screen (View)
    - Workflow Scheme

CONFIGURE SCREEN

Jira Admin	Yes
Jira Project Admin	Yes

1. NAVIGATE MAIN MENU BAR > ⚙ > **ISSUES**
2. IN THE ADMINISTRATION ISSUES VIEW, SELECT **SCREENS** FROM THE SIDEBAR
3. IN THE **VIEW SCREENS**, CLICK ON THE **CONFIGURE** LINK IN THE **ACTIONS** COLUMN FOR THE SCREEN YOU WANT TO CONFIGURE
4. IN THE **CONFIGURE SCREEN** PAGE YOU CAN:
    i. **ADD FIELDS** BY SELECTING A FIELD FROM THE DROP-DOWN **FIELD NAME** LIST AND CLICKING **ADD** BUTTON
    ii. **REARRANGE** THE FIELDS ORDER BY DRAGGING AND DROPPING. DO THIS BY CLICKING ON THE **HATCH MARK** TO THE LEFT OF THE FIELD NAME
    iii. **REMOVE** FIELDS BY HOVERING THE MOUSE ARROW OVER THE FIELD NAME AND CLICKING THE **REMOVE BUTTON** THAT APPEARS
    iv. **EDIT THE FIELD TAB NAME** BY CLICKING ON THE PENCIL ICON
    v. ADD ADDITIONAL TABS BY CLICKING ON THE **ADD TAB** BUTTON (PLUS ROUND BUTTON)
5. WHEN COMPLETE, SIMPLY EXIT THE PAGE, CHANGES ARE MADE AUTOMATICALLY

Copy Screen

Jira Admin	Yes
Jira Project Admin	Yes, but only within the project

1. Navigate Main Menu Bar > ⚙ > **Issues**
2. In the Administration issues view, Select **Screens** from the sidebar
3. In the **View Screens**, click the **Copy** link in the **Actions** column for the Screen you want to Copy
4. In the **Copy Screen** pop-up you can:
   i. Change the **Name** of the Screen, *or* accept the suggested name provided by Jira Core
   ii. Change the **Description** of the Screen
5. Click the **Copy** button

Edit Screen

Jira Admin	Yes
Jira Project Admin	Yes, if restricted to project

1. Navigate Main Menu Bar > ⚙ > **Issues**
2. In the Administration Issues view, Select **Screens** from the sidebar
3. In the **View Screens**, click on the **Edit** link in the **actions** column for the Screen you want to Edit
4. In the **Edit Screen** pop-up you can:
   i. Change the **Name** of the Screen
   ii. Change the **Description** of the Screen
5. Click the **Update** button

Delete Screen

Jira Admin	Yes
Jira Project Admin	No

1. Navigate Main Menu Bar > [gear icon] > **Issues**
2. In the Administration Issues view, Select **Screens** from the sidebar
3. In the **View Screens**, click on the **Delete** link in the **Actions** column for the Screen you want to Delete
4. In the **Delete Screen** pop-up, click the **Delete** button

CAUTION: You cannot delete a **screen** if it is **associated with** a **Screen Scheme** or a **Workflow Transition screen (View)**. You must delete the scheme and transition first.

Screen Schemes

Jira Admin	Yes
Jira Project Admin	No

Add Screen Scheme

1. Navigate Main Menu Bar > ⚙ > **Issues**
2. In the Administration issues view, Select **Screen Schemes** from the sidebar
3. In the View Screen Schemes, click on the **Add Screen Scheme** button
4. In the Add Screen Scheme pop-up:
   i. Enter the **Name** of the Screen Scheme
   ii. Enter the **Description** of the Screen Scheme
   iii. Select the Screen to be used as the **Default Screen** for the Screen Scheme (if not sure select the Default Screen)
   iv. Click the **Add** button
5. In the Configure Screen Scheme view:
   i. accept the **Default Issue Operation** by exiting this view, ***or***
   ii. Click the Associate an Issue Operation with a Screen button
6. In the Associate an Issue Operation with a Screen pop-up:
   i. Select the **Issue Operation** (**Create, Edit,** or **View**) from the drop-down list
   ii. Select the **Screen** to be **associated with** the **Issue Operation** from the drop-down list
   iii. Click the **Add** Button
7. Exit the Configure Screen Scheme view

What you also need to make it work

- ✓ Project
- ✓ Screen
- ✓ Issue Operation (Create, Edit, View)
- ✓ Issue Type Screen Scheme

Copy Screen Scheme

1. Navigate Main Menu Bar > ⚙ > **Issues**
2. In the Administration Issues view, Select **Screen Schemes** from the sidebar
3. In the **View Screen Schemes**, click on the **Copy** link in the **Actions** column for the Screen Scheme you want to copy
4. In the **Copy Screen Scheme** view you can:
   i. Change the **Name** of the Screen Scheme, ***or*** accept the suggested name provided by Jira Core
   ii. Enter a Description
5. Click the **Copy** button

Edit Screen Scheme

1. Navigate Main Menu Bar > ⚙ > **Issues**
2. In the Administration Issues view, Select **Screen Schemes** from the sidebar
3. In the **View Screen Schemes**, click on the **Edit** link in the **Actions** column for the Screen Scheme you want to edit
4. In the **Edit Screen Scheme** view you can:
   i. Change the **Name** of the Screen Scheme
   ii. Change The **Description**
5. Click the **Update** button

Configure Screen Scheme

1. Navigate Main Menu Bar > ⚙ > **Issues**
2. In the Administration Issues view, Select **Screen Schemes** from the sidebar
3. In the **View Screen Schemes**, click on the **Configure** link in the **Actions** column for the Screen Scheme you want to configure
4. In the Configure Screen Scheme view you can:
   i. accept the **Default Issue Operation** by exiting this view
   ii. Add a new association by clicking the **Associate an Issue Operation with a Screen** button
5. In the Associate an Issue Operation with a Screen pop-up:
   i. Select the **Issue Operation** (**Create, Edit,** or **View**) from the drop-down list
   ii. Select the **Screen** to be **associated with** the **Issue Operation** from the drop-down list
   iii. Click the **Add** Button
6. To **Delete** an **Issue Operation** associated with the **Screen Scheme,** or **Screen**, or both, click the **Delete** link in the **Actions** column

   CAUTION: You can only Delete an Issue Operation **if** a) it is **not the Default scheme**, and b) it is **not associated with any projects**

Delete Screen Scheme

1. Navigate Main Menu Bar > ⚙ > **Issues**
2. In the Administration Issues view, Select **Screen Schemes** from the sidebar
3. In the **View Screen Schemes**, click on the **Delete** link in the **Actions** column for the Screen Scheme you want to delete

4. In the **Delete Screen Scheme** view, click the **Delete** button

CAUTION: You can only delete a **Screen Scheme** if it is ***not* associated** with an **Issue Type Screen Scheme**

Issue Type Screen Scheme

Jira Admin	Yes
Jira Project Admin	No

Add Issue Type Screen Scheme

1. Navigate Main Menu Bar > ⚙ > **Issues**
2. In the Administration Issue view, Select **Issue Type Screen Scheme** from the sidebar
3. In the Issue Type Screen Schemes view, click on the **Add Issue Type Screen Scheme** button

CAUTION: This is a two-part operation, many people complete the first part, but exit before completing the critical second part. **Please follow the instructions** carefully

4. **Part 1**: In the Add Issue Type Screen Scheme pop-up:
   i. Enter a **Name** for the Issue Type Screen Scheme
   ii. Enter a Description
   iii. Select a **Screen Scheme** from the drop-down list
5. Click the **Add** button
6. Part 2: In the Configure Issue Type Screen Scheme view, click on the Associate an Issue Type with a Screen Scheme button
7. In the Associate an Issue Type with a Screen Scheme pop-up:
   i. Select the **Issue Type** from the drop-down list
   ii. Select the **Screen Scheme** from the drop-down list
8. Click the **Add** button

What you also need to make it work

- ✓ Project
- ✓ Screen Scheme
- ✓ Issue Type

Copy Issue Type Screen Scheme

1. Navigate Main Menu Bar > ⚙ > **Issues**
2. In the Administration issues view, Select **Issue Type Screen Schemes** from the sidebar
3. In the **Issue Type Screen Schemes** view, click on **Copy** link in the **Actions** column for the scheme you want to copy
4. In the Copy Issue Type Screen Scheme view:
   i. Enter the **name** for the new scheme, ***or*** accept the suggested scheme name provided by Jira Core
   ii. Enter a Description
5. Click the **Copy** button

Edit Issue Type Screen Scheme

1. Navigate Main Menu Bar > ⚙ > **Issues**
2. In the Administration Issues view, Select **Issue Type Screen Schemes** from the sidebar
3. In the **Issue Type Screen Schemes** view, click on **Edit** link in the **Actions** column for the scheme you want to Edit
4. In the Edit Issue Type Screen Scheme view:
   i. Enter the **name** for the new scheme
   ii. Enter a Description
5. Click the **Update** button

Configure Issue Type Screen Scheme

1. Navigate Main Menu Bar > ⚙ > **Issues**
2. In the Administration Issues view, Select **Issue Type Screen Schemes** from the sidebar

3. In the **Issue Type Screen Schemes** view, click on **Configure** link in the **Actions** column for the scheme you want to configure

NOTE: This will take you to the Configure Issue Type Screen Scheme view where you can...

...Associate an Issue Type with a Screen Scheme

1. In the Configure Issue Type Screen Scheme view, click on the Associate an Issue Type with a Screen Scheme button
2. In the Associate an Issue Type with a screen Scheme pop-up:
   i. Select the **Issue Type** from the drop-down list
   ii. Select the **Screen Scheme** from the drop-down list
3. Click **Add** button

...Edit an Issue Type Screen Scheme

1. Click on **Edit** link for the Issue Type Screen Scheme you want to Edit
2. In the **Edit Issue Type Screen Scheme Entry** view, select a new **Screen Scheme** from the drop-down list
3. Click the **Update** button

...Delete an Issue Type from the Issue Type Screen Scheme

1. Click on Delete link for the Issue Type you want to Delete

CAUTION: You cannot delete the Default Issue Type

Delete Issue Type Screen Scheme

1. Navigate Main Menu Bar > ⚙ > **Issues**
2. In the Administration Issue view, **Select Issue Type Screen Schemes** from the sidebar

3. In the **Issue Type Screen Schemes** view, click on **Delete** link in the **Actions** column for the scheme you want to delete
4. In the Delete Issue Type Screen Scheme view, click on the **Delete** button

CAUTION: You cannot delete an **Issue Type Screen Scheme** if it is **associated with a Project**. See the note at the end of following **Associate Issue Type Screen Scheme with a Project** for details on how to 'disassociate'.

Associate Issue Type Screen Scheme with a Project

1. Navigate Main Menu Bar > ⚙ > **Projects**
2. In the Administration Projects view, in the **Project List** click on the **project** (in the Project column) you want to associate with the Issue Type Screen Scheme
3. In the Project's **Project Settings Administration** view, select **Screens** from the sidebar
4. In the **Screens** view, click on the **Actions** button in the upper right corner
5. Click on **Use a Different Scheme** from the Actions drop-down list
6. In the **Issue Type Screen Scheme Association** view, Select the Issue Type Screen Scheme you want to associate from the Scheme drop-down list
7. Click the **Associate** button

TIP: If you want to delete an **Issue Type Screen Scheme** but it is **associated with a Project**, then follow the steps above and in step 6 switch the Project's Issue Type Screen Scheme to the **Jira Default Issue Type Screen Scheme.**

Custom Fields

Add Custom Field

Jira Admin	Yes
Jira Project Admin	No

1. Navigate Main Menu Bar > [gear icon] > **Issues**
2. In the Administration Issues view, select **Custom Fields** from the sidebar
3. In the **Custom Fields** view, click on the **Add Custom Field** button
4. In the **Select a Field Type** pop-up, click on the **Field Type** you want to use
5. Click the **Next** button
6. In the **Configure Field** pop-up:
   i. Enter a **Name** for the Field
   ii. Enter a **Description** for the Field
   iii. Enter **Options** if requested
      a. Enter an option and click **Add.** Options become the choice list from which you or your user(s) will select
      b. You can rearrange the order of the options by dragging and dropping them. Do this by hovering the mouse arrow over the hatch mark to the left of the option name. When your mouse arrow turns into a four-direction arrow you can drag the option up or down
      c. Delete an option by clicking the “x” next to the option name
7. Click the **Create** button

What you also need to make it work

✓ Screen

Configure Custom Field

Jira Admin	Yes
Jira Project Admin	No

1. Navigate Main Menu Bar > ⚙ > **Issues**
2. In the Administration Issues view, select **Custom Fields** from the sidebar
3. In the **Custom Fields** view, navigate to the **COG** wheel in the Action column for the Custom Field you want to **Configure**
4. Click on the **Custom Field Cog** and select **Configure** from the drop-down list

NOTE: While there are a number of things you can do on the **Configure Custom Field** view, we will limit ourselves to changing the **Default Value** and **Field Options**

5. Click on **Edit Default value** link in the Default Value Field
6. In the **Set Custom Field Defaults**, select a value (option) you want to use as the field's default value
7. Click on **Set Default** button
8. Click on **Edit Options** link in the **Options** Field
9. In the Edit Options for Custom Field view you can:
   i. Sort Options alphabetically by clicking on the link
   ii. **Add a New Custom Field Option** by inserting a value (option) into **Add Value** field at the bottom of the view, and then Click **Add** button

iii. Rearrange the sequence of the options by clicking on the appropriate **Arrow** in the **Order** column, ***or*** by entering a value's position number in the **Move to Position** column and then clicking on the **Move** button
iv. **Edit** the name of the Value
v. **Delete** the Value
vi. **Disable** the Value (useful if you don't want to use it at the moment but want to keep a record of the value in the database)

10. Click **Done**

Edit Custom Field

Jira Admin	Yes
Jira Project Admin	No

1. Navigate Main Menu Bar > > **Issues**
2. In the Administration Issues view, select **Custom Fields** from the sidebar
3. In the **Custom Fields** view, click on **Edit** in the **Cog** drop-down for the Custom Field you want to edit
4. In the Edit Custom Field Details view you can:
   i. Change the **Field Name**
   ii. Change the **Description**

CAUTION: Do not change the **Search Template** value

5. Click the **update** button

Translate Custom Field

Jira Admin	Yes
Jira Project Admin	No

1. Navigate Main Menu Bar > > **Issues**
2. In the Administration Issues view, select **Custom Fields** from the sidebar
3. In the **Custom Fields** view, click **Translate** in the **Cog** drop-down for the Custom Field you want to translate
4. In the **Translate Custom Field** view, choose the **language** you want from the drop-down list
5. Enter the <u>Translated</u> **Name** into the **Field Name**
6. enter a <u>translated</u> **description** into the **Description** field
7. Click the **update** button

CAUTION: Jira Core will not translate the field name for you – you must do that yourself; however, it will store the translated field name for different screens. For example, you may have a default Screen where the fields are in English, but you may have another version of the Screen where the fields are in French.

Associate Field to Screen(s)

Jira Admin	Yes
Jira Project Admin	Yes

1. Navigate Main Menu Bar > > **Issues**
2. In the Administration issues view, select **Custom Fields** from the sidebar
3. In the **Custom Fields** view, click on **Screens** in the **Cog** drop-down for the Custom Field you want to associate
4. In the **Associate Field to Screens** view, check the box in the **Select** column for the Screen or screens you want to associate with this custom field

TIP: If a screen has more than one Tab, a drop-down list will appear in the Tab Column. Select the tab where you want the custom field to be placed

5. CLICK THE **UPDATE** BUTTON

DELETE A CUSTOM FIELD

Jira Admin	Yes
Jira Project Admin	No

1. NAVIGATE MAIN MENU BAR > [cog icon] > **ISSUES**
2. IN THE ADMINISTRATION ISSUES VIEW, SELECT **CUSTOM FIELDS** FROM THE SIDEBAR
3. IN THE **CUSTOM FIELDS** VIEW, CLICK ON **DELETE** IN THE **COG** DROP-DOWN FOR THE CUSTOM FIELD YOU WANT TO DELETE
4. IN THE **DELETE CUSTOM FIELD** VIEW, CLICK THE **DELETE** BUTTON

CAUTION: If you delete a custom field, it will delete all the values for that field in all of your other issues. If you simply wanted to **remove** the custom field from the screen, follow the Instructions in the Associate field to Screen section and **uncheck** the box(s) in the **Select** column for the screen(s) you no longer want associated with the custom field.

Priorities

Create Priority

Jira Admin	Yes
Jira Project Admin	No

1. Navigate Main Menu Bar > ⚙ > **Issues**
2. In the Administration Issues view, select **Priorities** from the sidebar
3. In the **Priorities** view click on **Add Priority** button
4. In the Add New Priority pop-up:
   i. Enter a **Name** of a new priority
   ii. Enter a **Description** (optional)
   iii. Select an **image**
   iv. Select **color**
5. Click **Add** button

CAUTION: With versions 7.5 and earlier you can only have one priority scheme; consequently, when you add or delete a priority you affect every project in your Jira Core system. So, **this is an item that should only be managed by the System Administrator** or by the most Senior Jira administrator in your organization.

Starting with Jira Core version 7.6 you can create priority schemes for specific projects.

Edit Priority

Jira Admin	Yes
Jira Project Admin	No

1. Navigate Main Menu Bar > ⚙ > **Issues**

2. In the Administration Issues view, select **Priorities** from the sidebar
3. In the **Priorities** view click on **Edit** link in the **Action** column
   i. In the **Edit Priority** view you can change:
   ii. Priority **Name**
   iii. Description
   iv. Icon URL (**image**)
   v. Color
4. Click **Update** button

Create Priority Scheme

Jira Admin	Yes
Jira Project Admin	No

1. Navigate Main Menu Bar > ⚙ > **Issues**
2. On the Administration Issues View, select **Priority Schemes** in the sidebar
3. On the **View priority Schemes** click on the **Add Priority Scheme** button in the upper right corner
4. In the Add Priority Scheme view you can **name** a Scheme and determine which priorities you want in your new scheme by dragging and dropping them from/to Available Priorities and Selected Priorities boxes. Of course, if you want new, different priorities, you first need to create them in the Priorities view.
5. Click **Add** button
6. In the **View Priority Schemes** click the **Associate** link in the Actions column
7. Associate the priority scheme to one or more **Projects**

Time Tracking

Activate Time Tracking

Jira Admin	Yes
Jira Project Admin	No

1. Navigate Main Menu Bar > ⚙ >**Issues**
2. On the Administration Issues view, select **Time Tracking** in the Sidebar in the Issue Features section:
   - If the Top of the view reads, "Time Tracking is Currently ON.", all is good
   - If the Top of the view reads, "Time tracking is currently OFF.", then click on the **Activate** button at the bottom of the view

Change Default Time Tracking settings

Jira Admin	Yes
Jira Project Admin	No

NOTE: If you change the current Time Tracking settings, you will affect every Jira Core project. So, if there are multiple Jira Admins in your organization, make sure you have consensus before making any changes.

1. Navigate Main Menu Bar > ⚙ > **Issues**
2. In the Issue Features area of the Administration Issues view sidebar, select **Time Tracking**
3. Click the **Deactivate** button
4. In the Time Tracking is **Currently OFF** view you can:
   i. Change **Hours** per day

   ii. CHANGE **DAYS** PER WEEK
   iii. CHOOSE THE **TIME FORMAT**
   iv. CHANGE THE DEFAULT UNIT
   v. SELECT LEGACY MODE
   vi. COPY **COMMENTS** TO WORK DESCRIPTION
5. CLICK THE **ACTIVATE** BUTTON WHEN DONE
6. **RE-INDEX** THE PROGRAM

LOG TIME

Jira Admin	Yes
Jira Project Admin	Yes

1. OPEN AN **ISSUE**
2. IN THE **ISSUE DETAILS VIEW**, CLICK THE **MORE** BUTTON AND SELECT **LOG WORK**
3. IN THE LOG WORK POP-UP, IN THE **TIME SPENT** FIELD ENTER NUMBER OF WEEKS, DAYS, OR HOURS SPENT WORKING ON THE ISSUE
4. CHOOSE A DATE IN THE **DATE STARTED** FIELD (USE A CALENDAR)
5. IN THE **WORK DESCRIPTION** FIELD, ENTER A DESCRIPTION
6. CLICK THE **LOG** BUTTON

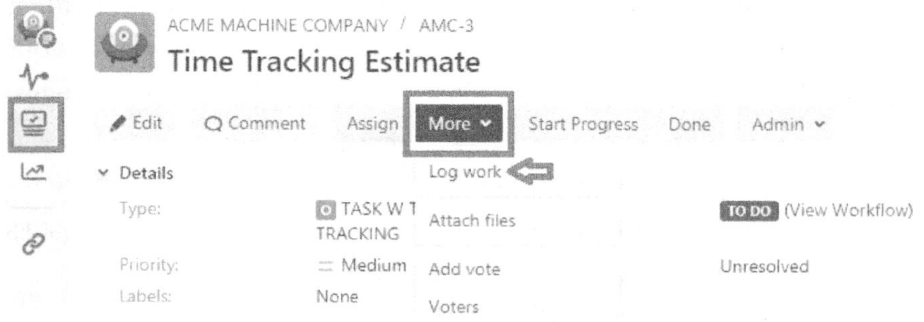

Logging Work using the Remaining Estimate fields in the Log Work pop up

Jira Admin	Yes
Jira Project Admin	Yes

1. Open an **Issue**
2. In the **Issue Detail View**, click the **More** button and select **Log Work**
3. In the Log work pop up, in the **Time Spent** field enter number of weeks, days, or hours spent working on the issue
4. In the **Remaining Estimate** area, choose one of the option (click on the radio button):
   i. Adjust automatically
   ii. Use existing estimate of
   iii. **Set to** and enter number of weeks, days, or hours in the **Set to** field
   iv. **Reduce by** and enter number of weeks, days, or hours in the **Reduce by** field
5. Click the **Log** button

Create a Time Tracking Function (add Time Tracking field to the Create, Edit, and View screens)

Jira Admin	Yes
Jira Project Admin	Yes

I. Creating the Time Estimate Issue Type and Associating it with an Issue Type Scheme:

1. Navigate Main Menu Bar > ⚙ > **Issues**
2. In the opened **Issue Types** view, click on **Add Issue Type** button (located in the upper right corner)
3. In the Add Issue Type pop-up, enter a name in the **Name** field
4. Click **Add**
5. In the Administration Issues sidebar, select **Issue type schemes**
6. In the **Issue type schemes** view, locate a Project in the **Projects** column and click on **Edit** link in the related **Actions** column
7. In the **Modify Issue Type scheme** view, locate newly created Issue Type in the **Available Issue Types** list and then drag & Drop it over to the **Issue Types for Current Scheme**
8. Click **Save**

II. Creating a Screen with the Time Estimate function:

1. In the Administration Issues sidebar, select **Screens**
2. In the View Screens page, click **Add screen** button (in the upper right corner)
3. In the Add screen pop-up, enter a name in the **Name** Field
4. Click **Add**
5. In the **Configure Screen** page, Add the following fields in the **Field Name** area:
   i. Summary
   ii. Reporter
   iii. Assignee
   iv. Due Date
   v. Time Tracking
   vi. Add any other fields you think you will need for your screen

6. In the Sidebar click on **Screens**

III. Creating Screen Scheme in order to manage the screen operations:

1. In the Administration Issues sidebar, select **Screen Schemes**
2. In the View Screen Schemes, click on **Add Screen Scheme** button (in the upper right corner)
3. In the Add Screen Scheme pop-up enter a Name in the **Name** Field
4. select the newly created screen (from Part II) as the **Default Screen**
5. Click **Add**
6. In the Configure Screen Scheme page, click on **Associate an Issue Operation with a screen** button (located in upper right corner)
7. In the Associate an Issue operation with a screen pop-up, select *Create Issue* as the **Issue Operation**, and the newly created screen (from Part II) as the **Screen**
8. Click **Add**
9. In the Configure Screen Scheme page, click on **Associate an Issue Operation with a screen** button (located in upper right corner)
10. In the Associate an Issue operation with a screen pop-up, select *Edit Issue* as the **Issue Operation**, and the newly created screen (from Part II) as the **Screen**
11. Click **Add**
12. In the Configure Screen Scheme page, click on **Associate an Issue Operation with a screen** button (located in the upper right corner)
13. In the Associate an Issue operation with a screen pop-up, select *View Issue* as the **Issue Operation**, and *the newly created screen* (from Part II) as the **Screen**

14. Click **Add**

IV. Associating Screen and Screen Scheme with the Issue Type and the Project:

1. In the Administration Issues sidebar, select **Issue Type Screen Schemes**
2. In the opened Issue Type Screen Schemes, locate the Project in the **Projects** column, and click on **Configure** link in the related **Actions** column
3. In the Configure Issue Type Screen Scheme page, click on **Associate an issue type with a screen scheme** button (in the upper right corner)
4. In the Associate an Issue Type with a Screen Scheme pop-up, select the Issue Type (created in the Part I) as the **Issue Type**
5. Select the Screen Scheme (created in the Part III) as the **Screen Scheme**
6. Click **Add**

V. Review:

1. Open the **project**
2. Create an **Issue**
3. In the **Create Issue** pop-up, ensure that opened project is selected as the **Project**
4. Select the Issue Type created in the Part I as the **Issue Type**
    - If everything is done correctly, you should see the two **estimate fields (Original Estimate and Remaining Estimate)** at the bottom of the pop up.

NOTE: If you do not see those fields, click the **Configure Fields** button in the right up corner and select Time Tracking.

! NOTE: **Time Tracking is a complex topic. For more details regarding Remaining Estimate fields options, and Log Work interaction with the Estimated and Remaining fields please see the Chapter 10 of this book.**

Create a Work Log Report

Unfortunately, there is no built in method to create a Jira Work Log Report. You can either purchase a 3rd party plugin or use one of the methods below.

1. Open the **Issue**, and click on the **Work Log tab** in the **Activity** area of the Issue's Details view
2. With the **Work Log tab** open, and work log details showing, use your web Browser's Print method to print the page (or use a snipping tool to cut and save an image)

Create a Project Time Tracking Report

Jira Admin	Yes
Jira Project Admin	Yes

1. Open the **Project** for which you want a report
2. In the Project's sidebar, select **Reports**
3. In the **All Reports** view, scroll down and click on *Time Tracking Report* link in the **Forecast and Management area**

4. In the **Configure – Time Tracking Report** view select options from the drop-down lists of the following fields:
    i. Fix Version Drop-down
    ii. **Sorting** Drop-down
    iii. **Issue** drop-down
    iv. Sub-task inclusion drop-down
5. Click **NEXT**

Users

Create User

Jira Admin	Yes
Jira Project Admin	No

1. Navigate Main Menu Bar > ⚙ > **User management**
2. In the **Users** view, click the **Create User** button
3. In the **Create New User** pop-up:
   i. Enter a user's **email address**
   ii. Enter the User's **Full Name:** Use the Organization's naming convention (e.g. First Name, Last Name, or Last Name, First name, etc.)
   iii. Enter the User's **Username**
   iv. Enter a **Password** (Optional)
   v. Check the Send **Notification** Email box
   vi. Check the Application access
4. Click the **Create User** button

What you also need to make it work

- ✓ User's email address

Invite Users

Jira Admin	Yes
Jira Project Admin	No

1. Navigate Main Menu Bar > ⚙ > **User management**

2. In the **Users** view, click the **Invite Users** button
   i. In the **Invite Users** pop-up, enter the user's **email address**
   ii. Enter multiple email addresses by either separating the addresses with a comma, or entering the email addresses on separate lines
3. Click the **Invite Users** button

What you also need to make it work

- ✓ Outgoing Mail Server
- ✓ User's email address

Edit User Profile

Jira Admin	Yes
Jira Project Admin	No

1. Navigate Main Menu Bar > ⚙ > **User management**
2. In the **Users** view, Click on **Edit** link in the Actions column for the User you want to edit
3. In the **Edit User Profile** pop-up you can:
   i. Change the **Username**
   ii. Change the **Full Name**
   iii. Change the **Email** address
   iv. Change the status from **Active** to **Inactive** by removing the check mark in the check box
4. Click the **Update** button

Edit User Groups

Jira Admin	Yes
Jira Project Admin	No

1. Navigate Main Menu Bar > ⚙ > **User management**
2. In the **Users** view, Click on the tree dots in the **Actions** column and choose the **Edit User Groups** option for the User you want to edit
3. In the **manage User groups** pop-up you can:
   i. **Add the User to other group:** Start to type a group name in the "Type to start searching" text box to see available groups, then select that group/s from the drop-down list and click on the **Join selected groups** button
   ii. **Remove the User from the Current Groups** to which s/he belongs by selecting that group and clicking on the **Leave selected groups** button

Delete User

Jira Admin	Yes
Jira Project Admin	No

1. Navigate Main Menu Bar > ⚙ > **User management**
2. In the **Users** view, Click on the three dots button in the Actions column and choose the **Delete User** option for the User you want to Delete
3. In the **Delete User** pop-up, click the **Delete** button

CAUTION 1: This action cannot be undone. Instead of deleting a User you may want to keep the user in Jira's Core database by simply making the user **Inactive**. Follow the instructions in the Edit User section, specifically **point 3.iv** (an added bonus is that ***inactive users do not count against your total License count)***

CAUTION 2: A user cannot be deleted if s/he has been assigned issue(s). You must first either delete the issue or assign the issue to someone else.

Project Roles

Add Project Role

Jira Admin	Yes
Jira Project Admin	No

1. Navigate Main Menu Bar > ⚙ > **System**
2. In the **Administration System** view, select **Project Roles** from the sidebar in the **Security** section
3. In the **Project Role Browser**, navigate to the **Add Project Role** section at the bottom of the view
4. Enter a project Role in the **Name** field
5. Enter a Description
6. Click the **Add Project Role** button

What you also need to make it work

- ✓ Project
- ✓ User

Edit Project Role

Jira Admin	Yes
Jira Project Admin	No

1. Navigate Main Menu Bar > ⚙ > **System**
2. In the **Administration System** view, select **Project Roles** from the sidebar in the **Security** section

3. In the **Project Role Browser**, click on **Edit** link in the **Actions** column for the **Role** you want to edit
4. In the **Edit Project Role** view you can:
   i. Change the **Name**
   ii. Change the **Description**
5. Click the **Update** Button

Manage Default Members

Jira Admin	Yes
Jira Project Admin	No

1. Navigate Main Menu Bar > > **System**
2. In the **Administration System** view, select **Project Roles** from the sidebar in the **Security** section
3. In the **Project Role Browser**, click on **Manage Default Members** link in the **Actions** column for the **Role** you want to manage
4. In the Edit Default Members for Project Role view, click on **Edit** link in the Default Users column or in the Default Groups column
5. In the opened **Assign Default Users/Groups to Project Role** view, enter the **names** of the default Users/Groups for the project role in the **Add User(s)/Group(s) to Project Role** text box

TIP: Separate user names/groups with a comma

6. Click the **Add** Button

Delete Project Role

Jira Admin	Yes
Jira Project Admin	No

1. NAVIGATE MAIN MENU BAR > [gear icon] > **SYSTEM**
2. IN THE **ADMINISTRATION SYSTEM** VIEW, SELECT **PROJECT ROLES** FROM THE SIDEBAR IN THE **SECURITY** SECTION
3. IN THE **PROJECT ROLE BROWSER**, CLICK ON **DELETE** LINK IN THE **ACTIONS** COLUMN FOR THE **ROLE** YOU WANT TO DELETE
4. CLICK THE **DELETE** BUTTON

CAUTION: Deleting a project role will delete it from **ALL** projects and schemes

EDIT USER PROJECT ROLE

Jira Admin	Yes
Jira Project Admin	Yes

1. NAVIGATE MAIN MENU BAR > [gear icon] > **USER MANAGEMENT**
2. IN THE **ADMINISTRATION USER MANAGEMENT** VIEW, CLICK ON THREE DOTS BUTTON IN THE **ACTIONS** COLUMN AND CHOOSE **VIEW PROJECT ROLES** OPTION FOR THE **USER**
3. IN THE VIEW PROJECT ROLES FOR USER, CLICK THE **EDIT PROJECT ROLES** BUTTON
4. IN THE EDIT PROJECT ROLES FOR USER VIEW:
   i. FIND THE **PROJECT** YOU WISH TO ASSOCIATE WITH THE USER
   ii. FIND THE **ROLE** YOU WISH THE USER TO PLAY
   iii. CLICK THE **CHECK BOX** AT THE INTERSECTION OF THE PROJECT AND ROLE
5. CLICK THE **SAVE** BUTTON

What you also need to make it work

✓ Project

- ✓ User

Groups

Jira Admin	Yes
Jira Project Admin	No

Add Group

1. Navigate Main Menu Bar > ⚙ > **User Management**
2. In the **Administration User Management** view, Select **Groups** from the sidebar
3. In the **Groups** view, navigate to the **Add Group** section
4. Enter a **Name** for the Group in the Name text box
5. Click the **Add Group** button

What you also need to make it work

✓ Permission Scheme

Edit Group Members

1. Navigate Main Menu Bar > ⚙ > **User Management**
2. In the **Administration User Management** view, Select **Groups** from the sidebar
3. In the **Groups** view, click the **Edit Members** link in the **Actions** column for the **Group** you want to edit
4. In the Bulk Edit Group Members page:
    i. If you select another group or multiple groups (in the left **Selected groups** column) in order to edit them, you must click **Refresh the group members list** to make the members appear in the Center Column **(Croup Member(s))**

CAUTION: When you open this page, your group is already highlighted and you will not see this refresh option

ii. **Remove** group members in the **center column** by clicking on their **name** and then clicking the **Remove Selected Users** button
iii. **Add** members to selected group, in the **right column**, by entering their **name** and clicking the **Add Selected Users** button

Giving a Group Global Permissions

1. Navigate to Main Menu Bar > ⚙ > **System**
2. In the Administration System sidebar click on **Global Permissions** in the security section
3. Go to the Bottom of the **Global Permissions** view to the **Add Permission** area
4. Select the type of Permission you want to grant in the **Permission** drop-down list

!IMPORTANT: do not select Jira SYSTEM Administrators

5. Select a *Group* in the **Group** drop-down list
6. Click the **Add** button

Delete Group

1. Navigate Main Menu Bar > ⚙ > **User Management**
2. In the **Administration User Management** view, Select **Groups** from the sidebar
3. In the **Groups** view, click on **Delete** link in the **Actions** column for the **Group** you want to delete
4. In the **Delete Group** view, click on the **Delete** button

TIP: You will not delete any users if you delete a group

Permission Schemes

Jira Admin	Yes
Jira Project Admin	No

Use a Default Permission Scheme (granted to any logged in user)

1. Navigate Main Menu Bar > > **Issues**
2. In the Administration Issues Sidebar, Click on **Permission Schemes** (should be the last option in the Sidebar)
3. In the Permission Schemes view, locate the **Default Permission Scheme**, and click on **Permissions** link in the Actions column
4. In the Default Permission Scheme view you can Edit or Remove a Project permissions, an Issue permissions, Voters & Watchers permissions, Comments permissions, Attachments permissions, and Time Tracking permissions by clicking on Edit or remove links

CAUTION: Be careful when editing the default permission scheme as it will affect all projects using this scheme. It may be wiser to create a project specific Permission scheme.

Create a Project Permission Scheme

1. Navigate Main Menu Bar > > **Issues**
2. In the Administration Issues Sidebar, Click on **Permission Schemes** (should be the last option in the Sidebar)
3. In the **Permission Schemes** view, click on **Add Permission Scheme** button (in the upper right corner)
4. In the Add permission scheme view, enter a Name of the Permission Scheme in the **Name** field (required), and a **description** (optional)

5. CLICK **ADD**
6. BACK IN THE **PERMISSION SCHEMES** VIEW, FIND YOUR NEWLY CREATED PERMISSION SCHEME AND CLICK ON **PERMISSIONS** LINK IN THE **ACTIONS** COLUMN
7. IN THE OPENED PERMISSION SCHEME VIEW, CLICK **EDIT** LINK IN THE **ADMINISTER PROJECTS** ROW
8. IN THE **GRANT PERMISSION** POP UP, CLICK **SHOW MORE** LINK
9. IN THE EXTENDED "**GRANTED TO**" LIST, CHOOSE THE OPTION (RADIO BUTTON)
10. CLICK **GRANT**
11. BACK IN THE **PERMISSION SCHEME** VIEW CHECK *WHO* NOW HAVE THE PERMISSION TO ADMINISTER THE PROJECT

ASSOCIATE A PERMISSION SCHEME WITH A PROJECT

1. OPEN A **PROJECT**
2. CLICK ON THE **PROJECT SETTINGS** FOUND IN THE PROJECT SIDEBAR
3. IN THE **PROJECT SETTINGS** VIEW, SCROLL DOWN TO THE **PERMISSIONS** AREA, AND CLICK ON THE **DEFAULT PERMISSION SCHEME** LINK
4. IN THE **PROJECT PERMISSIONS** VIEW, CLICK ON **ACTIONS** BUTTON (IN THE UPPER RIGHT CORNER)
5. SELECT 'USE A DIFFERENT SCHEME'
6. IN THE **ASSOCIATE PERMISSION SCHEME TO PROJECT** PAGE, SELECT *YOUR PERMISSION SCHEME* IN THE **SCHEME** DROP-DOWN LIST
7. CLICK **ASSOCIATE** BUTTON

Dashboards

Jira Admin	Yes
Jira Project Admin	Yes

Create New Dashboard

1. Navigate main menu bar > **Dashboards** > **Manage Dashboards**
2. In the Manage Dashboards view, click on **Create new dashboard** button located in the top right of the view
3. In the Create New Dashboard view, type the **name** of the new Dashboard in the name field
4. Write a brief **description** of the Dashboard, if you wish
5. In the **Start From** field, select the Dashboard from the drop-down list. A Blank dashboard means a dashboard without any gadgets
6. Click or unclick on the **Favorite star** to make the dashboard a favorite or not
7. Leave the **Viewers Icon** as is for now
8. In the **Add Viewers** drop-down list select Group, Project, Any Logged-in user, or Public
9. In the next box select a **role** from the drop-down list
10. Click the **+Add** button next to the **Add Viewers** fields
11. Ensure that your selected options is indicated in the **Shares** field above the Add Shares. If you are not happy with those who are now listed in the "Shares", click on **Garbage Can** icons next to the Shared fields until the Not Shared message appears
12. Repeat steps ## 7-11 for the **Editors**
13. Click on the **ADD** button at the bottom of the view

Copy Dashboard

1. Navigate main menu bar > **Dashboards**

2. Open the dashboard you want to copy
3. Click on the **Tools** button (three dots in the upper right of the dashboard's view) to open a list of the option. Select **Copy Dashboard**
4. Follow the steps 3 to 12 of the **Create new Dashboard** instruction. **NOTE:** in the **Start from** field the name of the copied dashboard has already selected

Edit Dashboard

1. Navigate main menu bar > **Dashboards**
2. Open the dashboard you want to edit

NOTE: If you are editing a newly created dashboard, a dashboard's view will appear with a couple of grey boxes each saying: ***Drag your gadgets here or add a new gadget.***
If, when creating a new dashboard, you had selected an existing project in the **Start From** field, then instead of the two grey boxes you would see the gadgets from the original dashboard.

3. To Edit the Layout click **Edit Layout** button in the upper right of the Dashboard view

4. In the Edit Layout pop up select the layout
5. To add a Gadget click **Add Gadget** button in the upper right of the Dashboard View
6. In the Add Gadget pop up select the Gadget and click on the **Add Gadget** button next to the gadget
7. Click on the 'X" to exit the pop up
8. To **Edit Gadget** hover your mouse over the Gadget Title Band. Three icons will appear near the right-side end of the band
   i. **To drag the gadget to another location** on the Dashboard click on a four-sided arrow icon
   ii. **To maximize the gadget** by hiding all other gadgets click on the maximize icon

iii. To **minimize** the gadget, **change the colour** of the band, **edit** the gadget, or **delete** the gadget click on the last three dots icon and select one of those options

Edit and Share Dashboard

1. Navigate main menu bar > **Dashboards**
2. Open the dashboard you want to Edit or Add/Remove Shares
3. Click on the **Tools** button (three dots in the upper right of the dashboard's view) to open a list of the option. Select **Edit Dashboard** OR **Share Dashboard**
4. In the Edit and Share Dashboard view you can:
   i. Change the **name** of the dashboard
   ii. Change the **description**
   iii. Make the Dashboard as **favorite or unfavorite**
   iv. Add or Remove **Shares**
5. Click **Update** button

Delete Dashboard

1. Navigate main menu bar > **Dashboards**
2. Open the dashboard you want to Delete
3. Click on the **Tools** button (three dots in the upper right of the dashboard's view) to open a list of the option. Select **Delete**
4. In the Delete Dashboard pop up click **Delete** button

Find Dashboard

1. Navigate main menu bar > Dashboards > **Manage Dashboards**
2. In the Manage Dashboards view select **Search** from the sidebar

3. On the **Search Dashboards** page you can filter your search by key words in the dashboard's name and description, by ownership, or by Sharing
4. Click **Search** button

View as Wallboard

1. Navigate main menu bar > **Dashboards**
2. Open the dashboard you want to see as **wallboard**
3. Click on the **Tools** button (three dots in the upper right of the dashboard's view) to open a list of the option. Select **View as Wallboard**
4. The gadgets of the Dashboard will be displayed as a series of slides

Set up Wallboard Slideshow

1. Navigate main menu bar > **Dashboards**
2. Open the dashboard you want to set up as **wallboard Slideshow**
3. Click on the **Tools** button (three dots in the upper right of the dashboard's view) to open a list of the option
4. Select **Set up Wallboard Slideshow** (this option allows you to set up a slide show of your dashboards and gadgets. You can select one, some, or all of your dashboards and you have a number of display options to choose from. meaning the gadgets will be displayed as a series of slides)

Modify the System Dashboard

Jira Admin	Yes
Jira Project Admin	No

1. NAVIGATE MAIN MENU BAR > ⚙ > **SYSTEM**
2. IN THE ADMINISTRATION SYSTEM SIDEBAR, FIND THE USER INTERFACE SECTION AND CLICK ON **SYSTEM DASHBOARD**
3. IN THE OPENED **CONFIGURE SYSTEM DASHBOARD** MAKE YOUR CHANGES

CAUTION: Notice the warning below the view header, "You are now configuring the SYSTEM dashboard. Changes made here will affect all users using the default system dashboard."

Filters and Reports

Jira Admin	Yes
Jira Project Admin	Yes

Quick Search

1. Navigate main menu bar > **Search**
2. In the Search drop-down list click on the **View all Issues** link or **View all Projects** link

Current Search

1. Navigate main menu bar > **Issues** > **Current Search** (last search you performed)
2. In the opened **Issue Navigator (Search)** view find your issue(s)

Search for Issues (Basic Search)

1. Navigate main menu bar > **Issues** > **Search for Issues**
2. In the opened **Issue Navigator (Search)** view use the **filter** menu bar to narrow your search

NOTE: Jira Core builds searches in the order that the filters were selected**,** meaning **those filters in the filter menu bar are subsets of other filters.** Therefore, when building a multi-filter search, remember to build the search in the proper filter order.

Advanced Search

1. Navigate main menu bar > **Issues** > **Search for Issues**
2. In the opened **Issue Navigator (Search)** view, in the filter menu bar click on the **Advanced** link

NOTE: Using the Advanced function involves **Jira Query Language (JQL).**

Save Search

1. Navigate main menu bar > **Issues** > **Search for Issues**
2. In the opened **Issue Navigator (Search)** view, find your Issue(s) using the Basic search (the filter menu bar) or using the Advanced search
3. Click on the **Save As** button
4. Type in a **Filter Name** in the **Save Filter** Pop Up
5. Click **Submit**

Build Custom Filter

1. Navigate main menu bar > **Issues** > **Search for Issues**
2. In the opened **Issue Navigator (Search)** view, find your Issue(s) using the Basic search (the filters menu bar) or using the Advanced search
3. Click on the **Save As** button
4. Type in a **Filter Name** in the **Save Filter** Pop Up
5. Click **Submit**

NOTE: Once you click the submit button your Search (really a filter) will be saved in the **Favorite Filters** sidebar

Subscribe to a Filter

1. Navigate Main Menu Bar > **Issues** > **Manage Filters**
2. Select **Favorite, My, or Popular** option in the Manage **Filters** sidebar
3. In the Favorite, My, or Popular Filters, in the **Name** column Find a filter you want to subscribe, then click on the **Subscribe** link in the **Subscriptions** column
4. In the **Filter Subscription** pop-up, select:
   i. the **Recipients** from the drop-down list
   ii. the Schedule
   iii. the **Interval** from the drop-down lists
   iv. Check or leave "email this filter, even if there are no issues found"
5. Click Subscribe

Create a Project Report

1. Navigate Main Menu Bar> **projects**
2. Select any project
3. Navigate to the project's sidebar and click on **Reports** icon on the **All Report** view
4. click any report
5. **Configure** the Report

Create Dashboard Filter Report

1. Navigate Main Menu Bar > **Dashboards**
2. Select any **Dashboard** (except for the System Dashboard)
3. Click on **Add Gadget** button in the upper right corner of the Dashboard
4. In the Add a Gadget pop up find **Favorite Filters**
5. Click **Add Gadget** button
6. In the Add a Gadget pop up find **Filter Results**
7. Click **Add Gadget** button
8. Click on the "X" to exit the pop up

Export a Filter's Results

1. Navigate Main Menu Bar > **Issues**
2. Select My Open Issues, Reported by me, or any other Filter
3. click on the **Export** drop-down list in the upper right corner of the opened Filter's view
4. Select one of the 11 **export options**:
    i. Printable
    ii. Full Content
    iii. RSS (Issues)
    iv. RSS (Comments)
    v. CSV (All fields)
    vi. CSV (Current fields)
    vii. HTML (All fields)

viii. HTML (CURRENT FIELDS)
ix. XML
x. WORD
xi. DASHBOARD CHARTS

Source Material

The JIRA CORE User's Guide is an excellent source for technical instructions:

https://confluence.atlassian.com/alldoc/atlassian-documentation-32243719.html

About Toreno Information Solutions

Toreno Information Solutions is a specialty software vendor and solution provider.

Our purpose is to help companies utilize low-cost, user-friendly technology to:

- Work easier and more efficiently with Workflow and Project Management software
- Manage information better through Database Design and Maintenance
- Enable teams to work together more effectively with Collaborative Workspaces

Working with Toreno I.S., allows you and your team to focus on core operations instead of being distracted by your technology. **Think of us as the non-technology, technology company.**

Located in Reno USA and Toronto Canada, our partners have decades of experience with data systems, systems management, document management, task, process, and project management, change management, analytic and operational report design.

Don't hesitate to email us at ContactUs@TorenoIS.com

Let's talk about how we can help your organization.

Our technology solutions

makes your life easier!

Made in United States
Orlando, FL
18 March 2025